Medieval French Romance

Twayne's World Authors Series
French Literature

David O'Connell, Editor

Georgia State University

TWAS 838

MANUSCRIPT PAGE, PARIS ARSENAL 3142, FOLIO 73 RECTO

Medieval French Romance

Douglas Kelly

University of Wisconsin–Madison

WITHDRAWI

Twayne Publishers • New York
Maxwell Macmillan Canada • Toronto
Maxwell Macmillan International • New York Oxford Singapore Sydney

Twayne's World Authors Series No. 838
Medieval French Romance

Douglas Kelly

Twayne Publishers   Maxwell Macmillan Canada, Inc.
Macmillan Publishing Company   1200 Eglinton Avenue East
866 Third Avenue   Suite 200
New York, New York 10022   Don Mills, Ontario M3C 3N1

Library of Congress Cataloging-in-Publication Data

Kelly, Douglas.
    Medieval French romance / Douglas Kelly.
        p. cm. — (Twayne's world authors series ; TWAS 838. French literature)
    Includes bibliographical references and index.
    ISBN 0-8057-8282-6
    1. French literature—To 1500—History and criticism. 2. Romances—History and
criticism. I. Title. II. Series: Twayne's world authors series. TWAS 838. III. Series:
Twayne's world authors series. French literature.
PQ201.K46 1993
840.9'001-dc20   93-6760
                                                                            CIP

The paper used in this publication meets the minimum requirements of American
National Standard for Information Sciences—Permanence of Paper for Printed Library
Materials. ANSI Z3948-1984. ∞ ™

10 9 8 7 6 5 4 3 2 1

Printed in the United States of America

Contents

Abbreviations

Journals, series, and other collections cited more than once in notes or bibliography.

AA	Ausgaben und Abhandlungen aus dem Gebiete der romanischen Philologie (Marburg)
AB	Altfranzösische Bibliothek
AESC	*Annales: économies sociétés civilisations*
AL	*Arthurian Literature*
AnnUA	Annales Universitatis Aboensis
ANTS	Anglo-Norman Text Society
AR	*Archivum Romanicum*
ARB	Académie Royale de Langue et de Littérature Françaises de Belgique: Textes anciens
AS	Arthurian Studies
ATSL	Accademia Toscana di Scienze e Lettere "La Colombaria": Studi
AY	*Arthurian Yearbook*
BB	Biblioteca Bodmeriana: Textes
BBSIA	*Bulletin Bibliographique de la Société Internationale Arthurienne / Bibliographical Bulletin of the International Arthurian Society*
BDA	*Bien dire et bien aprandre*
BEHE	Bibliothèque de l'Ecole des Hautes Etudes
BFR	Bibliothèque Française et Romane
BibAR	Biblioteca dell'*"Archivum Romanicum"*. Ser. 1: Storia-letteratura-paleografia
BLVS	Bibliothek des litterarischen Vereins in Stuttgart
BRPM	Beiträge zur romanischen Philologie des Mittelalters
BUL	Bibliothèque de la Faculté de Philosophie et Lettres de l'Université de Liège

BXV	Bibliothèque du XVe siècle
BZRP	Beihefte zur *Zeitschrift für romanische Philologie*
CCM	*Cahiers de Civilisation Médiévale*
CFMA	Classiques français du moyen âge
CGFT	Critical Guides to French Texts
CN	*Cultura neolatina*
CSML	Cambridge Studies in Medieval Literature
DMTS	Davis Medieval Texts and Studies
ECAMML	Edward C. Armstrong Monographs on Medieval Literature
ECr	*L'esprit créateur*
Emon	Elliott Monographs (Princeton)
EurH	Europäische Hochschulschriften/Publications Universitaires Européennes/European University Studies
FauxT	Faux Titre
FMLS	*Forum for Modern Language Studies*
FrF	*French Forum*
FrFM	French Forum Monographs
GAG	Göppinger Arbeiten zur Germanistik
GLML	Garland Library of Medieval Literature
GRL	Gesellschaft für romanische Literatur
GRLH	Garland Reference Library of the Humanities
GRLMA	*Grundriß der romanischen Literaturen des Mittelalters*
HICL	Histoire des idées et critique littéraire
LCT	*Legacy of Chrétien de Troyes*
Lit	*Littérature*
M&H	*Medievalia et Humanistica*
MAE	*Medium Aevum*
MFra	*Le Moyen Français*
MHRADS	Modern Humanities Research Association Texts and Dissertations Series
MLov	Mediaevalia Lovaniensia

MLR	*Modern Language Review*
MP	*Modern Philology*
MPLL	University of Michigan Publications: Language and Literature
NBMA	Nouvelle Bibliothèque du Moyen Age
NLH	*New Literary History*
PAPS	Proceedings of the American Philological Society
PerM	*Perspectives médiévales*
PIFOU	Publications de l'Institut d'Etudes Françaises et Occitanes de l'Université d'Utrecht
PQ	*Philological Quarterly*
PRF	Publications romanes et françaises
PSFM	Università di Pisa: Studi di filologia moderna
PSTE	Publications de la Faculté de Lettres de l'Université de Strasbourg: Textes d'études
PUF	Presses Universitaires de France
RBC	Research Bibliographies and Checklists
RF	*Romanische Forschungen*
RH	Romanica Helvetica
RHL	*Revue d'histoire littéraire de la France*
RPh	*Romance Philology*
RR	*Romanic Review*
SATF	Société des Anciens Textes Français
SRUD	Studia Romanica Universitatis Debreceniensis ser. litteraria
TAPS	*Transactions of the American Philosophical Society*
TCFMA	Traductions en français moderne des Classiques français du moyen âge
TLF	Textes littéraires français
TrB	Travaux de la Faculté de Philosophie et Lettres de l'Université de Bruxelles
TSMO	Typologie des sources du moyen âge occidental
TWAS	Twayne's World Authors Series

UNCSRLL	North Carolina Studies in Romance Languages and Literatures
UPAL	Utrecht Publications in General and Comparative Literature
VMPG	Veröffentlichungen des Max-Planck-Instituts für Geschichte
VR	*Vox Romanica*
WB	Wissenschaftliche Buchgesellschaft
Wol	Brian Woledge, *Bibliographie des romans et nouvelles en prose française antérieurs à 1500*
YFS	*Yale French Studies*
ZRP	*Zeitschrift für romanische Philologie*

Preface

Medieval French Romance is an introduction to one of the major genres of the European Middle Ages. It contains a description of romance, including a history of romance as it emerged and evolved from the twelfth into the sixteenth century as well as a literary history of subgenres in rough chronological sequence. It also identifies the traditions that contributed to the emergence of romance in France: patronage, oral and written sources, medieval rhetoric and poetics, and medieval historiography. Finally, it treats a number of critical and scholarly issues in current critical studies of romance.

Although intended as an introduction to medieval French romance, this book treats many works that have been neglected in modern scholarship. The focus on twelfth-century Arthurian romance has declined lately in favor of a broader view of the genre from its beginnings into the Renaissance. But many romances still lie unopened on library shelves, and still others await modern editions. We shall understand romance better when not only the masterpieces but also the less-than-masterful specimens (by current tastes and standards) are known and evaluated. The latter are particularly promising objects for doctoral dissertations and studies by younger scholars.

I should like to especially thank Sandra Ihle and Norris Lacy for having read earlier drafts of this book. P. G. Holthaus did an admirable job as copy editor for Twayne by identifying and correcting all manner of inconsistencies and errors; for all his care and patience I am most grateful. I claim responsibility for all surviving errors and infelicities.

Chronology

Romance chronology can be only approximate and tentative. Moreover, because it is on occasion difficult to determine where a given romance ends and another begins, adaptations are listed together with the probable originals in approximate chronological sequence. Furthermore, some selection has been necessary, since there are over 200 extant titles dating from before 1500 that are commonly identified as romances.

Regarding medieval chronology, one should bear in mind two important caveats. First, the chronology of major authors, upon which most work has been done, is still very controversial.[1] Dates have often been assigned by a single scholar using dubious or outdated techniques and evidence. Second, even when the chronology, or at least the chronological sequence, can be established with some certainty, this is not sufficient evidence that the earlier author influenced the later one. Indeed, earlier literary fashions may survive in one place after others have been adopted elsewhere. For example, the *Roman d'Alexandre* attributed to Alexandre de Paris retains a style of versification closer to oral epic, whereas the earlier *Roman d'Eneas* evinces qualities of *conjointure* attributed to the masterpieces of Chrétien de Troyes.[2] Authors may not have known their predecessors, or they may have ignored them. Furthermore, new versions and interpolations may make a given manuscript quite different from others, as in the case of the *Perceval Continuations* or the different versions of the *Roman de Thèbes*.

• • • • •

Alexander the Great Romances

ca. 1110–30	Albéric de Pisançon, *Alexandre*
1155–1165	Eustache, *Fuerre de Gadres*
ca. 1160	*Alexandre décasyllabique*
1170–1180	Lambert le Tort, *Alexandre dodécasyllabique*
ca. 1180	Thomas of Kent, *Roman d'Alexandre anglo-norman*, or *Roman de toute chevalerie*
1180–1190	Alexandre de Paris (de Bernay), *Alexandre*
Interpolations:	
ca. 1180	Jehan le Nevelon, *Vengeance Alexandre*

ca. 1185–1190	Gui de Cambrai, *Vengement Alixandre*
before 1257	*Prise de Defur*
1270–1350	*Voyage d'Alixandre au paradis terrestre*
1312	Jacques de Longuyon, *Vœux du paon*
before 1327	Jean le Court, dit Brisebare, *Restor du paon*
1340	Jean de la Mote, *Parfait du paon*
13th–15th c.	Five prose versions, plus fragments of others

1135	*Lai d'Haveloc*
ca. 1140	Geffrey Gaimar, *Geste des Bretuns* (lost) and *Estoire des Engleis*

Floire et Blancheflor
ca. 1147–1160	"Aristocratic" version
ca. 1180–1200	"Popular" version

Thèbes
ca. 1150–1155	First version[3]
13th c.+	Six prose versions

Apollonius de Tyr
ca. 1150–1160	Verse version
13th–15th c.	Six prose versions

ca. 1150–1165	Robert Biket, *Le lai du cor*

Bruts
ca. 1150	Harley *Brut*
after 1150	Munich *Brut*
ca. 1155	Wace's *Brut*
early 13th c.	Anglo-Norman *Brut*
13th–15th c.	Prose *Bruts*

ca. 1155–1160	*Eneas*
no date	prosification, perhaps directly from *Aeneid*

Amadas et Ydoine
1160	Anglo-Norman
1190–1220	Continental
ca. 1160	*Lai de Narcisus*

Sept Sages de Rome
ca. 1160   Verse version
13th c.   *Prose Sept sages de Rome*
                          Sept sages Proper

      ca. 1225   Version L
      ca. 1230–1265   Version A
      13th c. end   Version M
      15th c.?   Version D
      1450–1500?   Version H
   1228–1250   *Marques de Rome*

   1250–1270   *Laurin*

   1270 ca.   *Cassidorus*

   ca. 1285–1289   *Helcanus et Peliarmenus*

   ca. 1290   *Kanor*

ca. 1160   Wace, *Rou*

Benoît de Sainte-Maure
ca. 1160–1165   *Troie*

                          Five distinct prose versions, all with subversions or
                          adaptations, with diverse dates
ca. 1170–1175   *Chronique des ducs de Normandie*

Chrétien de Troyes
1160–1165   *Philomena* (Chrétien li gois?)
ca. 1165–1170   *Erec et Enide*
   1450–1468   *Burgundian Prose Erec*
ca. 1170–1177   *Cligès*
   ca. 1454   *Burgundian Prose Alexandre et Cligès*
ca. 1174–1179   *Le Chevalier de la charrette* (*Lancelot*)
ca. 1175–1179   *Yvain* (*Le Chevalier au lion*)
   15th c.   *Prose Yvain* (See Pierre Sala, below, p. xxiii)
ca. 1179–1191   *Le Conte du graal* (*Perceval*)
   1530   *Perceval en prose* (combines prose versions of
                          Chrétien's *Conte du graal* and its continuations
                          and additions)

Gautier d'Arras

1160–1181	*Eracle*
1170–1184	*Ille et Galeron* (2 versions)

ca. 1165–1187	Beroul, *Tristan*
1169–1170 or ca. 1225	*Jaufre*
before 1170	*Tristrant* (lost French version of Eilhart von Oberg's *Tristrant*)
1170	*Piramus et Tisbé*
ca. 1170	Thomas, *Horn et Rimenhild*
ca. 1170–1175	Thomas d'Angleterre, *Tristan*
ca. 1170–1180	Marie de France, *Lais*
ca. 1172–1176	Chrétien (Chrétien de Troyes?), *Guillaume d'Angleterre*
late 13th–early 14th c.	*Dit de Guillaume d'Angleterre*

Hue de Rotelande

ca. 1180–85	*Ipomedon*
ca. 1185–90	*Protheselaus*

ca. 1182–85	*Partonopeu de Blois*
ca. 1185–95	Renaut de Beaujeu or Bagé, *Bel Inconnu*
1188	Aimon de Varennes, *Florimont*
15th c.	Four prose versions

ca. 1190–1230	Anonymous Lays: *Graelent, Guingamor, Desiré, Tydorel, Melion, Tyolet, Espine, Doon, Trot, Lecheor, Nabaret, Ignauré*

Perceval Continuations and Other Additions:
Pseudo-Wauchier, *First or Gauvain Continuation*

ca. 1190–1200	(short version)
1227–37	(long version)
13th c. (2nd half)	(mixed version)
ca. 1190–1200	Wauchier de Denain, *Second Continuation* (short and long versions)

1200–10	*Bliocadran*
1205–1215	*Elucidation*
ca. 1214–1235	Manessier, *Third Continuation*
ca. 1226–30	Gerbert de Montreuil, *Fourth Continuation*

Robert de Boron
Verse version

1191–1212	*L'Estoire dou graal* (*Joseph d'Arimathie, Merlin* fragment, Lost *Perceval?*)

Prose version

ca. 1210–30	*Livre du graal*, or Robert de Boron cycle (*Prose Joseph d'Arimathie*, or *Le petit saint graal*; Prose *Merlin*; *Didot-Perceval*, or *Perceval en prose*)
before 1194	*Lancelot* (lost French version of Ulrich von Zatzikhoven's *Lanzelet*)

Robert le diable

ca. 1195	Verse version
13th c. (end)	Prose version (in *Chronique de Normandie*)
14th c.	*Dit de Robert le diable*
15th c.	Prose version of *Dit de Robert le diable*
12th c. (end)	*Guillaume de Palerne*

Perlesvaus

1192–1211	First redaction
1212 ca. or 1225–30	Second redaction
ca. 1200	*Aucassin et Nicolete*
ca. 1200	*Folie Tristan de Berne* and *Folie Tristan d'Oxford*
13th c.	*Melior et Ydoine*
13th c.	*Merlin* (Occitan fragment)

Jean Renart

1200–1202	*L'Escoufle*
1217–22	*Lai de l'ombre*
ca. 1228	*Le Roman de la rose* or *Guillaume de Dole*

ca. 1215–25	*Lancelot Proper*
ca. 1220–25	*Queste del saint graal*
ca. 1225–30	*Mort le roi Artu*

Late redactions

15th c.	*Histoire du saint graal abrégée*
1516 & 1523	*Hystoire du saint graal* (contains the *Estoire*, *Perlesvaus*, and *Queste*)
16th c.	*Histoire de Lancelot du Lac* (abbreviated)

ca. 1215–20	*Durmart le Galois*
ca. 1215–27	*Florence de Rome* (two redactions)
ca. 1227–30	Gerbert de Montreuil, *Violette*
ca. 1435–64	*Prose Gerard de Nevers*
1230	Renaut, *Galeran de Bretagne*

Roman de la rose

ca. 1230	Guillaume de Lorris
after 1230	Anonymous 60-line conclusion
1290–1300	Gui de Mori: first adaptation[6]
ca. 1270–80	Jean de Meun
1300–10	Gui de Mori: second adaptation
15th c. (end)	*Prose Roman de la rose*
before 1500	Jean Molinet, *Roman de la rose moralisé*
ca. 1230–1250	*Chevalier aus deus espees* or *Meriadeuc*

Prose Tristan

ca. 1230	Luce del Gat, *Tristan en prose* (first version)
ca. 1240–1250	Helie de Bron, *Tristan en prose* (second version)
late 13th–early 14th c.	*Alexandre l'Orphelin* (interpolation)
ca. 1350	*Ysaÿe le Triste*

ca. 1230–1240	*Roman du graal* Post-Vulgate[7]
	Estoire de Merlin and *La Suite de Merlin*
	Folie Lancelot

Balain

Queste del saint graal Post-Vulgate

Mort Artu Post-Vulgate

1232–1242   *Gui de Warewick*

14th c. (beginning) *Prose Gui de Warwick*, by Walter of Exeter?

15th c.   Anonymous *Gui de Warwick*

1234   Huon de Mery, *Tornoiement Antechrist*

1235–1240   *Comte de Poitiers*

1235–1240   *Guiron le courtois* or *Palamède*

1235–1240   *Livre d'Artus*

ca. 1241   Huon le roi, *Vair palefroi*

ca. 1250   *Atre périlleux*

ca. 1250   *Floriant et Florete*

15th c.   *Prose Floriant et Florete*, or *Le Chevalier qui la nef maine*

ca. 1250   *Gautier d'Aupais*

ca. 1250   *Hunbaut*

ca. 1250   Jehan, *Merveilles de Rigomer*

ca. 1250   *Le roi Flore et la belle Jehanne*

ca. 1250   Thibaut, *Roman de la poire*

Robert de Blois

ca. 1250   *Beaudous*

ca. 1250   *Floris et Liriopé*

1250–1260   *Sone de Nausay*

13th c. (3rd quarter) Requis, *Richart le beau*

ca. 1250–1270   *Joufroi de Poitiers*

ca. 1250–1275   *La belle Hélène de Constantinople*

before 1448   Jean Wauquelin, *La belle Hélène de Constantinople* (first version)

1448   Jean Wauquelin, *La belle Hélène de Constantinople* (second version)

ca. 1250–1290   *L'empereur Constant*
1256–1264   *Verse Fouke Fitz Waren* (lost)
    early 14th c.   *Prose Fouke Fitz Waren*
1258   Alexandre du Pont, *Mahomet*
1260–1280   *Abladane*
before 1268   *Cristal et Clarie*
before 1268   *Reinbert*
1268   *Claris et Laris*
1270   *Tournoiement aus dames*
1270–1280   Heldris de Cornüälle, *Silence*

Philippe de Remi, sire de Beaumanoir
1270–1279   *La Manekine*
    15th c. (middle)   Jean Wauquelin, *Prose Manekine*
1274–1279   *Jehan et Blonde*

1270–1280   *Flamenca*
1270–1292   Pierre Gencien, *Tournoiement des dames de Paris*
1271–1288   *Châtelaine de Vergi*
    end 14th–early 15th c.   *Prose Châtelaine de Vergi*
1272–1298   Rusticien de Pise, *Le roi Artus* (compilation)
1276–1312   *Artus de Bretagne* (*Artus de la Petite Bretagne* or *Artus le Restoré*)
1278   Sarrasin, *Hem*

Girart d'Amiens
ca. 1280   *Escanor*
1285–1291   *Meliacin* or *Le cheval de fust*

1285   Jacques Bretel, *Tournoi de Chauvency*
ca. 1285   Jakamés, *Le châtelain de Couci et la dame de Fayel*
    before 1469   *Prose Châtelain de Couci*
1285–1290   Adenet le Roi, *Cleomadés*
    1430–1460   Philippe Camus, *Prose Cleomadés* (abridgement)

Antoine de la Sale
1442   *Paradis de la reine Sibylle*
1456   *Jehan de Saintré*

1447–1448   Perrinet de Pin, *Philippe de Madien*
ca. 1450   *Gillion de Trazegnies*
15th c. (2nd half)   *Nouvelles de Sens*
15th c. (3rd quarter) *Rambaux de Frise*
1450–1470   *L'Abusé en court*
1453–1467   *Le Comte d'Artois*
1454–1456   Philippe Camus, *Olivier de Castille et Artus d'Algarbe* (see also under Adenet le Roi p. xxi)
by 1456   Rasse de Brunhamel, *Floridan et Elvide*
1456   *Sires* (or *Seigneurs*) *de Gavres*[8]
1456–1467   *Cent nouvelles nouvelles*
1457   René d'Anjou, *Livre du cuer d'amours espris*

Raoul Lefevre
ca. 1460   *Histoire de Jason*
ca. 1464   *Recueil des histoires de Troyes* (revisions after 1467)

ca. 1460   Sebastian Mamerot, *Histoire des neuf preux et des neuf preues* (various versions)
ca. 1460   *Teseide*
1465–1468   *Jehan d'Avennes* [9]
1470   Michot Gonnot's Arthurian compilation
1494–1495   *Jehan de Paris*
late 15th   Symphorien Champier, *Palanus*
–early 16th c.

Pierre Sala
15th c. (late)   *Chevalier au lion*
16th c. (early)   *Tristan*

16th c.?   *Trois fils de rois* (attributed to David Aubert)
16th c. (early)   Claude Platin, *Giglan fils de Gauvain et Geoffroy de Maïance*
ca. 1540   Nicolas de Herberey, *Amadis de Gaule*

Introduction

In the eleventh and twelfth centuries the word *romanz,*[1] a plural noun, designated the French language as distinguished from Latin. The word also referred to any work written in French. For example, in 1155 Wace called his *Brut* "cist romanz"[2] (work in French); after Thomas à Becket's death in 1170, Guernes de Pont-Sainte-Maxence lauded his *Vie de Saint Thomas Becket* in these terms: "Ainc mais si bons romanz ne fu faiz ne trovez"[3] (never was such a good work made or invented in the French language).

Chrétien de Troyes, it seems, was the first to use *roman* in the special sense of "romance" or *roman médiéval*. In *Cligés* he still uses it in the sense of language: "Ce est Cligés an cui mimoire/Fu mis en romans ceste estoire" (ll. 2345–46)[4] (this is Cligés in whose memory this story was put into French). But in his next romance, the *Chevalier de la charrette*, the more nearly generic sense "romance" emerges in the first lines: "Puis que ma dame de Chanpaigne/vialt que romans a feire anpraigne"[5] (Since my lady of Champagne wants me to undertake to write a romance). *Roman* comes to mean almost exclusively "romance."

However, Chrétien may have intended an even more specific sense for *roman* than the modern English word implies. In the prologue to *Erec et Enide* he distinguishes his version of Erec's story—his "molt bele conjointure"[6]—from those told by other storytellers. His version is superior to others, he asserts, because other versions are dismembered and incomplete whereas his version of the story is whole and complete. Toward the end of the twelfth century Renaut de Beaujeu adapted Chrétien's words, replacing *conjointure* with *roman*: "veul un roumant estraire/D'un molt biel conte d'aventure"[7] (I wish to extract a romance from a very beautiful tale of adventure). It would appear that romance as a genre is remarkable for the quality of its combination of diverse materials.[8]

Chrétien also refers to the meaning or signification of a romance's *conjointure*. In the *Erec* prologue he says that an author is obliged to put what he knows ("s'escience," *Erec* l. 20) into writing. Marie de France makes a similar claim in the prologue to her *Lais* (ll. 1–8).[9] Moreover, in the *Charrette* prologue Chrétien claims that his romance expresses the *san*, or meaning, of the story as he received it from his patroness Marie de Champagne (ll. 26–27). The audience should be able to elicit that meaning from the story he tells. The romance plot will therefore have to be construed in such a way that its meaning will be readily perceptible to its audiences. It follows, therefore, that a well-written romance narrative will elegantly combine diverse elements so as to convey a significant meaning to its audiences.

Chapter 1
Emergence and Evolution

Medieval romance can be traced from its emergence in the twelfth century to its final absorption in the late medieval *dit*, a combination of vision and treatise,[1] and the novella, a precursor of the classical novel.[2] We may schematize the evolution by different names that, in chronological succession, designate the romance writer and his (or occasionally her) art: *jongleur*, *clerc*, *scribe*, *trouvère*, and *poète*. These titles fit certain chronologiocal periods and kinds of romances.

The twelfth-century *jongleur* was an oral performer.[3] The performance was based on memory and improvisation. To be sure, nothing remains of oral improvisations except some documentary references. The closest French examples are early epic (*chanson de geste*). Memories of bygone names, places, and events provided the *jongleurs'* raw material. By an art of improvisation they conjoined these remembered pieces into narrative units, or "blocks," based on commonplace motifs like battle, counsel, festivity, and the like.[4] Epic was composed in verse. Other stories were transmitted in prose, especially those based on Celtic or Arthurian material. These features of oral composition are perceptible in a few early romances still close to the oral tradition in style, notably Beroul's *Tristan*, *Aucassin et Nicolete*, and the earliest version of the *Gauvain* or *First Perceval Continuation*.

The *clerc* as romancer appears after 1150 in the works of literate, educated authors such as Chrétien de Troyes, Benoît de Sainte-Maure, Marie de France, and Thomas d'Angleterre. Unlike *jongleurs*, clerical authors applied a sophisticated art of composition they had learned in medieval schools to the composition of vernacular narratives. Their romances tend to elaborate sources so as to illustrate a general idea or principle that provides a context for a narrative drawn from diverse sources. Their works made audiences aware of *roman* as a distinct genre. The clerical tradition in romance underwent a striking development in the thirteenth century, when scribes rewrote earlier verse romances as prose romances, often infusing them with Christian morality. Prose romances are usually much longer than verse romances, for they acquired additions, multiple plots, and cyclical increments as they circulated and were copied.

1

While prose romance was emerging early in the thirteenth century, verse romance was accommodated to the secular, lyric tradition of the troubadours and the *trouvères* either by elaborating on a common folktale plot with inserted lyric poems or by allegorical redefinition of the lyric contents in exemplary dream or dreamlike narratives by poètes. The protagonists themselves sometimes appear as *trouvères*, authors, or performers.

Romance continued to thrive in the fourteenth and fifteenth centuries, especially in the form of prose romances that scribes not only copied, but also added to and rearranged. There was a tendency, later abetted by the emergence of printing and the importation of the novella, to return to shorter narrative. This permitted the emergence of the novel.

Protoromance

Several kinds of vernacular writing contributed to the emergence of romance up to and during the time Chrétien de Troyes flourished. *Roman* as romance is preceded by protoromance.[5] There are three varieties: vernacular chronicles and hagiography, antique romances based on Latin sources, and narrative lays.

Vernacular Chronicles and Hagiography

Several historical works written in French before and during the time romance was emerging influenced its development. These included chronicles on British (that is, pre–Anglo-Saxon) and English history and saints' lives. Geoffrey of Monmouth's Latin *History of the Kings of Britain* became an important source for vernacular histories. Its chronicle of British kings extended from the days of Troy to those of King Arthur.[6]

Geffrey Gaimar's *Engleis*, originally a history of the British and English nations, is the earliest extant French chronicle. Only the part on the English kings survives today. It purportedly began with the Trojan War, relating the stories of those who, like Aeneas in Vergil's epic, escaped the destruction of Troy and founded new nations in western Europe. Remarks by Gaimar in the extant partial text indicate that the chronicle began with Jason's Argonautic expedition, an episode of which caused the Trojan War, then followed the flight of some Trojans to the West, probably including the adventures of Brutus as related by Geoffrey of Monmouth, and continued down to King Arthur, the destruction of his kingdom, and the Anglo-Saxon invasion. This lost part—the so-called *Geste des Bretuns*—was followed by the surviving second part, the *Geste* or

Estoire des Engleis. This part relates the history of the English nation until the reign of Henry I Beauclerc in the early twelfth century.

Gaimar's *Engleis* may not have been widely known or influential. But some of its features suggest new tastes, tastes that anticipate later twelfth-century romance. First, the marvelous is important, as in most medieval historiography. The marvelous embraces a wider range of phenomena than in modern French and English, owing principally to the fact that medieval notions of cause and effect often differed radically from our scientific understanding. Much occurs by chance or by fortune, without apparent reason or rationale. The Havelok episode in Gaimar's *Engleis* illustrates this characteristic.[7] Havelok reveals his royal nature when a beam of light issues from his mouth. (This episode also survives as an anonymous narrative lay.[8]) Second, Gaimar says chronicles should record not only military and dynastic events, but other aspects of chivalric civilization like love and sport (*Engleis*, ll. 6505–11).[9]

Another chronicler is Wace. His *Brut* is based almost exclusively on Geoffrey of Monmouth's *History*. His unfinished *Rou* is about the Norman nation from the time of Rou (Rollo, the Danish invader of Normandy) to its conquest of the British Isles. Benoît de Sainte-Maure, who also wrote the *Roman de Troie* on the Trojan War, undertook again to write the history of the Norman people from its beginnings in his *Chronique des ducs de Normandie*. It too is incomplete. It recounts in chronological sequence the history of the Norman rulers from their alleged Trojan origins. All chronicles focus on the adventures and marvels that make up the careers of consecutive individual rulers. In doing so they approach the biographical form typical of hagiography.

Wace wrote several saint's lives, the most notable of which is his *Sainte-Marguerite*. Other examples from the period include the anonymous *Saint Brendan*, a vernacular adaptation of a Latin tale about a sea voyage to Purgatory; the *Espurgatoire Saint Patrice*, attributed to Marie de France, which relates a knight's descent into Purgatory; and Guerne de Pont-Sainte-Maxence's *Thomas Becket*, which relates the life and martyrdom of Thomas à Becket. The saint's life is usually construed as Christlike; accordingly, the events modeled on his life include commitment to chastity, suffering, and martyrdom. However, the life of the saint is rarely imitable by laypersons, especially the nobility and the rising class of horseman or knights (*chevaliers*), the principal character types in medieval romance.

The heroes of chronicle perform marvels rather than miracles during adventures of war and intrigue, marvels that demonstrate noble qualities like prowess, magnanimity, and other commonplace features of the ideal ruler and knight. The historical works thus anticipate romance by combining an extraordinary narrative with exemplary personages who illustrate the tastes and ideals of the anticipated audience. In particular, the chronicles served as literary propaganda for the English Crown.

Chronicles bequeathed two narrative models to romance. Construing history as a sequence of marvelous adventures, they either related the dynastic succession of rulers, and within each reign a series of marvelous adventures—usually conquests—that constitute the ruler's biography; or they focused on a single ruler and, as in the saint's life, provided a biography emphasizing his or her virtues or vices. These kinds of history anticipated three kinds of romance: classical verse romance as the story of a major episode—a single *aventure merveilleuse*—in one knight's life; ancestral romance as a chain of romances relating in succession the story of a family; and, finally, cyclic romance as a vast panorama of adventures of large, even universal historical scope.

Two narrative subjects require special mention: Trojan origins and Arthur and the Round Table. Wace and perhaps Gaimar were influential in bringing Arthurian legend into vernacular history and literature by their adaptations into French verse of Geoffrey of Monmouth's *History*. As far as is known today, Wace was the first author to mention the Round Table (*Brut,* ll. 9747–60)[10]; Geoffrey of Monmouth does not mention it. Yet Wace says he had heard many tales about the Round Table and Arthur. Since Geoffrey did not include them, Wace rejected them as being too fabulous for his "history" (*Brut,* ll. 9788–98); indeed, he claims to have tried and failed to substantiate Arthurian marvels at the fountain of Barenton in the Breton forest of Brocéliande, the magic fountain in Chrétien's *Yvain*.[11] Wace required eyewitness confirmation.

Wace's *Brut* is a work that straddles the border between chronicle and romance. Like Geoffrey of Monmouth, his source, Wace relates, in chronological succession, the history of British kings, from Brutus ("Brut" in French) to the overthrow of the dynasty during the reign of Cadwallader, the last ruler after Arthur's death. The long Arthurian segment, beginning with the history of Uterpendragon, Arthur's father, and Merlin, and concluding with Arthur's war with Mordred, is the epoch of the Matter of Britain in later Arthurian romances. But the extensive Romano-Trojan beginnings as well as the adaptation from Latin into French relates the *Brut* to the antique romances. It remains chronicle by virtue of its link to the *Rou,* which is a kind of Anglo-Norman continuation of Trojan history, but with the intervening "English" history of Britain left out.

The Arthurian segment of the *Brut* relates the birth of Arthur after Uterpendragon falls in love with Ygerne, the wife of Gorlois, duke of Cornwall. Disguised as her husband by Merlin's aid, Uter succeeds in making love to her, as a result of which Arthur is conceived. The story of Arthur's wars in the north of the island and his European conquests established the Arthurian legend in French romance. The scheme is completed in the great war with Rome. Victory over the Romans in Gaul and a proposed march on Rome by Arthur's armies is cut short by Mordred's revolt. Left to guard Britain while Arthur was on the Continent, Mordred formed a liaison with Guenevere, Arthur's wife, and seized power. Arthur returns and in a great battle kills Mordred. Severely wounded himself, Arthur disappears, establishing the legend that he did not die, but would some day return to reclaim the throne and champion the British peoples again (*Brut*, ll. 13275–93).

Wace makes several allusions to tales he had heard concerning the Round Table, "Dunt Bretun dient mainte fable" (*Brut*, l. 9752) (about which the Britons relate many stories). He names major knights of the Round Table, including Gawain and Kay. Wace also knew numerous other tales probably related by *jongleurs*, but he refused to report them (*Brut*, ll. 9795–98). Wace set their stories in the time of a great *pax arthuriana*, just before the Roman wars, when Arthur peacefully ruled over a European empire (*Brut*, ll. 9731–34). A later scribe inserted precisely at this point the corpus of Chrétien de Troyes's Arthurian romances to suggest how peacetime was spent.[12]

Finally, Wace followed Geoffrey of Monmouth as well as Gaimar by indicating that love and prowess in arms are mutually beneficial: a knight must prove himself in tournaments three times before winning a lady's love (*Brut*, ll. 10493–520). When the Roman wars begin in Geoffrey, Cador, one of Arthur's vassals, expresses satisfaction that war has returned, since, he says, peace is debilitating for good knights. In Wace, Gawain, Arthur's nephew, counters this idea, stressing the values of peace for courtly society and for chivalry (*Brut*, ll. 10767–72). Following Gaimar's lead, Wace foreshadows the ethos of twelfth- and early thirteenth-century verse romance.

Subsequent works in this tradition also retain Geoffrey's chronicle form. The anonymous Harley, Munich, and Anglo-Norman versions of *Brut* are independent of Wace. It has been suggested that one or the other represents part of Gaimar's lost *Geste des Bretuns*, but there is no convincing evidence for this supposition. All are fragments.

The Antique Romances (*romans d'antiquité*)

The link with the Arthurian legend in Geoffrey and his French-language adapters established the legitimacy of the British Crown, a legitimacy subsequently claimed by their English successors—most notably Henry II, for whom Wace wrote—by right of conquest and the transmission of empire from one people to another (*translatio imperii*). Legitimacy is the foundation for Jehan Bodel's distinctions among the three *matières* (matters, or subject areas) of Britain, Rome, and France on dynastic precedence. Both antique romances and vernacular chronicles foster a worldview based on dynasty and dominion.

The so-called *romans d'antiquité* begin with two anonymous works: the earliest version of the *Roman de Thèbes* and the *Roman d'Eneas*, adaptations of Latin epics written by Statius and Vergil, respectively. Benoît de Sainte Maure's *Roman de Troie* amplifies the brief prose pseudohistories attributed to Dares and Dictys, which the Middle Ages took to be eyewitness reports of the Trojan War. The Alexander cycle emerges even earlier in the twelfth century in the version of Albéric de Pisançon; through various adaptations it expands into the dodecasyllabic *Roman d'Alexandre*, a lengthy cyclic romance in rhyming alexandrine *laisses* written by Alexandre de Paris (or de Bernay). Adaptations of Ovidian and pseudo-Ovidian sources also appear, notably the anonymous *Pirame et Tisbé* and *Narcisus* as well as *Philomena*, which was probably written by Chrétien de Troyes. The subject of antique romances is love and martial prowess, with more emphasis placed on combat than on love except in the Ovidian adaptations.

The most ambitious undertaking among romances based on ancient matter is the cycle of works devoted to Alexander the Great. The fragment by Albéric de Pisançon was subsequently adapted, added to, and modernized in versification, content, and ethos. Although the sequence of works that fit the modern title *Roman d'Alexandre* is not certain, a rough outline can be constructed based on what has survived.[13] Circa 1136–37, when Geoffrey of Monmouth wrote his *Historia*, Albéric de Pisançon had already written an *Alexandre* in octosyllabic, eight-line rhyming stanzas. It survives as a fragment today either because the last part is lost or because it was never completed.[14] An imitation made about 1160, cast in rhymed *laisses* of 10-syllable lines, focuses on Alexander's youthful exploits. Later, about 1170, Lambert le Tort de

Châteaudun continued the story to Alexander's death in dodecasyllabic or "alexandrine" *laisses*. His version related the entire career of Alexander from birth to death.

Lambert's version does not survive intact: what remains of it was interpolated into later versions. The final development came after 1180, when Alexandre de Paris (or de Bernay) wrote a complete *Roman d'Alexandre* by combining and reworking these antecedents. Later adaptations and additions were made to include accounts of Alexander's trip to Paradise and the three *Paon* (Peacock) additions in the fourteenth century.

Alexandre de Paris's *Alexandre* is later than the earliest versions of the other antique romances. But in many ways it is closer to the *chanson de geste* than they are. It is written in monorhymed *laisses* and stresses knightly prowess far more than love; it also evinces fascination for the marvelous, notably the marvels encountered by Alexander during his invasion of India. In addition, certain interpolations introduce the themes of destiny and immoderation, common in all antique romances, as Alexander searches out the secrets of nature undersea, in the sky, and at the gates of Paradise. His downfall comes from exceeding human limitations, first, by trying to know too much, and, second, by elevating serfs to positions of responsibility.

Thomas of Kent wrote an Anglo-Norman *Roman d'Alexandre*, also known as the *Roman de toute chevalerie*. Although nearly contemporary with Alexandre de Paris's version, it is an independent romance. Nonetheless, like its continental analogue, it is written in rhyming alexandrine *laisses*. Its almost 8000 lines describe at length the marvels Alexander encounters during his march into India. Although the romance corroborates the view that the "alexandrine" or dodecasyllabic line was early associated with Alexander romances, the peculiarities of Anglo-Norman versification and the apparent failure of Thomas of Kent's version to cross to the Continent before the thirteenth century make it an unlikely candidate for being the origin of the French alexandrine. An expanded 12,000-line version written in the thirteenth century interpolated extracts from the continental *Roman d'Alexandre*.

The romances about Alexander the Great constitute one of the great romance cycles. They illustrate human decline from optimism and glory to immoderation and destruction. Alexander's auspiciously marvelous birth and early accomplishments even inspired Albéric de Pisançon to question Solomon's "Vanity of vanities, all is vanity": "Solaz nos faz' antiquitas / Que tot non sie vanitas" [15] (May antiquity console us in the fact that not all is vanity). Alexander the Great was to provide that consolation. Yet the vanity of human greatness and pride came to the fore in succeeding adaptations in which Alexander, greedy for land, power, and knowledge, not only invaded the whole world but also stormed the skies, Hell, and Paradise. Alexander's early death brings his career and empire to nothing in both Alexandre de Paris and Thomas of Kent.

Alexander was a warrior, but he was also a cleric because of the exemplary education Aristotle gave him. Love plays a very minor role in the romances about him. Alexander had too many worlds to conquer to have time for love or romance. This is not so in the earlier antique romances, where prowess and love are reciprocal and mutually beneficial, as in Wace's *Brut*. But, although love serves a civilization where women as arbiters of achievement and reward replace God or the feudal lord, such idealism is evident in the antique romances only when knighthood serves chivalry that is itself at the service of a dynasty.

The so-called Classical trilogy designates the major antique romances: the *Roman de Thèbes*, the *Roman d'Eneas*, and Benoît de Sainte-Maure's *Roman de Troie*. Each of these protoromances begins with a castoff: Œdipe in *Thèbes* because of the prophecy of his incest and patricide, Eneas in *Eneas* after the Greek destruction of Troy, and Jason in *Troie*, whose uncle sends him in search of the Golden Fleece out of envy and fear that he might seize the throne. Each also develops love themes in the narrative. The incest of Œdipe and Jocaste prefigures the deadly war between their sons Etiocle and Polynice after their father's curse; each son, like other knights, has a love—sometimes across lines of combat, like Antigone and Partonopé in the *Thèbes*. Paris's reward in the Judgment of Paris at the beginning of *Eneas* leads to the abduction of Helen, the Trojan War, and Eneas' life as an outcast; the work relates Eneas' arrival at Carthage, his affair with Dido, the voyage to Latium, and the war for the land and love of Lavine. *Troie* concludes with the scattering of the Greeks, the difficult return of the conquerors after the war, and the deaths of Agamemnon and Ulysse.

The result in all cases is the passage of empire (*translatio imperii*) from one nation to another, in effect re-creating a lost homeland: to Athens in *Thèbes*, to Rome in *Eneas*, and, by anticipation, to the Trojan colonies of Eneas and Antenor in *Troie*. Wace's *Brut* fits into this scheme, anticipating by the Trojan settlement in Britain the British nation and the eventual succession of the English nation recounted in Gaimar's *Engleis*, Wace's *Rou*, and Benoît's *Chronique*.

Love is an impulse to and a source of chivalric worth in Geoffrey of Monmouth and the *Brut*. In *Thèbes* it is a potential corrective to fratricidal conflict. But the passions of Antigone and Partonopé, Ismène and Athon, and Salamandre and Eteocle do not prevent disaster. Œdipe's curse works itself out in the deaths of all these knights. Love is no more beneficial in *Troie*. It is a passionate source of discord in the episodes describing Paris's abduction of Helen and the love of Achille for Polyxène. In the last analysis, Benoît, who expresses misogynist prejudices in his representation of woman,[16] simply causes women to pass more or less willingly from one camp to the other, as with Medea, Helen, and Briseida, or abandons them to concubinage or death, as happens to Hesione, Polyxène, and other Trojan wives and daughters. Destiny is stronger than any kind of love in the somber world of the antique romances.

Each antique romance in the trilogy emphasizes the notion of "destiny" (Schöning, *Thebenroman*, 317–31). Destiny is the fate of a civilization or a dynasty worked out through conflict among nations or peoples, but impelled by obscure forces—pagan gods who are not credible in the Christian worldview professed by all the authors, but nonetheless effective in deciding the fate of nations. The will of the gods, whether a curse or a command, transfers empire from one people to another. When men acquiesce in their destiny, they succeed in finding love and empire, as in *Eneas*; when they resist or violate the will of the gods, they destroy such hopes, as in *Thèbes* and *Troie*. Empire passes ultimately from East to West. The war between the armies of Argos and Thebes destroys both in *Thèbes*, as does that between Greeks and Trojans in *Troie*. The destruction of Troy permits Eneas to found Rome after the defeat of Turnus in *Eneas*, and Brutus to found Britain in *Brut*, which we must include here as well. The Trojan destiny passes to the English after the overthrow of Cadwallader, and thence to the Normans and Angevins in the vernacular chronicles.

Eneas goes furthest toward the realization of romance as Chrétien de Troyes will write it. The anonymous author has rearranged and reworked Vergil and other sources to such an extent that it is possible to speak not of the chroniclelike sequence characteristic of the other antique romances, but of the *conjointure* common to twelfth-century verse romances (Petit, *Naissances*, 483–98). Dido is a victim of destiny. But in a lengthy amplification—one-third of the work—the love of Eneas and Lavine is consummated happily because their marriage serves the ends of destiny. However, the composite picture of these works—antique romances, the various versions of *Brut*, and chronicles—in explicit and implicit intertextual references, bears witness not only to textual, but also to historical worldviews. This corresponds to manuscript reality. Chronicles and antique romances were often bound together and even explicitly connected by some scribes. Moreover, they figure as interpolations like the *Troie* in a vernacularization of the Bible (see *Troie*, vol. 4, p. 435, and vol. 6, pp. 34–40).

Narrative lays

Lay is a term used rather loosely to designate a number of real and hypothetical texts in medieval literature.[17] In the twelfth century the authors of narrative lays refer to compositions in music played on the harp, viol, and other instruments by Breton and British musicians; they also refer to presumed actual events —"adventures"—the memory of which the lays keep alive. It is not clear whether such adventures were told to the accompaniment of music or whether the lays served to explain the adventures the music recalled, as in program music. In any case the story was turned into verse narrative in French lays.

Marie de France is the best-known author of lays. However, a number of anonymous lays survive together with a number of analogous shorter works: Ovidian adaptations such as *Philomena*, *Floire et Blancheflor*, the *Folie Tristan de Berne*, and the *Folie Tristan d'Oxford*.

The lay is a short narrative work. It usually employs "Briton" or Celtic material as story matter and shares with romance a common basic structure.[18] A marvelous adventure draws a hero or heroine to an encounter. Usually love plays a central role in the encounter, which may turn out well or ill. Most narrative lays recount the love of a male mortal for a beautiful woman, occasionally identified as a fay, encountered in the woods, beyond a river, or in some analogous otherworld setting away from court. For example, in Marie's "Lanval" a disconsolate knight wonders into the woods where he meets a beautiful woman who gives him her love and showers him with gifts. Similar schemes are found in analogues to "Lanval" like the anonymous *Graelent*, *Guingamor*, and *Désiré*. The lay may also relate the appearance of an otherworldly being in a conventional setting, as in "Yonec," where a splendid hawk responds to a lady's wish for a lover, transforms himself into a human and a Christian, and grants the lady her desire. *Tydorel* is an anonymous analogue.

Other lays evince no clear otherworld features. Marie's "Chaitivel" merely recounts the disastrous failure of a tournament as a love test; her "Deux amants" concerns a hero who refuses supernatural assistance in a test for love and consequently fails; and "Equitan" relates the disastrous results of adultery and betrayal. Still other lays move toward the farce, scatology, or misogyny of the fabliau, as in the *Lecheor*, various lays *Du con*, and chastity-test lays like the *Cor* or the *Mantel*. The more marvelous the adventure related, the more likely the conclusion is to be idealized as a happy ending.

Marie seeks in her lays to extract hidden meaning (*surplus de sen*) that glosses the adventure with a contemporary "French" meaning or context.[19] For example, in "Yonec" the hawk that metamorphoses into a handsome knight in response to the lady's wish for a lover is Christian and loves with what we might call a courtly love. He lives in a world beyond a kind of tumulus reminiscent of Celtic burial mounds, but otherwise his world seems in no way different in kind from the lady's world: its castle and walled city have a French shape, sheen, and rationale.

Nonetheless, Marie de France, like the "Ancients" she imitates, leaves some obscurities of her own: there is no rational explanation of the metamorphosis in "Yonec" or of the Avalon Lanval goes to at the end of his lay. Not that Marie could not provide explanations of marvelous adventures when she wanted to: the message-bearing swan in "Milun" moves between the lover and his lady impelled by hunger and a homing instinct. Did Marie emulate the "Ancients" by providing or retaining some marvelous mystery as part of the aesthetic of the lays? Or did she invite her readers or adaptors to contribute their own understanding of her marvelous lays?

Lays are usually called "Breton lays" today. Other kinds existed, but they emerged only in the thirteenth century. Shorter narratives like *Pyrame et Tisbé*, *Narcisse*, and *Philomena* sprang from the Latin tradition on which the antique romances drew. Marie herself may have been thinking of them when she alluded to the popularity of works based on Latin sources (*Lais*, "Prologue," ll. 28–32). They resemble lays in their relative brevity and in their focus on a single dramatic or tragic adventure. Marie's "Deux amants" suggests the drama of *Pyrame et Tisbé*, Guigemar's initial disinterest in love makes him a brother of Narcissus, and *Philomena* is a crueler mirror of the violence in "Equitan" and "Laüstic."

Other kinds of short narrative poems—whether we designate them lay or romance—belong to a phase in which the shorter narrative lay is in transition to lengthier romance. *Floire et Blancheflor*, for example, survives both in an "aristocratic" version and in a "popular" version, the latter in only one manuscript. The aristocratic version offers some variety among its four surviving manuscripts, including an "insular" version in one fragment and a "continental" version in three rather disparate manuscripts.

The "popular" version was probably written after the "aristocratic" one. It is closer to the anonymous lay in its paratactic combination of narrative parts. It contains the basic plot of the legend: the idyllic love of two children that blossoms into sexual, romantic, and, finally, conjugal love, as in the anonymous Breton *Lai de l'espine*. The two children are conceived and born at the same time. Floire is the son of a pagan, whereas Blancheflor is born a Christian; Floire becomes a Christian upon his marriage to Blancheflor at the end of the work.

The "aristocratic" text evinces clerical influence much like the antique romances. The Christian family of Blancheflor belongs to the lineage of Charlemagne and his mother, Berte au grand pied. The anonymous author says he heard two damsels telling the story to one another after they read it in a book. The typical length of a lay is 1000 lines or less, but this version of *Floire* expanded into a near-romance of over 3000 lines. The variety of sources that contribute to the aristocratic *Floire* makes it another early example of a narrative *conjointure* like that found in Chrétien de Troyes.

Floire illustrates the motif of the Handsome or Beautiful Pagan who, for love, converts to Christianity. The miraculous circumstances earlier associated with the birth of saints and heroes (for example, Alexander, Paris, and Œdipe) here prefigure a marvelous constancy and even security in the face of threats to fidelity.[20] Separated by his parents from Blancheflor, who is sold into slavery, and, finally, the sultan's harem, Floire succeeds nonetheless in finding and joining her there disguised as a woman. The sultan discovers them, but moved by their tender affection he pardons them and unites them in marriage. The fortuitous death of Floire's father leaves him the throne, to which he returns with his wife and, after Floire converts, the two live happily ever after. The happy ending is a tribute to constancy's triumph over misfortune.

Another specimen in the transition from lay to romance is Gautier d'Arras's *Ille et Galeron*. It survives in two manuscripts; like *Floire*, the manuscripts are different in length. *Ille* preserves in both manuscripts explicit connections with the lay. The author actually calls this work a lay,[21] although both versions contain more than 6000 lines. The plot is analogous to that in Marie de France's "Eliduc": both describe a man with two wives who is unable or unwilling to remain with his first wife. Lays differ little from romances other than in length, since romances also relate marvelous adventures that are significant for the context or ethos of the work. But Gautier rejects the dreamlike quality characteristic of lays in favor of a kind of exemplary realism (*Ille*, ll. 931–36). Marie de France thought that lays could yield a credible truth by skillful glossing of the narrative; Gautier claims as much for his "lay," *Ille et Galeron*. Short lays were later combined to make the composite *conjointures* of verse and prose romance. *Ille et Galeron* thus illustrates a transitional stage in the transformation of lay into romance.

Chapter 2
Twelfth-Century Verse Romance

The major achievement of twelfth-century French literature is verse romance, especially romance that treats Arthurian subjects or the Matter of Britain (*matière de Bretagne*). These romances establish *roman* as a designation for "romance." Almost all use the octosyllabic rhymed couplet.

The Tristan Romances

There are two main kinds of Tristan romances: the common redaction (*version commune*), illustrated by Beroul, and the courtly redaction (*version courtoise*), illustrated by Thomas d'Angleterre.[1] There are also some episodic versions in lay form, like the *Folie Tristan de Berne*, which stems from the Beroul tradition, and the *Folie Tristan d'Oxford*, which derives from Thomas's version of the legend.[2] The two *Folies* tell how Tristan disguises himself as a fool in order to visit Iseut. Like Marie de France's lay "Chievrefoil," they are episodic accounts of a clandestine encounter.

All versions of the legend of Tristan and Iseut have major episodes in common. These include the death of both of Tristan's parents, an occurrence that explains his name, "Tristan," suggestive of the tragic sadness of his orphanhood (from French *triste*, "sad"). An annual tribute paid to the Irish by the Cornish—Marc, Tristan's uncle, is king of Cornwall—explains the enmity between the Irish and the Cornish. Tristan defeats and mortally wounds the Morholt, Iseut's uncle, who collects the annual tribute. When Tristan arranges a marriage between Iseut and King Marc, Iseut's mother concocts a love potion for Iseut and Marc in order to unite the two enemies by an indissoluble love bond. When Tristan and Iseut happen to drink the potion the tragic love triangle is produced that lasts until the love-death at the end of the extant romances. Every version of the Tristan legend, including the episodic ones, presumes this scheme.[3] No doubt, for medieval audiences the tragedy of the legend lay in the way in which a feudal marriage, a common source of harmony among peoples, produces strife within the family—the uncle against the nephew—which is unavoidable, either because of the magic, superhuman force of the love potion in the *version commune*, or because of the fine, constant love between Tristan and Iseut described in the *version courtoise*.

Other French-language works on Tristan and Iseut may have existed in the Middle Ages. Eilhart von Oberg, a twelfth-century German romancer, claims to have translated a French romance that has not survived, and Thomas, Beroul, and Marie all refer to oral and written versions they knew, but that subsequently disappeared.[4]

Beroul's *Tristan*, like other examples of the *version commune*, makes the love potion responsible for Tristan and Iseut's love. They inadvertently drink the potion while Tristan is bringing Iseut to marry Marc, Tristan's uncle. However, the potion's full force is of limited duration. Thomas d'Angleterre's *version courtoise* may be a deliberate response to the loss of self-control occasioned by the potion in the *version commune*. He makes the potion into an image of a love that began earlier in Ireland when Tristan first met Iseut (*Tristan*, manuscript Douce, ll. 1214–20). But the love potion is central to the conception of the love in both versions. If Tristan and Iseut love only because the magic power represented by the potion compels them to fall in love, they are not responsible for their action. Beroul brings this idea out when a hermit tells Tristan and Iseut that they are beyond repentance and therefore virtually dead. This is because the potion deprives them of free will and thus responsibility for their actions.[5] They recover their sense of responsibility when the force of the potion declines after three years (Beroul *Tristran*, l. 2140). However, the love does not end. But when in Thomas the potion becomes an image of the powerful love that unites the lovers, matters of social responsibility, sin, and fidelity loom large in narrative elaboration.

The interpretation of Beroul's *Tristan* is complicated by three factors. First, its beginning and end are missing. Thus, second, we cannot know for sure whether the lovers eventually separate, leaving out the love-death, or whether Beroul included their death. Third, a change from the more tragic first part to a more farcical second part of the extant text suggests that there may have been two "Berouls," each having contributed to the extant manuscript a part that existed separately before.

The methods of narrative composition in Beroul's and Thomas's versions distinguish the two as much as does their conception of love. Beroul combines narrative blocks that are loosely coordinated or not connected at all.[6] This narrative style, termed parataxis, does not attempt to integrate narrative blocks or segments; each has a certain autonomy within the traditional scheme for the narrative. However, in

Thomas's fragmentary *Tristan*, there is evidence of coherent narrative elaboration analogous to Chrétien's notion of *conjointure*. In his adaptation Thomas tries to harmonize as many versions of the legend as he can. However, he rejects matter that does not conform to his conception of the story and his idealization of love.[7]

Chrétien de Troyes

Chrétien de Troyes is the most original romancer of the twelfth century. He appears to have been the first author to treat the chivalric quest, the love of Lancelot and Guenevere, and the Grail. He wrote five major romances, whose probable chronological order is *Erec et Enide*, *Cligés*, *Le Chevalier de la charrette* or *Lancelot*, *Le Chevalier au lion* or *Yvain*, and *Le conte du graal* or *Perceval*. The last 1000 lines of the *Charrette* appear to have been completed according to Chrétien's plan by a scribe, Godefroi de Leigni.[8] The *Conte du graal* is incomplete; perhaps Chrétien died before finishing it or he halted work on it after the death of his patron, Philippe of Flanders. It soon acquired continuations, presumably encouraged by its unfinished state. *Philomena* by "Chrétien li gois," an adaptation from Ovid, and *Guillaume d'Angleterre* by "Chrétien," a kind of hagiographic romance, have also been attributed to him.

In the prologue to *Cligés* Chrétien says that a civilization based on chivalry and learning (*chevalerie* and *clergie*) was transmitted from Greece and Rome to France (*translatio studii*). That civilization is exemplified in his romances. Love is especially important. It brings together exemplary knights and ladies whose achievements in quests, combats, and court realize the civilization. However, problems may arise in the acquisition and retention of love. Many of these problems stem from one's perception of the lover's intention and the relative merits of other demands besides love, such as prowess in arms, family obligations, or feudal service. *Erec* and *Yvain*, for example, offer apparently contrasting solutions to the problem of the relative worth of prowess in arms and chivalry, on the one hand, and conjugal love, on the other.

Chrétien's originality is suggested by his alternate use of incognito, pseudonyms such as "Chevalier de la charrette" and "Chevalier au lion," and delayed identification of a character's name until a significant moment, as with Enide, Lancelot, and Perceval. Since his romances are vehicles for presenting problems and suggesting their solutions, identification is a sign of self-realization. One of the major problems he evokes, especially in *Cligés*, is the love of Tristan and Iseut.[9] Their love is decried in that romance because Iseut shared her body with two men. Furthermore, Tristan and Iseut's love arose not from natural inclination or free choice, but because of the magic, superhuman power of the love potion. Chrétien's emphasis on choice and free will in deciding to love is tempered in the romances by the emotional impact on the lover of the qualities of the person with whom he or she falls in love. Thus both Erec and Yvain fall in love with the women they marry because their beauty, both outer and inner, shines through surface defects like poor clothing and grief. These women in turn consider the family and prowess of the men they love as much as their handsome looks—which are, in the last analysis, a manifestation of inner worth in an aristocratic world.

In *Cligés*, which is modeled on the main features of the Tristan legend, Fenice objects to an adulterous liaison like Iseut's. She seeks a love wherein the constancy of Tristan and Iseut is perfected by means of sexual fidelity. For Chrétien, sincere love, whether in marriage, as in *Erec* and *Yvain*, or in adultery, as in the *Charrette* and *Cligés*, promotes the equality of the lovers, not the traditional authority of the husband over his wife or of the seducer over the seduced. *Erec* illustrates this theme best. When Erec and Enide love well, she is both wife and *amie*; when problems arise, she is merely a wife. Although today this ideal of marital love may seem conventional, it would have seemed new and original in the twelfth century. Chrétien foregrounds love that is founded on constancy, equality, and the advantages that accrue to the lovers, their families, and civilization because of their love.

In Chrétien's problem romances the characters are not always aware of the wrongs they commit, and thus of the problems they cause. Perceval shows no concern about his mother when she faints at the moment he takes leave of her; only after a complex sequence of adventures does he begin to understand the meaning and consequences of this *pechié*, or sin. In the meantime this first wrong prefigures later ones, including his failure to ask the right questions at the Grail Castle, because of which he brings shame on himself, grief to others, and desolation in the world. Less dramatic, but no less problematic, are the errors of omission or commission attributed to both Lancelot and Guenevere, to Enide, to Yvain, and to Yseut as Fenice describes her in *Cligés*.

In *Erec et Enide*, his first romance, Chrétien established a basic narrative structure that he used in all of his Arthurian romances except the *Charrette*. The narrative of each romance is about 7000 lines long, except for the *Conte du graal*; it contains about 10,000 lines in the surviving text, but Chrétien may have intended a tale of about 14,000 lines.[10]

Each plot is divided into two relatively independent sequences. The first sequence takes up about one-third of the total, with the remainder of the text devoted to developing the second sequence. For example, the first sequence in *Erec* interlaces two episodes: the hunt for the white stag and the sparrowhawk contest. The conclusion of the first episode identifies Enide as the most beautiful woman at court; her marriage to Erec marks the conclusion of the second episode. The second sequence usually relates a quest composed of discrete adventures leading to a marvelous goal and the denouement of the plot.

Chrétien enunciated the principle of romance *conjointure* as a combination of previously scattered or incomplete narratives (perhaps including one or more lays) into a marvelous adventure made coherent by an informing idea or context. I can illustrate this idea by reference to *Erec*'s two narrative episodes, called *vers*, which are conjoined by analogous goals.

When Erec brings Enide to court after the sparrowhawk contest, she is beautiful enough to win the kiss from the successful hunter for the white stag; this completes the white stag episode or first *vers* (l. 1798). Enide as prize of both "beauty contests"—the white stag kiss and the sparrowhawk combat—brings the two episodes together. Her name is revealed when she marries Erec at the end of the second episode in the first sequence. The two interlaced episodes effect the *conjointure* of the romance's first sequence. In the second sequence of the romance a misunderstanding between husband and wife leads to a lengthy quest interspersed with diverse adventures, and eventual reconciliation, with, as happy ending, the coronation of the couple as king and queen. The sequences and episodes, analogous to the brief plots of many lays, are conjoined in the two-part narrative of Chrétien's first Arthurian romance.

Cligés has the same 1:2 pattern for its two narrative sequences, except that the first sequence relates the love and marriage of Cligés's parents, Alexandre and Soredamors, whereas the second relates the more problematic affair of their son Cligés with Fénice the empress of Constantinople. *Yvain* follows even more closely the *Erec* model of marriage sequence followed by quest sequence.

The *Charrette* is different from the other Chrétien romances in several ways. First, it presents an adulterous love that cannot end in marriage. Second, it confines itself to only a single sequence in the career of the titular hero and heroine and thus does not have the two relatively independent sequences of the other romances. Third, it doubles the quest by having both Lancelot and Gauvain set out to liberate Guenevere from abduction (although very little of Gauvain's unsuccessful quest is related).

In some ways *Yvain* is actually a continuation or mirror of the *Charrette*.[11] *Yvain* does not have a real prologue; instead it opens in medias res; moreover, certain episodes in *Yvain* are explained by reference to Gauvain's quest for Guenevere in the *Charrette*. Whether Chrétien intended *Yvain* as a continuation of the *Charrette* and thus envisaged a romance of approximately 14,000 lines is uncertain. Donald Maddox has noted Chrétien's tendency to build each succeeding romance he wrote on the data of his earlier ones, thus anticipating a compilation of interrelated works and even the coherence of a cycle.[12] In any case, the principle of tangential development would be followed in the *Perceval Continuations* of the early thirteenth century; it anticipates thirteenth-century prose cycles as well.

Other Arthurian Romances

Chrétien's Arthurian model—Arthur's Round Table from which prominent knights set out in quest of adventures—occurs elsewhere. Raoul de Houdenc based his *Meraugis de Portlesguez* on the qualities of lovers as judged by Arthur's court. Meraugis and Gorvain Codruz both love the same woman. Meraugis's love is founded on the lady's inner worth, Gorvain's on her physical beauty. The ensuing adventures demonstrate, by victory in combat or success in achieving marvelous adventures, that the former's courteous conception of love is preferable to the latter's preoccupation with beauty. It therefore upholds the aristocratic ideal according to which nobility expresses itself as both exterior and interior perfection. Like Chrétien, Raoul de Houdenc assigned a role to Arthur's nephew Gauvain, presenting him as Meraugis's companion and counterpart.

The *Vengeance Raguidel*, which has also been ascribed to Raoul, makes Gauvain the central figure. It thus inaugurates a series of "Gauvain romances"[13] that focus on the social distinction and courtesy of Arthur's nephew, his many loves, and his occasional propensity to excess and even madness. In the intricate plot of the *Vengeance* Gauvain follows a very indirect route to achieve the vengeance that gives the work its title. Gauvain's character—his "casual" approach to adventure, whether amorous, knightly, or social (Busby, *Gauvain*, 284)—often leads him to digress from his goal, and even to forget it for a time. Comedy is a frequent by-product of his encounters. Nonetheless, despite sometimes topsy-turvy adventures, Gauvain always manages to land on his feet and complete his initial quest honorably.

In the thirteenth century Gauvain continued to figure prominently in verse romance, in part perhaps because Chrétien did not devote an entire romance to him.[14] This lacuna was to be filled not only by romances centering on Arthur's illustrious, yet problematic nephew, but also by those in which he figures prominently, or in which his son or his brother is the protagonist.

Renaut de Beaujeu's (or de Bagé's) *Bel inconnu* is an example of the "Gauvain-family" kind of romance. It relates the adventures of Guinglain, or the "Fair Unknown," the son of Gauvain and a wood fay named Blancemal. Guinglain's quest involves him in the marvelous rescue of the Blonde Esmeree, a maiden whom a magician has transformed into a serpent and who can be released from the evil spell only by a kiss. She falls in love with her rescuer and later marries him at Arthur's court. But another maid, the Pucelle aux blanches mains, had fallen in love with Guinglain earlier; indeed, she had inspired the quest that led him to find and disenchant the Blonde Esmeree. She is Guinglain's real love. The romance is incomplete, although the narrator says that he could tell how Guinglain and the Pucelle renewed their love. The narrative breaks off, so Renaut tells us, because the lady he himself loves and for whom he was writing the romance pays him no attention.

The *Bel inconnu*, like other incomplete romance narratives, problematizes denouement and closure in the context of romance *conjointure*. We can never know whether the autobiographical explanation for the tale's termination is true, or whether the author is playing games with his audience or even inviting a different reading of narrative closure. The *Bel inconnu*, an apparently incomplete romance, raises questions about literary history, narratology, and patronage,[15] questions that are not unique to it.

Grail Romances

There are two major traditions in twelfth-century Grail romance. The first begins with Chrétien's *Conte du graal*, the second with Robert de Boron's *Estoire del saint graal*. Since neither romance was completed by its original author, each invited continuations, amalgamations, and adaptations in verse and prose.

Chrétien de Troyes

From the modern perspective the most fascinating invention of Chrétien de Troyes was the Grail. His *Conte du graal* or *Perceval* is virtually two romances in one. The *Conte du graal* centers in the first sequence on Perceval's misadventure at the Grail Castle; the incomplete second sequence relates his quest to discover that castle in order to right the wrong he had earlier committed there. It also contains a novelty adumbrated in the *Charrette*: the parallel quests of two knights, Perceval and Gauvain. Gauvain must defend himself when accused of murder, and in addition he must achieve the quest for the Bleeding Lance that is part of the Grail scenario in Perceval's visit to the Grail Castle. The first sequence, devoted almost exclusively to Perceval's adventures, corresponds to the usual first part in Chrétien's romances, except that it is twice the usual length. The second sequence contains only two Perceval episodes, the initial one in which he and numerous other knights set out on quests, and the meeting with his uncle the hermit; the rest is devoted to Gauvain's adventures. Although the romance is incomplete, it is far longer than any of Chrétien's other romances.

The first sequence begins with Perceval living in a solitary woods with his widowed mother, or *Veve dame*, who wants to prevent her son from knowing about knighthood lest he die a violent death like his father and brothers. The charmingly described encounter of the ingenuous boy and some knights dashes her hopes, and she herself dies when Perceval leaves for Arthur's court to be knighted. There he meets Arthur while Kay violently rebukes signs and predictions of his future greatness. He acquires a knight's armor after slaying the Scarlet Knight, then is dubbed by Gornemant de Goort, who shows him how to wear armor and handle a sword and spear properly. He next rescues the beautiful Blancheflor, besieged by Clamadeu because she refuses to marry him. He discovers love at Blancheflor's castle, Belrepaire, or at least apparently enjoys a sexual encounter with her; certainly, at a later point in the story, when three drops of blood fallen on fresh snow remind him of the face of Blancheflor and he muses on the image until the snow melts, he is in love with her.

After leaving Blancheflor, Perceval has a marvelous encounter: he happens upon the Fisher King, a maimed king fishing in a river, who directs him toward a castle where Perceval sees the Grail and the Bleeding Lance.

This is the first time in any extant text that the Grail and the Bleeding Lance appear, and therefore Chrétien is usually credited with their invention. However, the origins of the two objects are complex and obscure. There is no doubt that there was a Celtic tradition concerning a marvelous platter possessing magic powers not unlike a cornucopia.[16] Yet the French word *graal* was a common word; it referred to a low-bottomed bowl, as in the *Alexandre décasyllabique*.[17] But Chrétien's "grail" is no ordinary one: made of precious metals and embellished with precious stones, it holds a sacred host. The host sustains the life of the Fisher King's mysterious father, who resides in a room into which the Grail procession goes.

The Bleeding Lance[18] is related implicitly to the Fisher King's wound. He was "maimed," that is, emasculated, and can bear the painful wound only by fishing or by being gently transported about on a bed. His wound would have been healed had Perceval asked the so-called unspelling (disenchanting) questions: Whom does the Grail serve? And why does the Lance bleed? His failure to ask these questions has disastrous consequences, as he learns later from the Hideous Damsel, a messenger from the Grail Castle whose visit inaugurates the second sequence of the romance.

Perceval is a character type that will loom large in subsequent Grail romances: the inadvertent or unsuspecting wrongdoer. In the second sequence of the *Conte du graal* a hermit who is also Perceval's uncle and the brother of his dead mother explains that his failure can be traced back to the so-called *pechié de ta mere*,[19] or sin committed against his mother. When Perceval left her to become a knight at Arthur's court, his mother collapsed. Perceval ignored her fall, even though he knew that he should help widows in distress. His mother died of grief and, the hermit tells him, Perceval is responsible for her death. His failure to do his duty initiates a chain of disasters like the failure to ask the unspelling questions at the Grail Castle, which results in a waste land of orphans, widows, and disconsolate maidens, as the Hideous Damsel tells Perceval (ll. 4642–83). The final calamity—Perceval forgets God for more than five years during which he unsuccessfully seeks the Grail—culminates in the hermit episode. What Chrétien intended for his unfortunate hero after that episode is not known. Presumably his return to God on Easter Sunday while staying with his hermit uncle has advanced his quest for the Grail and points toward a happy resolution of the plot. But this is not at all certain, since some subsequent Grail romances relate the continuous downfall of protagonists once they go wrong. The Grail is always associated with violence and moral blindness in French romance.

Interpretation of the *Conte du graal* is therefore complicated by uncertainty as to the context within which it should be read. In Chrétien's earlier romances a chivalric context blends with an amorous one, and a noble or "courtly" love explains the actions of the protagonists and articulates narrative significance. But the introduction of the Holy Grail into the chivalric, amorous world of the Round Table subverts the ideals of love and chivalry that characterized Chrétien's earlier works. Confusion about what ethos should dominate is mirrored in Perceval's own misapprehensions and assumptions about right conduct. His passage from knighthood to love while in a state of sin and forgetfulness enhances suspense, but offers no clear scale of values by which to interpret the narrative. To be sure, Perceval receives a number of maxims about right conduct for knights from his mother, from Gornemant, and from the hermit. Nonetheless, although they overlap and complement one another, the maxims do not constitute a moral system within which Perceval himself (to the extent that he understands the maxims) or the audience may achieve moral discrimination.

Nowhere more than in the *Conte du graal* does Chrétien seem to disorient both his protagonists and his audience. Perceval passes from a foolish (*nice*) young man to an awareness of his guilt for the sin he committed against his mother, along the way discovering the values associated with knighthood, courtesy, and love. Yet the results of his growth in knowledge are disastrous or strangely inconclusive. The very spatial and temporal coordinates of the plot oscillate. In Perceval's first adventure after leaving his mother, involving the *amie* of the Orgueilleux de la lande, he unwittingly abuses the maiden's hospitality because he is unable to distinguish between obedience to his mother's admonitions and real courtesy and decorum. Later the emergence of the Grail Castle where there seemed to be nothing before—an effect of geographical perspective or grace?—culminates in Perceval's inability to perceive that the lessons in courtesy he received from Gornemant are useless when sin renders him speechless. More than five years later, after vainly seeking the Grail by combat, he is unable to distinguish between a typical Friday and Good Friday, a failure that provokes the astonishment of pilgrims when they see Perceval wearing armor on this day of peace. His folly operates on several levels, his memory seems uncertain, and his forgetfulness is often total.

Interpretation of the *Conte du graal* is further complicated by Gauvain's role in the second sequence. In his case as in Perceval's, the plot seems constantly to diverge from its path and its apparent context, enhancing a growing sense of temporal and spatial dislocation. At the same time Perceval sets out to correct the wrong he committed at the Grail Castle, Gauvain prepares to go forth to relieve the besieged castle of a maiden at Montesclaire—indeed, the entire Round Table is propelled into a variety of quests. But Gauvain's quest aborts when a knight accuses him of murder and he is obliged to go to Guiromelant's castle to clear his name. Then, after two curious adventures—the encounter with the maid of the narrow sleeves and an adventure of lovemaking with the granddaughter of the person he is accused of having murdered—Gauvain is obliged to seek the Bleeding Lance. This quest puts him on a path parallel to Perceval's. But the Lance is quickly forgotten—just as the problem of the maiden at Monstesclaire had been earlier—as Gauvain falls into another set of adventures beginning with the Orgueilleuse of Logres that leads to the Castle of Marvels. In that castle he finds King Arthur's mother, dead for 200 years, his own mother, dead for 100 years, and his charming sister Clarissant! The space-time coordinates are obviously askew. Gauvain's quest apparently lasts only a few days, yet it is interlaced with Perceval's after the latter has been wandering about for over five years! Are we peering into Alice's Wonderland?

Chrétien wrote the *Conte du graal* at the request of Philippe de Flandre, as he tells us in the prologue. Philippe inspired the romance in ways reminiscent of Marie de Champagne's patronage of the *Chevalier de la charrette*. First, he gave Chrétien the book that served as the source for the romance. Second, he may have inspired a meaning (*san*) by his Christian charity, much as the countess may have applied her own ideas on marriage to the love of Lancelot and Guenevere.[20] Philippe's charity, Chrétien avers, makes him superior to Alexander the Great, since the latter practiced only largess. Does this Christian addition to the noble ideal parallel the Christian ethic brought into romance by Chrétien's Grail and Lance, so different from the ideals proclaimed in the Alexander romances?

Such problems, and the very incompleteness of the *Conte du graal*, no doubt excited curiosity about its meaning and conclusion. But before taking up the continuations and other additions to and adaptations of the *Conte du graal*, we must look at another incomplete Grail romance in verse.

Robert de Boron

In Chrétien the Grail is holy because it contains the host. But Chrétien's Grail itself does not have the liturgical and biblical associations Robert de Boron gives to it in his *Estoire del saint graal*. Robert's *Estoire* began a cycle that linked the Arthurian Grail to the Last Supper, Joseph of Arimathea, and Merlin.

Robert's *Estoire* survives in a single manuscript as a verse fragment about 3500 lines long. It contains an apparently complete branch called *Joseph d'Arimathie* and an incomplete *Merlin*. The *Estoire* appears to have been planned as a poem of multiple parts. It was probably never completed as planned—at least not in verse form. The *Joseph* relates the death of Christ. Blood from his body is collected in the vessel used at the Last Supper, thereby transforming this common vessel into the Holy Grail. The family of Joseph of Arimathea establishes a Christian community in the Near East, and then miraculously travels to Britain to christianize the island. The 500-line fragment that follows in the manuscript begins the story of Merlin. Though nothing else survives in verse, a number of prose versions presumably based on Robert are extant. One, the *Prose Joseph d'Arimathie*, is followed by various prose *Merlins*, some of which are linked to the Vulgate *Lancelot-Graal* cycle, and, apparently, a prose *Perceval*. The last may be part of the "fifth branch" Robert announced at the end of the verse *Joseph*; it may begin with the *Merlin* fragment. It may also survive in a revised version known as the *Didot-Perceval*.

Robert's Perceval moves away from the chivalric exemplars of courtly romance. Chrétien's Perceval loses himself in a world whose temporal and spatial coordinates vary with the scale of values by which, in any given adventure, he is evaluated and thinks himself to be evaluated. Such uncertainty becomes, in Robert de Boron, willing but passive acquiescence to God's will. Thus Joseph of Arimathea is less a knight than an example of divine grace. He waits until called, and moves as directed; through him God achieves his will while protecting his faithful servant. The abnegation of human will in favor of God's will looms large in the evaluation of knights and ladies in thirteenth-century Grail romances.

In Robert's romance the Grail has acquired an existence independent of the original meaning of the word in Chrétien. Since it now designates the vessel from which Christ drank at the Last Supper, the *graal* as platter has become the Grail. It is also called a vessel, thus emphasizing its function as a drinking vessel rather than as a nourishing platter. In addition wordplay explains its meaning by the verb *agreer*—"to please": the Grail is that which pleases.[21] A fish, perhaps a symbol of Christ, is served at a solemn meal given by Bron, the husband of Joseph's daughter. It gives him his name, Fisher King, and associates the King with the Grail and Grail services; he is not maimed.

Narrator's interventions in the *Joseph* raise a number of questions. First, its primary source, alleged to be a great Grail book (*Estoire*, ll. 932–36),[22] if it ever existed, has been lost. Second, Robert's conception of the complete work is obscure. He states at the end of the *Joseph* that he is skipping over four intervening parts about Joseph's descendants in order to relate the fifth part, but that he intends to return to those parts later (ll. 3501–07). But there is no evidence that the four missing parts were ever written. However, whatever sense one gives to these statements, in the context of literary history they anticipate the cyclical elaboration of Grail history that eventually will reach from the death of Christ to the death of Arthur in the multifarious branches and parts of the great thirteenth-century prose romances.

The sanctity of the Grail in Robert's *Estoire* firmly imposes on Arthurian romance a moral context inconsistent with the vision of chivalry, courtesy, and love common in twelfth-century romance. Furthermore, the cyclic tendencies of Robert's *Estoire* point to a variety of romance that is no longer self-contained, as in Chrétien, but open to continuous expansion and adaptation within the context of divine history and morality.

The twelfth century ends, therefore, with two different Grail romances: Chrétien's *Conte du graal* elevates the humble bowl or platter called the *graal* to religious significance, while enshrouding it in mystery (in part no doubt because the romance is incomplete). Robert de Boron lifts some veils of obscurity from the Grail as vessel by tracing it back to the cup used at the Last Supper, and forward to Arthur and Merlin.

But what did the Grail mean to readers who read and audiences who listened to Chrétien's *Conte du graal* or Robert's *Estoire?* The low-bottomed but wide platter is sanctified by the host in Chrétien, the vessel by Christ's own blood in Robert. How may we explain this transformation from a flat object like a paten into a vessel like the chalice used in mass? Perhaps the simplest explanation is that illustrated by the shape of the chalice itself during the thirteenth century. The chalice could be a low-bottomed vessel or more vertical in shape.[23] The transformation from plate to vessel was reflected in the different versions and adaptations of the Grail romances that associate the Grail with the mass or an analogous religious ceremony.

Non-Arthurian Romances

Contemporary with Chrétien and on until the end of the twelfth century a number of romancers wrote on matters wholly or partially non-Arthurian. Their composition illustrates perhaps better than Arthurian romance itself experimentation with narrative forms, contents, modes, and styles. These romances thus contributed to the expanding horizons of expectation of medieval audiences. Chrétien himself inaugurated these developments in *Cligés*. Although the romance uses Arthurian settings and contrasts its plot and ideas about love with the plot and love themes in the Tristan legend, it also draws on non-Arthurian sources. Insurrection against the king and Ovidian casuistry are features of the first sequence on Alexandre and Soredamors, whereas the second sequence focuses on a palace liaison that, after a tournament and a violent episode involving a pretended death (*fausse mort*), concludes with the lovers' marriage. *Cligés* thus reveals affinities with *Floire et Blancheflor*. But it also adapts other traditions in the pretended death of the heroine.

For the most part, non-Arthurian verse romances belong to the tradition of the Matter of Rome in the broadest sense, that is, the plots and protagonists are Greco-Roman or Byzantine. Several names stand out among the non-Arthurian romancers: Gautier d'Arras, Hue de Rotelande, Aimon de Varennes, and the same Alexandre de Paris (or de Bernay) who wrote the dodecasyllabic *Roman d'Alexandre*. Major anonymous romances include *Partonopeu de Blois* and *Waldef*.

Like Chrétien in *Cligés*, Gautier d'Arras combines a variety of matters in *Eracle*: hagiographic features in the first narrative block, wherein Eracle, a gift from God to his parents, demonstrates his own gifts by identifying the best gems, horses, and women; a courtly love story in the second block concerned with the excessive jealousy of Lais, the emperor of Constantinople, and his wife's infidelity because of it; and crusading epic in the third centering on Eracle as heroic crusader. Gautier's *Ille et Galeron* appears to adapt a source from the Matter of Britain tradition, but much of the story transpires in Rome. Ille leaves Brittany and his wife, Galeron, because, after losing an eye in combat, he thinks she will no longer love him. Later, at the moment he is to marry the daughter of the emperor of Rome, his wife finds him again and they reunite; later still, when the first wife decides to enter a convent, Ille does marry the Roman princess.

Gautier has often been cast as Chrétien's rival, although there is little concrete evidence for this supposed rivalry. Gautier is associated with the court of Aelis de Blois, Marie de Champagne's sister. It has of late proven useful to treat Gautier as an original romancer interesting in his own right.[24] *Eracle* illustrates the passage of romance from an oral to a literary genre, that is, from emphasis on a text designed to be read aloud before an audience to one intended for private reading. Thus Gautier helps to mark the transition from oral modes of reception typical of early *chansons de geste* and founded on a community of knights to increasing emphasis on individual reception and focus on the single, exceptional hero. Eracle himself is literally a gift from God, or *enfant dieu donné*, who by his own virtue becomes emperor.

Eracle's three parts are so distinct that we may speak of narrative parataxis, that is, the abrupt juxtaposition of loosely connected narrative blocks. Gautier emphasizes this feature of the romance's composition. At the end of the first segment on Eracle's God-given gifts, Gautier announces the crusading successes that he will relate—but not before relating the second part on the infidelity of the empress.[25] *Eracle*'s disparate narrative parts are held together merely by the recurring presence of two major figures, Eracle and the emperor Lais.

Ille et Galeron, Gautier's other romance, illustrates the kind of interlace rejected in *Eracle*, but practiced by Chrétien in, for example, the interlacing episodes, or *vers*, of the first *Erec* sequence. Gautier interlaces the story of Ille's two marriages without the paratactic breaks of *Eracle*. The romance is remarkable for another reason. The two surviving manuscript copies are so different that they must be edited separately. Why? Is one manuscript the victim of successive scribal tampering? Or did Gautier himself invent a second version, perhaps to please a new patron?

Hue de Rotelande wrote two romances. In *Ipomedon* the male lover plays hard-to-get to a disconsolate lady to punish her for being overly slow about responding to his love. *Protheselaus* recounts in a traditional context the career and love of the titular hero. Both these romances are continuations, *Ipomedon* of the *Roman de Thèbes* and *Protheselaus* of *Ipomedon*. Both borrow from *Thèbes* names and motifs like the combat between two brothers. *Eneas* and Benoît's *Troie* also appear to have been used. Hue's audience was probably Anglo-Norman and Norman, which no doubt accounts for the author's use of Sicily as the location where most of the action takes place in both romances: Sicily was under Norman domination in the late twelfth century.

Ipomedon is the more problematic—or curious—of the two romances. Its reversal of conventional roles in love makes the man seem to take on attributes usually associated with the female beloved. Haughty, disdainful, capricious, and cruel, he ignores the woman (who herself was at first haughty—hence, her name, La Fière) until finally granting her desire for marriage and providing her with lusty sexual consummation. The romance has been variously read as exemplary of medieval misogyny, as an almost farcical parody of courtly love, or as a subtle critique of courtly love values.[26] Perhaps it also suggests that honesty in sex and love is the best policy. No doubt, for readers of the Middle Ages as for us today, individual interpretations of the romance depended on the reader himself or herself. In any case, none of *Ipomedon*'s problematic features survive in its sequel, *Protheselaus*. Protheselaus, the younger brother, defeats and slays his older brother after the latter wrongfully deprives him of his inheritance. Love in this romance is uncomplicated.

Partonopeu de Blois relates the love of the titular hero for Melior, the daughter of the emperor of Constantinople. Melior falls in love with Partonopeu and then uses the magic she has learned to meet him. The one condition for her love is that Partonopeu not see her until she comes of age; otherwise she will lose her magic powers and take back her love. They therefore meet only in the dark. All this recalls the "otherworld" adventures in Breton lays. But Partonopeu breaks the pact with Melior, impelled by his mother and the Church, who think Melior is a devil. He loses her and goes mad. However, he recovers and eventually wins her back by constancy and his success in a tournament held for her hand. In a continuation a sultan tries unsuccessfully to win Melior from Partonopeu.

Partonopeu combines the three Matters of Britain, Rome, and France. It conjoins Celtic otherworld features like the fay with magic powers and the legendary Trojan origins of the French crown. Partonopeu successfully defends France against pagans invading from the British Isles. Melior herself is daughter of the emperor of Constantinople. *Partonopeu* survives in two versions and a continuation. The first part of the continuation, a little over 1000 lines long, is written in octosyllabic rhyming couplets, like the romance proper itself. Its second part, which contains over 1500 lines, uses octosyllabic couplets for about 500 lines, then abruptly changes to rhyming dodecasyllabic *laisses*. The change was made, the narrator states, in order to improve the poem.[27] Later it passes to rhyming decasyllabic couplets for a letter, then returns to octosyllabic rhyming couplets in the last 750 lines.

Like the *Bel inconnu*, *Partonopeu* is offered by its anonymous author as a form of love service to a lady. The narrator intervenes to contrast his relation to his lady with that of the romance protagonists. Like Renaut de Beaujeu, he breaks off before the conclusion to see if his lady, whom he calls "Passe Rose" (*Partonopeu*, l. 3927), wishes him to continue—she need only give him a wink (*Partonopeu*, ll. 10622–23). The romance is among those whose patron the narrator says he loves, and on whose encouragement—whatever that may mean—the continuation of the romance depends. Apparently the author's lady did wink, since we do have a continuation.

Partonopeu struck some contemporaries with its marvelous beauty, others with its sinful attraction.[28] The plot is relatively simple. Apart from the excursion into "faery" that dramatically ends with Partonopeu's betrayal of Melior's confidence, the narrative focuses on combats, either in the war of the Christian king Clovis with the pagan invader Gormont, or in the tournaments for the love and hand of Melior. The magic of love for a fairy princess from Constantinople in the first part is restored by a human love inspired by a knight's unique excellence—just as, in the French royal line, the pagan gods of Troy are replaced by the Christian God of New Troy when Clovis converts to Christianity (*Partonopeu*, ll. 445–48).

Aimon de Varennes wrote *Florimont* because of his love for a certain Vialine,[29] although narrative interventions about that love do not figure so prominently as in *Partonopeu* or the *Bel inconnu*. Florimont is the grandfather of Alexander the Great. His story takes up anew the theme of Fortune to explain the rise, decline, and rise again of the titular hero. Florimont's initial rise is due to his love for the Maiden of the Hidden Isle, a fay who inspires love and prowess in him, as in Marie de France's "Lanval" and *Partonopeu*. But, from the point of view of lineage and nobility, such a love is totally unacceptable: it is private and cannot lead to marriage or the continuation of the family. When Florimont's relationship with the fay is discovered, he is forced to give her up. He then falls into lovesickness, abandons chivalry (*recreantise*), and neglects his noble potential. Later, however, he finds a new, worthier, and totally suitable love in the person of Romadanaple, daughter of the Macedonian king. As his love for the king's daughter grows, his prowess returns. They marry. Their first child, Philippe, will be Alexander the Great's father.

Florimont's career therefore adapts the Fortune model to include destiny.[30] Fortune condemns its victims to the rise and fall illustrated by

Florimont's decline while in love with the Maiden of the Hidden Isle. To correct himself, Florimont integrates love, marriage, and prowess in service of a lady, family, and nobility. He thus realizes a noble destiny not subject to Fortune.

As an ancestral romance *Florimont* fits implicitly into the Alexander cycle. It has a Mediterranean setting—besides Greece and Macedonia, the narrative geography includes Albania (where Florimont is born), Italy, and Carthage. In narrator interventions Aimon asserts that the story goes back to tales he heard while in Greece. He claims that he put them together in a Latin-language memorandum, then rewrote them as French verse for Vialine after returning to France (Kelly, *Art*, 100–101).

Alexandre de Paris's *Athis et Prophilias* is the tale of two friends, one from Rome, the other from Athens. A love rivalry between them is successfully resolved in a happy ending. The romance evokes the harmony of chivalry and learning, that is, the *chevalerie-clergie* paradigm enunciated in the prologue to Chrétien's *Cligés*. Rome trains its sons and those of Athens in chivalry and the knightly arts, whereas Athens provides them with the learning they need.

The anonymous *Amadas et Ydoine* belongs to the Matter of France. It involves a love triangle. A forced marriage is circumvented by the ingenuity (*engin*) of Ydoine and the prowess of Amadas, who outwit the count of Nevers, Ydoine's fiancé. Ydoine does not reject the match because her fiancé is old, impotent, ugly, or a coward. It is merely that she loves Amadas more. Ydoine convinces the count of Nevers that, by consummating the marriage, he will fall under a spell and die. The count agrees to abandon his marriage plans. Not one to pine long, he woos and wins the daughter of the count of Poitou, whom, unbeknownst to the reader, he had truly loved all the time!

Amadas et Ydoine illustrates the same concern as *Florimont* with a love in which inclinations conflict with social or moral priorities. The romantic, emotional side of the love is, however, supported by emphasis on qualities that permit one to discriminate among persons according to their worth. Nobility in *Amadas* derives not only from lineage—Amadas is socially inferior both to Ydoine and to the count of Nevers—but from inborn qualities that permit distinctions to be made apart from lineage. *Amadas* also illustrates conflicts stemming from the ostensible misogyny of the narrator, who corrects himself because of the worth of the ladies for whom he writes the romance.[31]

Apollonius de Tyr is the only so-called Greco-Roman romance that survived into the French Middle Ages. Only a fragment of the twelfth-century version is extant today. Its amalgam of incest, wanderings, sudden turns in fortune, shipwreck, and virtue that remains strong and constant even in the brothel evokes a world that has hardly been touched by Christian morality.

This is not so for verse romances based on the Seven Sages of Rome. Both the *Sept sages Proper* and the later *Dolopathos* are misogynist romances. Both relate how a wicked stepmother tries unsuccessfully to seduce her stepson, and then betrays him. The frame narrative focuses on a kind of trial wherein exemplary stories underscore arguments concerning the guilt or innocence of the stepson and stepmother. Although most twelfth-century verse romance tends to idealize the noble woman as an object of love and an inspiration to courtesy and prowess, the Seven Sages romances evince deep mistrust even of empresses.

Two Anglo-Norman romances belong to the Matter of England: *Horn* and *Waldef*. The *Roman de Horn*, attributed to a certain Thomas, is 5250 lines long and it uses Anglo-Norman rhyming in dodecasyllabic *laisses*. It is an ancestral romance. If the romance about Horn's father, the *Roman d'Aalof* referred to in the prologue existed, it has disappeared; nor is the sequel on Horn's son Hadermod extant, which the epilogue says Thomas's son Gilimol will write. The plot combines the military ethos of the *chansons de geste* with the love interest of most twelfth-century verse romances. However, this does not produce a moral dilemma for the characters or the author. Pride is Horn's major defect.

Waldef offers independent evidence for the existence of *Aalof*, which the anonymous romance refers to as well as to a *Brut* (by Wace?) and a *Tristan*. It too is an ancestral romance, but one that relates the story of the titular hero's parents, wife, and children in one work—an incomplete one today, since the sole surviving manuscript breaks off abruptly after 22,306 lines of octosyllabic rhyming couplets. It is replete with conflicts among petty English kings, including numerous wars, abductions, the nefarious doings of Saracens, and a search for Waldef's family after its dispersal in Europe and Africa. The anonymous author wrote for an *amie*, but we learn neither her name nor the author's because the latter promised to reveal them only in the missing conclusion. Despite analogies with *Partonopeu* and *Florimont*, *Waldef* is closer to *Horn* in its emphasis on a martial, feudal ethos rather than on courtesy and fine loving.

Twelfth-century verse romances bequeath to the thirteenth century a variety of issues of interest to the nobility. Besides the growing preoccupation with the moral and religious duties of knighthood reflected in the Grail romances, many treat social and amorous duties and the conflicts that may arise because of them. Moreover, in the secular realm the relationship between love and knightly prowess is still as problematic at the end of the century as it was in Wace's *Brut* when Cador and Gauvain disagreed on the relative value of war and peace for aristocratic civilization. A military ethos prevails in romances like *Horn* and *Waldef*, whereas love is prominent in *Partonopeu* and *Amadas*; the rejection of misogyny in *Amadas* contrasts with the dominant misogynist ethos of the Seven Sages tradition. All these issues loom large in thirteenth-century romances.

Chapter 3
Thirteenth-Century Prose Romance

Thirteenth-century French romance adapted verse romance in prose cycles. A cycle is a sequence of adventures that not only continues the story of several knights, but also interlaces their adventures and correlates the events of one time with those of another. Some cycles also add the careers of ancestors and descendants, as in ancestral romances in verse. Moreover, there was a tendency to integrate events into the design of Christian typology from the Fall through the Crucifixion to the Last Judgment. This typological framework eliminated the essentially episodic character of verse romance, which tended to isolate the narrative of one romance from that of another. Within this scheme of universal history recurrent patterns that distinguish events by type allowed the cycle to return back on itself, as it were, by modeling adventures on recurrent patterns like the quest, falling in love, combat, and so forth; thus a cycle's manifold interlacing branches mirror earlier events in later versions of them. The prose romancers were trying to bring all narratives together into a single œuvre, the great narrative cycle of world history and the virtual summa of all possible narratives.

Chrétien and Robert de Boron anticipated some of these developments. Chrétien linked the plots of the *Charrette* and *Yvain* and projected multiple quests at the beginning of the second sequence in the *Conte du graal*. For his part, Robert de Boron projected narrative branching and interlacing that would bring the story of the Grail up to an Arthurian present adumbrated in the *Merlin* fragment; his major innovation was to link Arthurian and Grail narrative with biblical history. Verse is not the medium of the new kind of romance, in part, no doubt, because the very magnitude of the new conception favored the less demanding medium of prose.[1] At the time it was also believed that the use of versification and rhyme forced an author to alter the truth, and therefore to introduce lies into the narrative. This was an unacceptable situation in works whose authors consciously intended to integrate romance plot elements and thematic motifs with the Christian worldview.

Prose romance explodes the notion of the single author, just as it blurs the distinction between author and scribe. The lack of a holograph makes every manuscript copy a variant version—and variation is the rule of the game.[2] While copying a given romance from a manuscript or amalgamating two or more romance manuscripts, scribes might combine elements from several manuscripts, add new segments, rewrite, or even re-create the text from which they had started. Hence, the differences among manuscripts are far more radical than would be expected by modern readers used to the finality of printed books. The fact that prose romances survive in great numbers, and continued to be recopied until after printing began, accounts for ongoing adaptation and "modernization" in no way hindered by constraints of rhyme and versification.

Arthurian Prose Romance

The Robert de Boron tradition in prose

Robert himself or an adapter turned his verse *Estoire du saint graal* into prose. There are three parts to the prose version: *Joseph d'Arimathie*, *Merlin*, and the two adaptations known as the *Didot-Perceval*. *Joseph* rather faithfully reproduces the surviving verse *Estoire du saint graal*.[3] The *Prose Merlin* is found in several redactions and sources, some of which are incorporated into later cycles. The prose version begins much as the verse one does, relating how the devils tried to produce an antichrist through the union of a devil with a sinful woman. The plan backfired, producing Merlin instead of an antichrist. Merlin inherits from his devil-father superhuman vision into the causes of marvelous adventures, and by God's grace he can also see into the future. He is thus able to facilitate Arthur's birth, his rise to power, and the establishment of the Round Table.

The *Didot-Perceval* is the third branch of the prose cycle attributed to Robert de Boron. The two extant versions agree on the main lines of the story, but differ in some important details. Both adapt material from Chrétien's *Conte du graal*, completing it, as in Geoffrey of Monmouth and Wace, with the death of Arthur after his wars with Rome and Mordred's and Guenevere's betrayal. Perceval as Grail hero amalgamates features of Robert's own invention with features found in Chrétien's *Conte du graal* and the *Second Perceval Continuation*. These include Perceval's initial failure to achieve the Grail adventure and heal the Fisher King. In a second attempt Perceval dutifully asks the unspelling question: whom does the

Grail serve? The *Didot-Perceval* also introduces a new element, the Perilous Seat which splits violently when Perceval first sits on it during the unsuccessful Grail episode, but joins together seamlessly again during his second, successful visit.

It is uncertain how the *Didot-Perceval* came to be written and incorporated into the prose trilogy attributed to Robert de Boron. Some believe that it represents the work by which Robert intended to complete the *Merlin*. Others have postulated various rewritings between his original plan and the two extant versions.[4]

The major thirteenth-century prose romance is the *Prose Lancelot*. But it appears to have gone through a number of redactions before achieving its definitive shape in the Vulgate or cyclic *Lancelot-Graal*.

Noncyclic Romances

There are two noncyclic Arthurian prose romances: the *Noncyclic Lancelot* and the *Perlesvaus*. Both are anonymous. There is disagreement as to the chronology of these romances and their relation to other romances and manuscript traditions. They are special cases: though related to the *Lancelot-Graal* Vulgate cycle, they are still independent of it. Their principal distinction is that in both Perceval is the Grail hero; in the *Lancelot-Graal* cycle, Galaad is.

The *Noncyclic Lancelot* begins a biography of Lancelot. It refers to a Grail quest with Perceval as the successful knight. However, it does not contain any of the material from Chrétien's *Charrette*. But like the *Charrette* it is not a complete biography of Lancelot, either because it was meant to be episodic, or because the new notion of Galaad rather than Perceval as Grail knight required a new work.

The *Noncyclic Lancelot* was identified and given that title by Elspeth Kennedy.[5] It begins with the birth of Lancelot and ends with the death of Galehaut, Lancelot's friend and companion. It is generally regarded as a distinct version of the Lancelot story, although its relation to the Vulgate *Lancelot* and to other Grail romances is disputed. It names Perceval as the Grail hero and does not seem to anticipate Galaad. Galaad is Lancelot's baptismal name; Lancelot is only a surname used by his father, as in the Vulgate cycle. The references to Perceval as the achiever of the Grail quest may be either to earlier romances like Chrétien's and Robert's, or they may be to an anticipated conclusion, never written, from which Galaad would have been absent. On this turns one's conception of the *Noncyclic Lancelot*. If the Perceval allusions are to earlier romances, then the *Noncyclic Lancelot* is an independent, partial—that is, episodic—biography of Lancelot; if they point to a conclusion never written, it is a first version of the Vulgate cycle subsequently expanded (by the same or another author?) to include the remainder of Lancelot's life and the Galaad episodes, and reworked to add the rigorous morality that characterizes the *Queste* and the *Mort* in that cycle.

The *Noncyclic Lancelot*'s worldview is analogous to that in Chrétien's *Charrette*. It is a prose romance with the standard themes and motifs of secular Arthurian verse romance—courtly love, Round Table chivalry, feudal relations and customs—and a structural interlace far more sophisticated than in Chrétien or even multiple quest verse romances, but already prominent in the *Perlesvaus* (Kennedy, *Lancelot*).

The *Perlesvaus*, also called the *Haut livre du graal*, appears to have gone through two redactions. It is clearly episodic. Like the *Noncyclic Lancelot*, it draws on both Chrétien and Robert de Boron, of whose Grail romances it is either a continuation or a variant version in prose—perhaps even a response to their incomplete works.[6]

The *Perlesvaus* fully incorporates Arthurian legend into a religious context. The hero's name is changed from Perceval to Perlesvaus.[7] The narrative illustrates the crusading ethos of the Church triumphant over the Old Law. It continues Chrétien's *Conte du graal*, beginning with the disastrous effects of Perceval's failure to ask the unspelling questions. Dismay darkens Arthur's realm. The king himself no longer shows largess. His desuetude leads to dispersal of the Round Table. Knights wander about seeking adventures, often engaging in unmotivated violent or murderous combat, a situation that recalls Perceval's adventures in Chrétien during the five to six years during which he sought in vain the Grail Castle.

The *Perlesvaus* is divided into 11 branches of variable, but increasing length.[8] The disparate adventures they contain are linked not only by the repercussions they have in various parts of the work, but also by a fundamental opposition between the forces of Good and the forces of Evil. The New Law wages war with the agents of evil who represent the Old Law. The Old Law is associated not only with Judaism, but also with paganism. The larger conflict is mirrored by strife within families (see Schmid, *Familiengeschichten*, chap. 5). Perlesvaus's family in particular is divided into those who, together with Perlesvaus, are on the side of the New Law, and those who support his uncle, the Seigneur des Mares, an unrepentant defender of the Old Law. Perlesvaus finally slays his evil uncle in combat. His sister, Dandrane, and Iglais, his mother (still very much alive, unlike her counterpart in Chrétien), are, like Arthur and the Grail Castle, often threatened and on occasion dominated by the forces of the Old Law.

Gauvain and Lancelot are also prominent in the story. Each has his own adventures and Grail experiences, and each fails because of moral defects. Lancelot's defects stem from his adulterous love for Guenevere, a love that endures even after she dies of unexplained causes. Only Perlesvaus has the requisite virginity and chastity to achieve the Grail quest. The romance is replete with violent and strange adventures, some of which are given rather alarming allegorical readings. It is, to be sure, readily possible to read the quest for the Grail as a struggle between the Old Law and the New Law, but it seems strained to make the violent murder of his wife by Marin le jaloux into an allegory of Christ's death, even if allegorical readings are necessarily "other," and must not therefore fit the literal sense.

Since the date of the *Perlesvaus* and its relation to other romances are disputed, it is difficult to assign it a fixed place in the emergence of thirteenth-century prose romance. As I noted above, it seems to follow Chrétien's version of the Perceval story. The "Latin" source it mentions has not been definitely identified. The reference to "Avalon," where Guenevere is buried and where Arthur is to be buried, suggests not the legendary island, but the Vaux d'Avalon or Glastonbury Abbey, where Arthur's and Guenevere's alleged tombs were "discovered" in 1191.[9] Differences between the *Perlesvaus* and both Chrétien and Robert de Boron, such as the changes in the name of the hero, perhaps his recovered virginity, the profound restructuring of his family along matrilinear lines, and the prominence of Lancelot in the plot, problematize the relationship. As a continuation, *Perlesvaus* is also a rewriting.

The Vulgate *Lancelot-Graal* Cycle

The cycle contains three main branches: the *Estoire del saint graal* relates the origin of the Grail in the Holy Land after Christ's death, its transference or "translation" to Britain, and the christianization of that island; the *Merlin* relates the births of Merlin and Arthur and the king's early years, including his Saxon wars and marriage to Guenevere; and the *Lancelot en prose* relates a variety of tales about Arthur's knights, especially Lancelot, covers the quest for the Holy Grail, and reports the destruction of the Arthurian world.

The *Lancelot en prose*, actually written *before* the other two branches, has three subbranches. The *Lancelot Proper* is the longest part of the whole cycle. It tells of Lancelot's birth, his love for Guenevere, and his adventures and those of other prominent knights, especially Boort, Lionel, Hector, Gauvain, and Galehaut, up to the beginning of the quest for the Holy Grail; it includes several visits to the Grail Castle and the births of Perceval and Galaad. The *Queste del saint graal* introduces Galaad to the Round Table and recounts the principal events in the quests for the Grail, especially those of Galaad, Perceval, Boort, Lancelot, and Gauvain. Almost all Round Table knights fail to achieve the quest because of their sins, especially their loss of chastity and virginity. The Grail therefore returns to the Holy Land, whence a hand lifts it into Heaven after Galaad passes away. The *Mort le roi Artu* recounts the breakup of the Round Table fellowship and the end of Arthur's kingdom. It includes Arthur's discovery of the love of Lancelot and Guenevere, his war with Rome, and Mordred's betrayal. In the end all the principals die (except, perhaps, Arthur, who is transferred to Avalon by Morgain).

Despite attempts both in medieval manuscripts and modern scholarship to subdivide further this mass of material into structurally rational and narratively coherent parts, there is no general agreement as to what kind of division this should be.[10] Apart from the central biography of Lancelot, which is recounted chronologically,[11] two features of the romance's composition stand out. They are the art of narrative branching and the drift from a courtly love context to a moral context.[12]

Presenting simultaneous but separate events as narrative is analogous to rendering three-dimensional objects in two dimensions: it requires structural adaptation. The narrative solution to the problem is interlace and encasement of episodes: either the author alternates one knight's adventures with those of others (interlace), or he or she inserts one narrative into that of another (encasement). All this takes place within carefully marked and consistent spatial and temporal coordinates. The resultant tangle (*enchevêtrement*) or weave of plots is made coherent by linking different branches and by evaluating contexts according to the often conflicting ideals to which different knights conform and by which they judge their success.

Branching is described in a passage found in both the *Noncyclic Lancelot* and the cyclic version. The quests and adventures of knights are recorded at Arthur's court by interlacing narrative sequences, like intertwining branches in a tree. The tree image not only mirrors the interlace of quests and adventures, it also gives the plot a vertical coherence and structure. Arthur's court chroniclers, it is said,

> mistrent en escript lez aventures mon seignor Gauvain tout avant, por ce que c'estoit li commenchemens de la queste de Lancelot, et puis les Hector, por chou que de cel conte estoient branche, et puis lez aventures a tous lez .XVIII. autres compaignons, et tout ce fu del conte Lancelot, et tout cil autre furent branche de chestui, et li contes Lancelot fu branche del Graal, si com il y fu ajoustés.[13]

> [put my lord Gauvain's adventures first because he began the quest for Lancelot, then those of Hector because they were a branch of that story, and afterward the adventures of all 18 other companions. All this was part of Lancelot's story, and all the others were branches of it. And Lancelot's story was a branch of the Grail story, as it was added to it.]

The Grail story provides the trunk narrative and a moral context, explaining the branches or quests that spring from it.

Another image that gives a coherent scheme to the cycle is that of the three tables: the table of the Last Supper, the Grail table, and the Round Table itself. The failure of the Round Table to meet the moral standards of the two other tables adumbrates the failure of the world's best to find redemption and meaning in the Christian religion they profess.[14] After removing the Grail from Britain, God finally lifts it from earth after Galaad's passing (*Queste*, p. 279 ll. 2–7). The counterpart to the ablation of the Grail is the fall of Arthur's sword Excalibur into a lake from which a hand emerges to seize it at the end of the *Mort Artu* (sec. 192 l. 82–sec. 193 l. 2).

The *Mort Artu* announces that the adventures of the Grail and indeed all knightly adventures as such have ceased in Arthur's "adventurous kingdom" of Logres. This is because the Grail, once the source of all adventures in the cycle, is gone. The multiplicity and diversity of earlier adventures prefigure the unfathomable significance of the holy vessel from which they emanate. The proliferation of adventures as the narrative of the *Lancelot Proper* advances toward the Grail quest is so great that the narrator cannot relate all of them.[15] In the *Queste* only the four knights who accept the ritual of contrition, confession, penance, and pardon may know adventures: these knights are Lancelot, Boort, Perceval, and Galaad. All the other Round Table knights fail. By and large, they encounter only misfortunes (*mescheances*) that lead to murder, shame, or martial impotence. In the *Mort* itself all events are meaningless *mescheances*, including the final destruction of Round Table knighthood in the apocalyptic battle on Salisbury Plain between Arthur and Mordred.

The *Lancelot-Graal* completes the amalgamation of traditional Arthurian material—the Round Table and its knights, the love of Lancelot and Guenevere, the Grail quest—with biblical history and morality. A complex but coherent chronology, careful interlacing of adventures and quests, and allegorical and typological interpretation of events hold the cycle together. The gradual revelation of moral truth makes for heightened suspense, as an essentially this-worldly ethic in the early parts of the *Lancelot Proper* is gradually undermined. Rigorous Christian morality triumphs in the end as Galaad achieves the Grail, just before it is removed from the sinful Arthurian world, which slides into decline and finally into extinction in the bloody carnage of Salisbury Plain. The biblical framework gives harsh answers to questions posed by potentially conflicting secular and spiritual ideals in earlier romances.

A caveat is in order: the coherent picture of the composition of the Vulgate cycle I just offered does not necessarily conform to the way it came to be written. There is no consensus on its authorship beyond the conviction that more than one author or scribe contributed to its elaboration. Does this mean, as most believe today, that the plan for the work was altered, or at least evolved, from an essentially secular idealism epitomized by Lancelot in the early parts of the *Prose Lancelot*? Or did the original plan use the secular context only to undermine it gradually as the truths of the *Queste* overwhelm the ideals of Round Table chivalry?

The historical facts of authorship will probably never be known for certain. Here I can note only the major changes that indicate a shifting moral perspective between the beginning and the end of the *Lancelot Proper*. Lancelot is the best knight in the world, despite his growing sinfulness as the plot advances. But when the Grail quest begins the moral order emerges unequivocally. A maiden tells Lancelot that he is no longer the best knight in the world (*Queste* pp. 12 l. 28–13 l. 2). How are we to understand the seeming contradiction between the valorization of Lancelot and Guenevere's love at the beginning of the *Lancelot Proper* and the radical condemnation of that love that characterizes the *Queste* and the *Mort*? Several explanations have been put forward. One is that the contradiction is real, either because of a change in authorship in the different parts of the cycle, or because the author or authors changed their conception and evaluation of the love as the writing progressed.[16] Another explanation is that the cycle contains a double truth, with each truth valid in its own exclusive framework.[17] One truth is that of courtly love as inherited from Chrétien; according to this view, Lancelot and Guenevere's love is a source of prowess and social good so great as to compensate for their sinful liaison. The other truth is that their love is indeed a sin that causes the destruction of Arthurian civilization.

After the springlike beginning of the cycle, when Lancelot falls in love, the narrative atmosphere gradually and continuously darkens as signs, interpretations, and prophecies suggest more and more insistently that his love is wrong. The adaptation of Chrétien's *Charrette* is an important moment in the change. The central episode of Lancelot's quest in Chrétien's *Charrette* takes place in a cemetery. There Lancelot lifts a tombstone that only that knight can lift who is destined to liberate Guenevere and Arthur's subjects held prisoner by Meleagant. He does the same deed in the prose version. But the cemetery in the prose version contains a second prophetic tombstone not found in the *Charrette*. It is to be lifted by the knight who will achieve the quest for the Holy Grail after achieving, that is, bringing to an end, the marvelous adventures in Arthur's kingdom. Lancelot cannot raise this tombstone because of his love for Guenevere. But Lancelot's as-yet-unborn son Galaad will lift it.

The juxtaposition of tombs in the cemetery figures a fundamental opposition in the Lancelot-Grail cycle and marks a major difference between it and the *Noncyclic Lancelot*: Lancelot's *fin'amour* for Guenevere, exemplified by his act of lifting the first tombstone, is incompatible with the morality required to lift the second stone and achieve the Grail quest. Warnings proliferate as the time for the Grail quest draws near, but no one heeds them. Lancelot knows that he sins by loving the queen, but he believes that his worth and achievements are enhanced by that love, and therefore that it allows him to become and achieve more than would otherwise have been possible (*Lancelot*, sec. 85, pars. 2–3). The belief that sin might accomplish more than grace is an obvious error, as the *Queste* points out. It completes the gradual revelation of the truth of Lancelot's life and the evaluation of his career in the cycle. Guenevere is the reason for his moral decay and relative lack of prowess (*Queste*, pp. 125–27). The emergence of this truth about his love from beneath its surface attraction is consistent with single authorship, with a single architect perhaps directing the work of scribes in a kind of manuscript workshop (Frappier, *Etude*, 142–46, 440–55), and with a new author who realigned the plot to fit a new morality.

Whether written by a single author, or conceived by a single master planner, or put together by the cumulative, even contradictory, efforts of different writers and scribes, the composition of the cycle doubtless passed through at least four stages: (1) the gathering of Arthurian material, especially from twelfth-century romances, to focus on Lancelot and a potential Grail quest to be completed by Perceval; (2) the replacement of Perceval by Galaad, as well as the subordination of all the quests and adventures in Arthur's realm to the Grail quest; (3) the linking of Arthurian history to biblical history, and the modeling of secular events on examples drawn from moral and typological interpretations of biblical events; and (4) amplification, abridgment, or rearrangement by scribal interventions.

Both the *Estoire* and the *Merlin* build on material already contained in the three major parts of the *Lancelot en prose*. The *Estoire* develops references and allusions to early Grail history in the *Queste*, including the life of Adam and Eve after their expulsion from the Garden of Eden, Cain's murder of Abel, the Ship of Solomon sent sailing through the ages as a message to Galaad, and the invention of the Grail and christianization of Britain. Similarly, *Merlin* relates Merlin's birth, the conception and birth of Arthur, and Arthur's childhood, discovery, and Saxon wars, all of which are alluded to in the *Lancelot Proper*, which was written before both the *Estoire* and *Merlin*.

Whatever precise relationship might obtain between the *Noncyclic Lancelot* and the *Perlesvaus*, on the one hand, and the cyclic or Vulgate *Lancelot-Graal*, on the other, the seeds of the moral conception that emerges in the cycle are already planted in them. The *Noncyclic Lancelot* suggests a connection between Lancelot and Perceval's quest. *Perlesvaus*, while introducing Lancelot into Grail romances as Guenevere's lover, also highlights the contrast between his morality based on love service and Perlesvaus's based on chastity. The *Noncyclic Lancelot* gives its titular hero two names: "avoit non Lanceloz en sorenon, mais il avoit non an baptaisme Galaaz"[18] (His byname was Lancelot, but his baptismal name was Galahad). Galaad is Lancelot's real name. The mysterious name in the *Noncyclic Lancelot* yields its meaning when the new cycle introduces Lancelot's son, Galaad.

Robert de Boron projected a historical cycle that fit Arthurian legend into sacred history by connecting the Grail with Christ's death. The *Noncyclic Lancelot* and *Perlesvaus* attempt, each in its own way, to maintain that link implicitly or explicitly. But neither is full and complete in itself. The completion of the task is the achievement of the cyclic prose romance. Both the *Noncyclic Lancelot* and the *Lancelot-Graal* cycle make Lancelot central. In following Lancelot's career from birth to death, the cycle points to Galaad, especially after the *Charrette* episode. Galaad's virginity and chastity make him eminently suitable for achieving the quest for the Grail.

Subsequent Cycles and Compilations

Just as there is no certain explanation of the cycle's relation to *Perlesvaus* and the *Noncyclic Lancelot*, there is no general agreement as to how the *Estoire* and *Merlin* were added to the Vulgate cycle. Just as problematic is the relation between the Vulgate cycle and subsequent cycles or branches added to or parallel with it, such as the Post-Vulgate *Roman du graal*, the different versions of the *Tristan en prose*, and the diverse compilations that were collected in different manuscripts from antecedent or new material from the thirteenth into the fifteenth century.

It is difficult today to perceive how authors and publics understood what specific manuscripts communicated to them, manuscripts typically characterized by unique or varied scribal additions, abbreviations, dovetailing, and scribal errors. The Middle Ages hardly concerned itself with generic definitions or precise closure. The extent to which different works and cycles overlap with, complement, or rewrite one another—and this includes scribal interventions in the transmission of discrete manuscripts and groups of manuscripts—is far too complex perhaps ever to be sorted out. Many manuscripts have been lost, and many of those that survive are fragmentary or incomplete.[19] How authors and scribes knew one another's work, and how well they knew it, is highly uncertain. However, it is certain that the mind that brought together Lancelot, Guenevere, and the Grail invented a story that was to evoke great astonishment, reflection, and narrative elaboration for the rest of the Middle Ages.

The so-called Post-Vulgate *Roman du graal* or pseudo–Robert de Boron cycle survives only in some lengthy fragments and foreign versions. It too begins with an *Estoire*, then goes on to relate events in the careers of Arthur and his kindred left out of the *Lancelot Proper*, including tales about Gauvain and his brothers and Mordred, as well as tales about figures borrowed from the *Prose Tristan*. The elaboration of this version is too complicated, and in some ways controversial, to detail here, especially because of the fragmentary state of the surviving manuscripts. However, two features stand out clearly.

First, the narrator in several fragments refers to a mathematical division of the entire work into three branches, each branch equal in length to each of the others. The division was intended to allow the reader to ascertain whether his or her copy was complete. Unfortunately, the fragmentary state of the surviving manuscripts is such that there is no way to verify the assertion. The division is not implausible, and, indeed, Fanni Bogdanow has made a convincing case for it (*Romance*, 60–63). The text even states that many episodes, especially those about Lancelot, were deliberately left out in order to keep the tripartite division balanced. For example, the reader is referred to the Vulgate *Prose Lancelot* for the Lancelot story. Thus the Post-Vulgate *Roman du graal* is grafted onto the trunk of the *Lancelot-Graal*.

Second, the morality of the Post-Vulgate *Roman du graal* is even harsher than that of the Vulgate *Queste*. *Mescheances* occur prior to the Grail quest. They befall even good knights, who may unwittingly do wrongs for which they are punished, but which still threaten the salvation of their soul after repentance (Bogdanow, *Romance* 216). Even the assertion that the Lord tries those who are good more than those who are evil offers precious little comfort in the face of virtual predestination.

Balain is the prime exemplar of such unhappy knighthood. During a combat with King Pellean at the Grail Castle, Balain's sword breaks. Rushing about seeking another weapon, he comes upon the Bleeding Lance. Seizing it with sinful hands, he deals the Dolorous Stroke to Pellean. Unwittingly guilty, like Perceval in Chrétien's *Conte du graal*, he may not atone for his error. The consequences of this act are devastating for himself, the Round Table, and Arthur's kingdom: the Grail Castle collapses into ruin, the king is maimed, and three lands are blighted. The maimed king and the waste land must wait until Galaad heals the king and removes the blight. Balain's own misfortunes continue until finally he and his brother slay one another in combat.

The intention of the anonymous author or authors of the *Roman du graal* seems to have been twofold. First, to complete the history of Logres, Arthur's kingdom, in three parts fitting the tripartite division: its history from the death of Christ until Balain's Dolorous Stroke; the history of Logres until the arrival of Galaad; and the Grail quest and destruction of Arthur's kingdom in adaptations of the Vulgate *Queste* and *Mort*. Their second intention was to add or complete parts left out of Lancelot's story in the *Prose Lancelot*, notably the careers of Arthur and his nephews Gauvain and Gaheriez.

The *Prose Tristan* identifies two authors: Luces del Gat and Hélie de Boron. They designate either a first author and a continuator, as in the *Perceval* Continuations and the *Roman de la rose*, or two different versions such that Hélie is an adaptation of Luces.[20] Although two major versions of the *Prose Tristan* have been identified, their relationship to one another and to antecedent material is not agreed upon. There survive, in addition, several unique or special versions—continuations, abridgments, and other adaptations—that appeared during the rest of the Middle Ages (Baumgartner, *Tristan*, 16–98). The two major versions and their later adaptations rely more or less on the Vulgate and post-Vulgate cycles, of which they describe themselves as branches, as well as on other works such as *Guiron le courtois*.

Emmanuèle Baumgartner has shown that the *Prose Tristan* shifts emphasis from the love of Tristan and Iseut, which was the focus of the verse romances, to Tristan and the Round Table. Tristan becomes one of the three best knights, inferior only to Galaad and Lancelot (*Tristan*, 88). Part of the narrative includes the basic plot from the verse romances, especially the *version commune*. Tristan and Iseut fall in love because of the potion they mistakenly drink. After banishment from Marc's court in Cornwall,[21] Tristan begins a new life as a Round Table knight. Henceforth Tristan's principal activity is the quest, despite brief episodes when he is reunited with Iseut or King Marc. In the end Tristan does not die because his wife, Iseut of the White Hands, lies about Iseut the Blond's arrival to cure his poisoned wound, as in the verse romances. He is murdered by Marc. Marc himself emerges as a villain, enemy not only of the lovers but also of the Round Table.

Tristan's death occurs during the Grail quest. Marc murders his nephew who has returned unsuccessful from the quest which he did not understand or even wish to take part in. The murder is therefore a meaningless *mescheance*, as are so many deaths in the *Queste*. Tristan's story is cast largely in the context of the failed ideals of earthly chivalry. As a branch of the Vulgate Grail trunk this is the appropriate broad context for it. However, within the secular context of the actual *Prose Tristan* itself, most conflicts occur because of the excesses of earthly chivalry—murders, rapes, betrayals. Rare is the moderation characteristic of bygone chivalric ideals of prowess, love, and rectitude.

The *Prose Tristan* expresses its theme of immoderation most strikingly through Dinadan.[22] Dinadan believes knights should uphold the tripartite ideals of prowess, love, and rectitude. To seek combat for combat's sake, he asserts, is folly, not prowess; the love of Tristan (and others) for Iseut is foolish, not noble. Dinadan's mockery of or despair about his peers derives from their ignoble actions.

The *Prose Tristan* in its various versions shows a perplexing, internally contradictory world. The idealization of Galaad, Lancelot, and Tristan as the three best knights contains an inherent contradiction regarding ethical worldviews that is not resolved. Although the *Prose Tristan* is made into a branch of the Lancelot-Grail cycle and although parts of the Vulgate and Post-Vulgate *Queste* are interpolated into it, Tristan's goals overshadow those of the Grail quest. Rather than providing a moral victory, the quest causes Arthur's downfall because so many of his knights die, including Tristan himself. It is indeed perplexing that one of the best knights in the quest, Palamède, is both a pagan and Tristan's unsuccessful, albeit worthy, rival for Iseut's love.

The *Prose Tristan* in all its versions focuses on the sinful knights, hence those who can have no real adventures in the Grail quest and are victims of *mescheances*. The narrator states in a brief digression that the archbishop of Canterbury told him to leave matters of religious doctrine out of his book because, he says, romance should not treat religious subjects; hence the *Prose Tristan* is a "livre de deduit e de cortoisie" (sec. 171) (book of amusement and courtesy). Has the morality of the earlier prose romances become too harsh and problematic even for the Church?

The *Prose Tristan* also links the story of Arthur, Tristan, and the Round Table to the Matter of France. The end of the cycle announces Charlemagne's invasion of England. The French emperor will destroy the Grail Castle and establish a new empire in Arthur's realm. This amalgam of matters, in Jehan Bodel's sense, occurs in subsequent prose compilations and in the *Sept sages de Rome* cycle.

Compilations written during the rest of the Middle Ages collect material from the earlier cycles and offer it in new combinations. Some additions offer a new knight's story (*conte*), either that of a well-known figure heretofore neglected, as in the *Prose Erec* in the Post-Vulgate *Graal*, or of a totally new figure, as in *Alixandre l'Orphelin*. These interpolations are not separate romances, but new branches grafted onto earlier material. Still other additions complete or fill out material not fully developed in earlier versions. The *Livre d'Artus* does so with the Vulgate *Merlin* and other parts of the Vulgate cycle. Like the Post-Vulgate *Graal* and *Prose Tristan*, it focuses on a particular knight, here Gauvain. The alleged author of *Guiron le courtois* or *Palamède* is Helie de Boron, one of the authors claimed by the *Prose Tristan* as well. The name also identifies the author of the so-called *Livre de Bret*,[23] a work referred to as well in the Post-Vulgate *Graal*; but if the *Bret* was ever written, it is no longer extant. *Guiron* itself as a branch of the Grail romances relates the careers of the fathers of the Round Table knights during the reign of Arthur's father Uterpendragon. Thus we follow the adventures of Tristan's father, Meliadus; Erec's father, Lac; Palamède's father, Esclabor; Lancelot's father, Ban, and his uncle, Boort; Yvain's father, Urien; and others. Compilations like the *Artus* and *Guiron* are best understood as the work of scribes.

The best-known scribe is Rusticien de Pise. Rusticien worked simultaneously as both scribe and compiler, collecting earlier material, excising, rearranging, and recombining to realize unique manuscript versions of Arthurian, Grail, Tristan, and other matters. But Rusticien admits that his compilation lacks the coherence and order of the works of his predecessors, so abundant and multifarious is the material that he includes. Chronological order as well as focus on a principal figure are sacrificed in favor of prolixity as marvelous adventures proliferate. Rusticien says he intends to relate as much as possible, presumably for audiences more interested in quantity of marvelous adventures than in quality of conception or composition. But, as with all the prose romances, even Rusticien's bounty did not preclude later scribal interventions. By the end of the thirteenth century prose romance, like verse romance, favors compilation over composition.

A major feature of prose romance is the change from the secular ethos of verse romance to a religious morality. Whereas verse romance tends to define its ideals in terms of secular nobility, prose romance judges the nobility according to the moral truths of Christianity. This even explains the change from verse to prose. An anonymous life of the French king Philippe-Auguste, of which only the prologue survives, states that the biography has been written in prose in order to preclude the lying that versifying, including rhyming, entails. Thus it will be true—like the *Prose Lancelot*![24] This astonishing comparison with the *Prose Lancelot* is comprehensible only if one understands by "truth" the historical and moral paradigms upon which the *Lancelot-Graal* bases its evaluation of narrative and character. Two prominent examples are the pattern of Fall and Redemption, and the typology of Christian history.

The Fall illustrates original sin. In the Garden of Eden Adam and Eve fell from grace when they disobeyed God's command and ate the forbidden fruit. Their sin figures prominently in both the *Estoire del saint graal* and the *Queste del saint graal* as well as in the Post-Vulgate *Graal*, but far less in the *Prose Tristan*. When Adam submits to his wife's will instead of to God's, he allegorically chooses sensual delights, imagining them to be good. The Fall becomes an image of any sinful act, for example, that of Lancelot with Guenevere. Lancelot imagines that his love for the queen is the source of his worth and the reason for his extraordinary accomplishments. When they learn that he will not achieve the Grail quest because of his love, Lancelot explains to Guenevere that it makes no difference because her love has made him better than he would have been otherwise (*Lancelot*, sec. 85, par. 3). But when Lancelot offers the same argument in the *Queste*, a hermit sets him straight. Lancelot could have achieved the Grail quest, but his sin with Guenevere denies him that achievement. If he did accomplish anything, it is not because of love, but rather because of the residue of his former virtues (*Queste*, p. 126 ll. 23–30). He actually achieved less than he would have had he not loved.

But redemption is possible to achieve by means of contrition, confession, penance, and pardon. Lancelot is again the prime example. When he learns the deleterious effect of his love for Guenevere on his virtues, he sincerely regrets his sin and, by confessing it, can do penance. He does penance in ways that humiliate him before others, much as he had heretofore humiliated himself in the eyes of others for Guenevere's sake. But now the rewards are real. Lancelot wins pardon and is able, at least from a distance, to experience something of the Grail at the end of his quest.

Sin fits into the typological scheme of world history. According to this scheme, three major events pattern and give meaning to history. They are the Fall, the Coming of Christ and his Crucifixion, and the destruction of the world and Last Judgment. The pattern is rehearsed or "postfigured" in Arthurian history: the sin of Lancelot and Guenevere rehearses the Fall, whereas Galaad's birth is analogous to Christ's coming (*Queste*, p. 38 ll. 2–28); but the achievement of the Grail is not enough to save the Arthurian world, which performed so poorly in that Quest because of sin. Therefore the Grail is removed to Heaven, much as Christ ascended after the failure of the world to recognize him, a failure signified by the Crucifixion. The destruction of the world is rehearsed in the destruction of Round Table knighthood at the end of the *Mort Artu*.

As the Post-Vulgate cycle and the *Prose Tristan* adapt the quest for the Holy Grail to their versions of Arthurian history, the moral imperatives come with them, although Tristan himself is even less prone to contrition than Lancelot; he perseveres in his love for Iseut to the end. His insensitivity to the moral demands of the quest are analogous to Gauvain's in the Vulgate *Queste*. The Post-Vulgate *Graal* evinces an even more pessimistic conception of grace than the other two cycles. Balain, although unwittingly doing wrong, can receive no pardon for having touched the Holy Lance. From one misadventure to the other he stumbles towards condemnation and Hell. His almost Pascalian world of grace and predestination darkens the Arthurian landscape beneath an almighty God.

There is, therefore, an important distinction between verse romance and prose romance in the first half of the thirteenth century. Whereas verse romances continue to represent secular ideals in which chivalry, courtliness, and noble love are sought after and exemplified, prose romances introduce Christian moral and eschatological truths into the romance world. They impose a reevaluation and, finally, a radical condemnation of secular values. Knighthood, chivalry, and love are meaningful only in God's scheme of things. This holds as well for non-Arthurian prose romance.

Non-Arthurian Prose Romance

Although the Arthurian legend was the best-known matter of prose romance, other matters treated in prose interested medieval publics. These were sometimes combined with Arthurian material.

The *Sept sages de Rome* Cycle

The Seven Sages prose cycle grew from the verse *Sept sages*, much as Arthurian prose romance emerged from Chrétien, Robert de Boron, and the Tristan verse romances. However, it did not grow in conformity with a single conception; its mode of elaboration and informing *san* changed remarkably from branch to branch. By and large, the *Sept sages* cycle begins with and evolves from the static trial-frame narrative of the highly misogynist first branch, the *Sept sages en prose*, through interlacing narrative patterns no doubt adapted from the Arthurian cycles, toward a less-harsh morality, especially in *Laurin*, which introduces Arthur and the Round Table. The careers of many major figures are followed through different ages in life and several generations, thus permitting considerable diversity in the representation of character in single individuals as well as in the variety of individuals followed through some six or seven generations. The emperor Cassidorus is a prominent example of the transformations that mark the separate stages in life between youth and old age. From brilliant young knight, he changes into an accomplished emperor, then completes his life as a hermit with a saintly end.[25] On the other hand, his sons Helcanus, Pelyarmenus, and Fastydorus illustrate extremes of character in their propensities toward good or evil: Helcanus is an admirable knight and ruler, Pelyarmenus rules by treachery and deceit, and Fastydorus is a stay-at-home, do-nothing emperor. Cassidorus's subsequent children and grandchildren also find their places in the broad spectrum of the so-called ages of man and morality.

Geographically, the cycle ranges over the Mediterranean world, as the Roman emperors at Constantinople and Rome extend their empire and influence over the entire basin and even into the Arthurian realm (*Laurin*) and Hungary (*Cassidorus*).

The cycle contains six major branches:

1. *Les Sept sages Proper* borrows the trial-frame motif from the verse versions. A stepmother tries to have her stepson destroyed after he resists her attempts to seduce him. A sequence of novellas is adduced as exemplary evidence in the trial frame. The empress attempts to destroy her stepson by having him condemned for various kinds of crimes. She illustrates the crimes by relating stories of wicked sons in order to frighten his father, the Roman emperor, and convince him of his son's guilt. Her efforts are countered by the Seven Sages and, finally, the young man himself, who tell stories of wicked stepmothers. There are a number of versions of this branch, with different tales used in each version. However, the misogynist intent and the trial frame are common to all versions.

2. *Marques de Rome*, the second branch, also contains a trial based on exemplary stories and is rigorously misogynist. But the trial motif is episodic in a plot that moves between the Roman and Byzantine realms. Marques himself is the son of one of the sages in the *Sept sages*. But his virtue and wisdom contrast with a new generation of sages, who grow jealous and treacherous. Marques successfully resists seductive women (but he does marry), unwise counselors, and the machinations of the sages to become emperor of a united Roman and Byzantine empire.

3. *Laurin* continues *Marques* (who remains a principal figure alongside his son, Laurin). But it moderates the misogyny of the preceding branches, partly by emphasizing more secular concerns and partly by linking the matter of the Seven Sages to the Round Table. Marques goes to Gaul and comes into contact with Arthurian chivalry, courtesy, and even love.

4. In *Cassidorus* the narrative returns to the Mediterranean basin to recount the life of Laurin's son, Cassidorus. His is a lengthy biography in which moral severity alternates with a courtly ethos, depending on what age in life Cassidorus has attained and the twists and turns of fortune.

5. *Peliarmenus* (also called *Helcanus et Peliarmenus*) relates the careers of Cassidorus's two sons, Helcanus and Peliarmenus. Peliarmenus opts for treachery and deceit in his struggle for power, emerging as a king like Richard III (without the physical defects). He is finally undone. Meanwhile, Cassidorus has more children, then becomes a hermit. A mysticism in some ways reminiscent of the *Queste del saint graal* enters the plot but does not dominate the context or restore the harsh misogyny of the first two branches of the cycle.

6. *Kanor*, the final branch, relates the careers of Cassidorus's last sons and others related to him. It ties together numerous interlacing narrative strands, depicting the larger family of Cassidorus in a final vision of universal peace and harmony. Some episodes imitate the allegorical mode, matter, and motifs in Huon de Mery's *Tournoiement Antechrist*. The branch ends with the crowning of Cassidorus's grandson Libanor as emperor of the four parts of the world.

The Seven Sages cycle provides interesting comparative and contrastive material for prose romance. It diverges in content and context from the Arthurian cycles in some branches, but approaches them in others. Its drift toward more secular values contrasts with that toward greater moral rigor in the Vulgate and Post-Vulgate cycles. The Seven Sages cycle uses interlace, but expands the genealogical branching more than the Arthurian cycles. It is therefore analogous to ancestral verse romances of the twelfth century.

The later branches of the *Sept sages* cycle reflect the reaction against the gloomy worldview of earlier thirteenth-century romance. After the pessimism about human morality and human freedom made manifest in the prose romances before midcentury, audiences seem to prefer a less morally rigorous romance (Van Coolput, *Aventures*). In the prose romances this is evident as early as the *Prose Tristan* itself. From Chrétien and Robert on, Grail romances are somber works; they offer knighthood as a community of hermits. But the *Prose Tristan*'s valorization of Tristan, a reprobate sinner in the context of the Vulgate and Post-Vulgate cycles, and its marginalization of Galaad and the Grail restore secular chivalry and love to a prominence they had lost. The author's assertion that he, as a knight, may not write of religious matters moves prose romance, like thirteenth-century verse romance, toward the adventuresome, indistinguishable careers of questing knights—as meaningless in their ceaseless rounds of combat as Dinadan claims, yet a source of pleasure and escape for audiences who delight in the multifarious variety and seeming endlessness of marvelous adventures. Now that the adventure is all, the identities and distinctions of unique excellence fade. Similarly, the last branches of the *Prose Sept sages*, written in the second half of the century, abandon the cruel misogyny still dominant in *Marques de Rome* in favor of a brighter, more "Arthurian" courtliness exemplified by the young emperor Libanor, a secular Galaad.

Other Thirteenth-Century Prose Romances

Three works stand out among noncyclic romances, each treating the Matter of France: *Aucassin et Nicolete*, the *Fille du comte de Pontieu*, and *Roi Flore et belle Jehanne*. *Aucassin* is a hybrid. It is called a *chantefable* in the single manuscript in which it is preserved, probably because it alternates verse (with music) and prose. It belongs to the *Floire et Blancheflor* kind of story, relating how a Saracen girl bought by a French nobleman and a young knight who are in love triumph over adversity and unite in a happy marriage.

The *Fille du comte de Pontieu* is less direct in its approach to a happy ending. A wife raped by robbers tries to kill her husband for not protecting her. She is put to sea in a barrel, picked up by pirates, and sold to the sultan of Tunis. She marries him and gives birth to Saladin. In the meantime her husband and father are captured by Saracens; she frees both and all three return to France. The story continued to be adapted in the fifteenth century.

Roi Flore et belle Jehanne includes an intended rape that does not take place. It is an example of the wager motif that recurs in a number of verse romances. Two men, here a husband and his friend, wager on the wife's fidelity. When the friend deceitfully pretends to have gained her favors, the husband is saddened and departs. The wife, in order to exonerate herself, follows her husband disguised as a man. The rather simple plot includes several commonplace motifs like disguise, a wager, attempted rape, and barren couples. Jehanne largely dominates the situation, even when, after the death of her first husband, she marries King Flore—but only after insisting that he court her properly.

These romances anticipate the breakup of cycles into shorter works in the later Middle Ages.

Chapter 4
Thirteenth-Century Verse Romance

Judging by the number of surviving manuscripts, verse romance sank into decline in the thirteenth century. To be sure, the number of twelfth-century verse romances still being copied tended to mask the decline; nevertheless, prose romance generally displaced verse as the major narrative medium. Perhaps this suggests a different audience from that of verse romance—one of readers rather than listeners. Earlier audiences may also have had more secular interests. Prose, as we have seen, emphasizes religious and moral truths.

But despite a falling off in the number of original verse romances, thirteenth-century verse romance evinces great variety in matters and contexts. There is experimentation with different modes and manners, perhaps because of diverse audience and patron tastes and preferences. Arthurian romances often feature Gauvain as a major protagonist. They also prolong or multiply quests while increasing the number of adventures, and add continuations to earlier, sometimes incomplete works. Continuations are themselves subject to adaptation and continuation at the hands of succeeding scribes and according to the tastes of different writers, courts, and even manuscript workshops (*ateliers*).[1] The epic Matter of France continues to adopt features from Arthurian romance that will eventually cause the two to coalesce in late medieval and Renaissance chivalric novels (*romans de chevalerie*). A more French, and thus "realistic," kind of romance appears, the so-called *romans roses* of Jean Renart—"realistic" because they mirror settings and "idealized" economies of the French aristocracy.[2] Many adventure romances relate a chain of adventures, disappearances, abductions, searches, and misunderstandings that punctuate and prolong plots frequently based on folktale motifs like the wager on a woman's fidelity (*conte de la gageure*). Ancestral romances continue to be written, reflecting the grouping of epic matter or *gestes* by families. Some romances are episodic, others are virtually cyclic. Arthurian verse romance, while continuing the tradition of twelfth-century verse romance, also fell under the influence of the prose romances. The escapist tendency that emerges in prose romance after 1250 is even more obvious in verse romance. Some publics no longer seem interested in moral issues or the opposition between secular and religious moralities. Immorality among contemporary nobility could not be treated for fear of the consequences.[3] However, this fear did not preclude romance plots that reflect contemporary political and social circumstances in support of a patron's interests. For this reason, thirteenth-century and later romances often seem to mirror the political, social, or religious convictions or ambitions of the time and milieu for which they were written.[4]

Original experiments occur in non-Arthurian and allegorical romances. In both subgroups the lyric mode manifests itself, either by the insertion of lyric pieces, themes, and images into plots or by the allegorization and personification of lyrical experience in dream narrative. Two authors initiated these developments: Jean Renart and Guillaume de Lorris, both of whom wrote romances called *Roman de la rose*. In this they reflect the change of the romancer from *clerc* to *trouvère*, and of romance from a learned to a vernacular tradition.[5]

Arthurian Romances

From their beginnings Arthurian narratives were set in the British Isles. Although these romances glorified a *British* king, the English king claimed to be the legitimate successor of the British line when it died out after Arthur's death. Henry II, in conjunction with Glastonbury Abbey, may have encouraged the identification of English royalty with Arthur in order to confirm English dominion throughout the British Isles as well as on the Continent vis-à-vis the French king, to whom, as count of Anjou and duke of Normandy, he was in theory a vassal.[6] Arthur in this way could glorify the Anglo-Angevin dynasty much as Charlemagne glorified the Capetian dynasty. These considerations would explain Henry II's patronage of Wace and Marie de France; Chrétien's *Erec* and *Cligés* may also have been written for the English court.[7]

Many thirteenth-century Arthurian romances were written for insular patrons. In England and Scotland they appear to reflect, in an Arthurian past, current dynastic rivalries and ambitions (Schmolke-Hasselmann, *Versroman*, 178–248; Crane, *Insular*, 83–91). If this is so, we should regard the survival of Arthurian verse romances as a conservative, Anglo-Norman phenomenon. Their conventional "happy endings" would express hope for the survival of local baronial prerogatives analogous to those contracted in the Magna Carta.

Continuations, Preludes, and Interpolations to Chrétien's *Conte du graal*

The *Perceval Continuations* continue the quests of Gauvain and Perceval which, in Chrétien's *Conte du graal* and the first two Continuations themselves, are incomplete. These Continuations include actual continuations and new beginnings.

The pseudo-Wauchier, or *Gauvain Continuation*, exists in three versions. The "short" redaction was perhaps originally an independent romance about Gauvain fitted to Chrétien's torso. The "long" redaction is a later adaptation of the short redaction, in part designed to accommodate the *Second Continuation*. The "mixed" redaction is an amalgam of the short and long redactions.

The *First Continuation* is by far the most complex of the four because of its three redactions. All continue the exploits of Gauvain begun by Chrétien. All are incomplete. Furthermore, variant narratives within the three redactions reveal extensive scribal intervention intended to adapt the received text to new tastes and audiences. The principal drift of the changes is from a version originally characterized by a chivalric, but non-courtly ethos, toward more conventional courtly romance (Pierre Gallais, *Imaginaire*).

Each redaction contains six major branches. All but the third and sixth focus on Gauvain. The third is the totally independent Caradoc Briebras branch; the sixth relates exploits of Gauvain's brother, Guerrehés. The first Guiromelant branch completes the Gauvain episodes in Chrétien's *Conte du graal*. Branch two relates a siege of Brun de Branlant's castle and Gauvain's sexual encounter with the Pucelle de Lis, including his combats with her father and brother. The third branch tells the story of Caradoc, son of the magician Eliavrés and Ysave[8]; it includes a beheading test best known in its Middle English analogue, *Sir Gawain and the Green Knight*, and a chastity test won by Caradoc's *amie*. Branch four links Gauvain to the adventure of the knight Girflet at the Chastel Orgueilleux, which began in Chrétien and is found as well in the *Second Perceval Continuation*. Branch five contains Gauvain's visit to the Grail Castle[9]; it includes a Bleeding Lance, a broken sword that Gauvain is unable to join perfectly again, signifying his failure, and a Grail that floats in the air dispensing nourishment. The episode has little in common with Chrétien's version of events at the Grail Castle. The sixth branch tells how Guerrehés avenges the death of a knight brought to Arthur's court in a swan-drawn boat; he first loses to, then defeats the Petit Chevalier, who also reappears in the *Second Continuation*.

Gauvain's Grail visit is probably the closest in the romances to the Celtic versions of the adventure that probably circulated orally in France in the twelfth century. As the Grail floats freely dispensing food, a stationary lance bleeds into a vessel. The text identifies this lance with the lance that pierced Christ's side on the Cross. Gauvain fails to rejoin perfectly the broken sword, which reveals that he is unworthy to achieve the Grail adventure. He falls asleep during an explanation of the Grail mysteries and awakens outside the castle later on.

The *Gauvain Continuation*'s abrupt juxtaposition of narrative branches recalls paratactic composition in chronicles and in Beroul. It probably reflects the sequence of "stories" which might make up a performance by *jongleurs*. Like Beroul's *Tristan*, it links disparate episodes less by an overall idea or arrangement like a *bele conjointure* than by the titular hero who reappears in each block or episode, or by a member of his family, as in the introduction of Gauvain's brother Guerrehés. It also includes entirely independent material like the Caradoc branch.

The *Second Perceval Continuation*, also known as the Wauchier Continuation, continues Perceval's adventures in the incomplete *Conte du graal*. It too is incomplete. Two redactions begin the continuation. The "short" redaction breaks off at l. 10268, after which it follows the "long" redaction in the manuscripts.[10] In both long and short redactions the narrative centers on Perceval's effort to correct his failure in Chrétien by returning to the Grail Castle to ask the right questions; this he does in the last episode, although the achievement is not perfect. The narrative breaks off just as Perceval is proclaimed "lord of the palace" by the Fisher King.

But Perceval's quest for the Grail Castle is hardly direct, nor is it always uppermost in his mind. Numerous sideroads and branching adventures suggest that he is wandering about (*errances*) rather than pursuing a single-minded quest. There are narrative links both with the *Conte du graal* and with the *First Continuation*; these include a short Gauvain section during which Arthur's nephew seeks Perceval, demonstrates his prowess in a tournament, meets his son Guinglain, or the Fair Unknown (Biaus Desconneus), and recalls his own visit to the Grail Castle in the *First Continuation*. Perceval, for his part, returns home to meet his sister and see his mother's tomb; he also stops at Beaurepaire to visit Blancheflor. He has adventures at the Chastel Orgueilleux, the Mont Doloreux—both announced in the *Conte du graal* and the *First Continuation*—as well as others with the Maiden of the Chessboard Castle, with whom he has a sexual encounter. Perceval fails to join the broken sword of Gauvain's visit to the Grail Castle in the *First Continuation*. He also encounters a Tree Child, a Burning Candle Tree, and the Black Hand Chapel—mysterious adventures that the incomplete Continuation does not elucidate despite Perceval's questions.

Manessier's *Third Perceval Continuation* completes the Perceval story and the sequence of continuations. Perceval becomes more saintly. The Grail itself passes from a low-bottomed bowl (Chrétien) and a semblance of a Celtic religious object (*First Continuation*) to the chalice associated with the Last Supper and, finally, the eucharistic chalice. These developments stem from Grail traditions different from Chrétien's, especially oral traditions and the Vulgate cycle, the latter of which Manessier draws on for some episodes.

Manessier uses interlace like the prose romances. Perceval's quest alternates with those of other knights, some of which (those of Sagremor, Gauvain, and Boort) are rather long. Several loose narrative threads are tied up, some of which had been dangling since the *Gauvain Continuation*. However, no Galaad supplants Perceval, who is still the best knight in the world. He leaves Blancheflor and returns to the Grail at Corbenic to enter upon a hermit's life. He dies in the odor of sanctity, sustained to the end by the Grail.

Gerbert de Montreuil's *Fourth Perceval Continuation* includes some new Tristan and Gauvain episodes, and lacks a conclusion in the two surviving manuscripts, one of which links it to the end of the Second and the beginning of the Third Continuation. Perceval is still in quest of the Grail after the two unsuccessful or at least incomplete visits in Chrétien and the *Second Continuation*. He achieves a series of heterogeneous adventures, some of which interlace with those of Tristan and of Gauvain[11]; there are also episodic encounters with other Round Table knights and with Arthur. Perceval's meandering quest for the Grail Castle is completed in the final episode when he successfully joins the broken sword, but the episode is cut short in order to attach it to Manessier's Continuation.

Besides the Continuations new material was also added to the beginning and interpolated at various places within the narrative of Chrétien's unfinished *Conte du graal*. Such additions and interpolations clarify matters like the origins of the waste land and the inaccessibility of the Fisher King (*Elucidation*), the death of Perceval's father and his mother's flight into the forest (*Bliocadran*), and the broken sword.[12]

The so-called *Elucidation*, an anonymous, 484-line text, elucidates very little in the course of its enigmatic prehistory of the Grail story. Like the *Gauvain Continuation*, it may be an originally independent narrative added to Chrétien's romance and the first two Continuations. It begins with the rape of beneficent fountain-fairies by King Amangon and his knights. The fountain fays terminate their hospitality after the rapes, the kingdom becomes a waste land, and the Fisher King's court becomes inaccessible. The knights of the Round Table, including Perceval and Gauvain, seek his court because the Grail is found in it. Mystery shrouds the destruction of Logres which it announces. Each of seven mysterious "Guardians" has a story that is said to proceed from the Grail, but none is told.

In 800 lines the anonymous *Bliocadran* develops sparse details in Chrétien on the violent deaths of Perceval's father and brothers and his mother's flight into solitude. The father, Bliocadran, whose eleven other brothers had died in wars, is himself killed in a tournament. Perceval is born at the same time. Lest the boy also die in combat, the mother flees with him into the waste forest so he will never know knighthood.

Although the first three *Perceval Continuations* survive in a large number of manuscripts by the standards of verse romance, the *Fourth Continuation*, the two preludes, and the interpolations do not. No manuscript contains all the additions to the *Conte du graal* (the most complete, Mons Bibliothèque Publique 331/206, lacks the *Fourth Continuation*). The Continuations, including scribal interventions and adaptations, begin with the paratactic structuring and knightly ethos of the short versions of the *Gauvain Continuation*. Subsequent versions and adaptations of it and the *Second Continuation* enhance the courtly veneer of the tales in more coherent, interlacing patterns of discrete adventures. A focus on the Grail and the adoption of the rigorous morality of the prose romances lead to greater emphasis on virginity and chastity in the last two Continuations. The moral ethos contrasts sharply with that prevailing in other thirteenth-century verse romances, whether Arthurian or not.

Discrete Arthurian Romances

Arthurian verse romance continued to be written after Chrétien and Raoul de Houdenc, and even after prose romance dominated the genre.

The verse romances concentrate on the quests and adventures of titular knights, most of whom enter the Round Table circle. They grew longer as well, so that the last examples (including Froissart's fourteenth-century *Meliador*) may extend to over 30,000 lines. But unlike the *Perceval Continuations* they are independent works. Even Girart d'Amiens's *Escanor*, 26,000 lines long, although episodic in many ways, inspired no known sequel or continuation.

Like the *Perceval Continuations*, thirteenth-century verse romances recycle traditional matter, motifs, conventions, and images to relate the adventures of various titular or prominent knights to whom each romance is devoted. But they are independent of one another, unlike the *Perceval Continuations*, the different branches of prose romance, ancestral romances, or, indeed, twelfth-century romances such as Chrétien's *Charrette* and *Yvain*. Each merely recounts another set of adventures radiating from and returning to Arthur's court.

Twelfth-century Arthurian verse romance and the *Perceval Continuations* rely by and large on the single quest plot of the titular hero. In the thirteenth century this motif is characteristic of most Arthurian romances, although some variants—as in Chrétien and Raoul—introduce additional, parallel questers like Gauvain, or even a multiplication of potential quests, as in the *Conte du graal* (ll. 4741–46). In single-quest romances a rather lengthy story is related, often containing more heterogeneous adventures than in Chrétien or Raoul. On the other hand, in the manner of the *Charrette*, episodic romances focus on a single adventure which in itself may be only part of a larger quest or *errance*. By midcentury Arthurian verse romances begin to adopt the interlace patterns adumbrated in Chrétien and fully deployed in prose romance. However, the unique excellence that identifies and distinguishes the protagonists of Chrétien's and Raoul's romances recedes before the pleasure of recounting marvelous adventures. The multiplication of heroes, quests, and multifarious adventures of interest principally for their marvels suggests anew a transformation in audience tastes from ethical and social idealism to adventure for adventure's sake.

Four kinds of verse romances stand out. Although there is a degree of overlap, common features distinguish single-quest romances, brief or episodic romances, Gauvain romances, and interlace romances.

Single-quest romances focus on the quests and wanderings of a single titular knight.

Durmart (15,998 lines) has three main parts of unequal length, but of different ethical significance. Each part corresponds to a stage in

Durmart's life. In the first he is guilty of *recreantise*, passing his time idly in adulterous dalliance with the wife of his father's seneschal. The father's admonitions bring Durmart to his senses, and in the second part he sets out in quest of the queen of Ireland. He finally demonstrates his superiority by sitting in the Perilous Seat. In the third part, after marrying the queen, Durmart goes to Rome to relieve the pope, who is besieged by pagans. He then finishes his life in peace and prosperity.

Durmart follows a clear line of development from idle young prince through demonstration of chivalric prowess and worth to defense of Christendom. The romance contains some motifs common in Perceval romances: the Perilous Seat as well as a candle tree in which a Christ-like child sits. The pope explains all these marvels: the tree is the world; good shines forth in the burning candles, whereas those that go out represent evil; the tree child is Christ. But allegorization goes no further. Durmart ends his life in the bosom of his family, not like Perceval in a hermit cell.

Guillaume le clerc's *Fergus* is a parody of the Perceval story.[13] Young Fergus is raised away from court, but not because his father is dead. The father is a peasant to whom his noble mother was wed. Unlike his base brothers, Fergus inherited his mother's noble disposition. He desires to become a knight after seeing Arthur and Round Table knights, including Erec and Perceval, returning from the hunt for the white stag. He is knighted, falls in love with the beautiful Galiene, then loses her. His quest for her contains numerous adventures, the happy conclusion to which is marriage. Although Guillaume alludes to Perceval's quest for the Grail in his prologue, *Fergus* contains no Grail narrative; the humor that pervades the romance recalls Perceval's own blunders, but the story lacks religious significance. Its parody of the Arthurian ideal may also satirize the aristocratic ethos.

Yder (6769 lines, but the beginning is missing in the only extant manuscript) criticizes Arthur himself. It relates Yder's adventures in search of his father. Like Perceval, Yder lived alone with his mother for 17 years before setting out on his search. His quest is crowned with success; he even reunites father and mother in marriage after his own marriage. Keu is prominent as a treacherous courtisan, and Arthur as a jealous, untrustworthy sovereign; perhaps he mirrors John Lackland (Schmolke-Hasselmann, *Versroman*, 204–5). The court is corrupt, whereas Yder, ever a source of courage and valor, restores social order based on love, fidelity, and trust.

Gauvain romances (including those about his brothers or sons) are a special variety of single- or double-quest romance. They evince fascination with Arthur's nephew. Numerous romances treat episodes in his life, following Chrétien's tendency to use him as a foil or contrast to the titular knight in the *Charrette*, *Yvain*, and the *Conte du graal*. The *Chevalier à l'épée* even faults Chrétien for not having written a romance about Gauvain.

Gauvain's character varies from romance to romance, although he retains certain conventional features. He is something of a womanizer and on occasion a violent knight. He often demonstrates mythical restoration of strength, usually at noon. On the positive side, he is a valued companion to other knights, and a model of chivalry who willingly identifies himself whenever asked.

Arthurian romances from Chrétien and Raoul to the end of the thirteenth century give more prominence to Gauvain than to other recurrent figures like Keu, Sagremor, or even Arthur himself. But in only a few is he the principal figure, notably the First *Perceval Continuation*, the *Chevalier à l'épée*, the *Mule sans frein*, the *Atre périlleux*, and *Hunbaut*.

Although *Hunbaut* is incomplete, the surviving fragment illustrates the alternation between Gauvain and the titular hero that is characteristic of Gauvain and other double-quest romances.[14] Hunbaut and Gauvain are companions in quest for about 1800 lines, then separate to pursue different adventures. Gauvain is with Arthur until the 3618-line fragment breaks off; Hunbaut's adventures were related in the missing part of the sole manuscript. In *Gliglois* Gauvain loses the love of Belté to Gliglois, his squire; the lady at first appears harsh and cruel toward the young squire, but this attitude proves to have been only a test to prove that Gliglois's love was superior to Gauvain's. On the other hand, the anonymous *Chevalier à l'épée* and Paien de Maisières's *Mule sans frein* relate only a single episode in the career of Arthur's nephew. Each resembles the lay in length, focusing on a marvelous amorous adventure.

Some verse romances adapt interlace from prose romance. However, Chrétien de Troyes had already set an example in the incipient multiplication of quests at the beginning of the second part of the *Conte du graal*. Although some of these romances may be quite long—Girart d'Amiens's *Escanor* has about 26,000 lines, *Claris et Laris* over 30,000— they do not reach the physical proportions of the prose cycles. However, the desire to relate the parallel quests of several knights necessarily entails the use of interlace to allow for chronological simultaneity. A number of romances use the principle of the multiplication of quests.[15]

The *Merveilles de Rigomer*, by an otherwise unknown Jehan, relates a large-scale attempt by the Round Table knights to liberate Lancelot after he is imprisoned in Rigomer. Gauvain and 57 other knights set out on separate routes to accomplish this goal. The romance records the parallel adventures of seven knights, with Gauvain being the one who finally liberates Lancelot. The potential for a very complex narrative is therefore only partially realized.

The same is true for Girart d'Amiens's *Escanor*, except that its complexity derives less from multiple quests than from multiplication of personages with their own plots, including several Bruns, several Escanors, Girflet (here Gauvain's brother), and others. Keu and Gauvain are the main protagonists. Love tempers Keu's usual irascibility. He achieves a number of adventures and wins a great tournament for his lady. Gauvain's adventures begin when Escanor le beau accuses him of murder. Among many other encounters, we learn how Gauvain won his horse, the Gringalet. There is much movement to and fro, but few actual quests. Instead narrative moves from court to combat in tournaments, sieges, open-field warfare, duels, and the like. *Escanor* belongs to those romances that favor the tournament as motif. These include the semi-Arthurian *Sone de Nausay*, as well as a subgenre that merely relates a tournament: Sarrasin's *Hem*, Jacques Bretel's *Tournoi de Chauvency*, and others.[16]

Claris et Laris is far and away the most striking example of systematic interlace. Three questing sequences mark three divisions in the plot. The first part is a double quest of Arthur's court by Claris and Laris. The second employs multiple quests: 12 knights set out in search of Laris, who has been abducted by a fay. The plot follows the separate quests by means of rudimentary interlace until Claris liberates his companion; on the way he also liberates some knights imprisoned during their own adventures. The third part is the most elaborate. Laris is abducted once again, this time by the king of Denmark. No fewer then 30 knights set out to liberate him. The author succeeds in relating something about each one, as in the second part. The plot focuses successively on three groups of 10 knights who then separate; all their quests are related one after the other. However, Claris criss-crosses the grid, freeing knights, joining up with others, and finally leading them into Denmark. The conclusion is predicted in one episode that features Merlin.

Arthurian verse romance thus moves from emphasis on the unique excellence of the titular knight or knights toward variety and proliferation of multifarious adventures. Identity as personification of a role, common in twelfth-century romance, gives way as knights are often distinguishable only by name, assumed name, or byname. In the *Atre périlleux*, Gauvain loses his name—he is said to be dead—and must recover his identity before returning to court. On the other hand, the *Chevalier aux deux épées* keeps the protagonist's name, Meriadeuc, a secret until he learns it himself at the end of the 12,353-line romance. However, his multifarious adventures identify features of his character and his past, thus giving substance to the name when we finally learn it.

Narrative Lays

A number of anonymous lays in the Matter of Britain tradition survive from the late twelfth century and the first half of the thirteenth century. They tend to focus on the love of a mortal for a fay or faylike maiden away from court, as in *Guingamor*, *Graelent*, and *Desiré*. An encounter of both lovers with the Otherworld occurs in the *Lai de l'espine*. A variant of this type addresses the inconstancy of women in this world; Robert Biket's *Lai du cor*, for example, centers on a chastity test. Other surviving lays mock idealized love, as in the *Lai du lecheor*.

Lays in the *roman rose* tradition like Jean Renart's *Lai de l'ombre* and the *Châtelaine de Vergi* retain the ethos and settings of the *roman rose*, but in shorter narratives. They treat themes like incipient love, conjugal and family conflicts, betrayal, and jealousy. But they do so in French settings, that is, in castles and towns with French names. The endings may be happy or unhappy, as with the longer *romans roses*. They may pose fascinating turns in plot, like that in Jean Renart's *Ombre*, where a gesture opens a lady's heart to love in spite of herself.

Romancing of Epic

Epics (*chansons de geste*) continue to show the influence of romance as oral improvisation gives way to literary epic. Rhyme appears with the octosyllabic couplet. Some original epic material like *Huon de Bordeaux* became so marvelous in its continuations as to obscure any distinction between epic and adventure romance in the cycle.[17]

Later epics were turned to prose and assumed the features, topics, and motifs of prose romance. Indeed, the two were amalgamated, much as in the amalgamation of Seven Sages with Arthurian matter in *Laurin*.

Non-Arthurian Romances

Other romances, such as *Galeran de Bretagne, Sone de Nausai*, and Heldris de Cornuälles's *Roman de Silence*, touch only tangentially on the Matter of Britain. Still others are set principally in France or French-speaking regions and thus represent the Matter of France; this group includes Jean Renart's *Escoufle*, his *Roman de la rose* (*Guillaume de Dole*), and his *Lai de l'ombre*; Philippe de Beaumanoir's *Jehan et Blonde* (partially set in England) and his *La Manekine*; and the anonymous *Joufroi de Poitiers*.

Some non-Arthurian romances introduce episodes and motifs from the ubiquitous Matter of Britain, much as the twelfth-century Tristan romances introduce Arthurian scenes. Renaut's *Galeran de Bretagne* (incorrectly attributed to Jean Renart) is analogous to Marie de France's lay "Fresne," much as Gautier d'Arras's *Ille et Galeron* is analogous to her "Eliduc." The heroine even retains her botanical name, "Fresne." The 7800-line work includes narrative sequences like love blossoming in childhood and lovers in search of one another as in *Floire et Blancheflor*, the *Lai de l'espine*, and Jean Renart's *Escoufle*. The ties of the Matter of Britain with other matters show that romance as genre has become a coat of many colors.

Sone de Nausai includes a few episodes set on an island off the coast of Norway, where one finds the Grail in a monastery founded by Joseph of Arimathea and preserved by monks there since that time. In Heldris's *Silence*, Silence is born a girl and an only child in a kingdom where no daughter may inherit. Disguised and raised as a boy, she accomplishes numerous exploits as squire, *jongleur*, and, finally, knight. After Merlin identifies Silence as a woman, the law is changed and she assumes the dress and manners of a woman, marries, and lives happily ever after.

Despite the Briton or Arthurian trappings of these romances, they belong by subject to the Matter of France. The image they offer of aristocratic mores conforms more closely to thirteenth-century practice and realia, however idealized these may be. This is apparent in court ceremonies and festivities like tournaments, feudal disputes, court intrigues, family structures and hierarchies, inheritance, marriage, and social order. Love is consummated in marriage; problems stem from conflicts about lineage and rank. Knights may go forth to show prowess, but they do so in tournaments and wars rather than alone in dark forests or on long quests. They retain contact with their lands and inheritance. There is no equivalent to the Round Table for which knights leave their lands more or less permanently. In the Matter of France knights remain attached to their place of origin or join a new family by marriage. The marvelous stems from extraordinary twists in the narrative caused by fortune or chance.

The *roman rose*, or sentimental romance (also called "realistic" and "lyric" romance), is the most original subgenre in thirteenth-century romance. Examples include Jean Renart's *Escoufle*; the *Roman de la rose*, usually known as *Guillaume de Dole* so as not to confuse it with the *Roman de la rose* by Guillaume de Lorris and Jean de Meun; and the non-Arthurian *Lai de l'ombre*. Other works in this subgroup are Gerbert de Montreuil's *Roman de la violette*, Philippe de Beaumanoir's *Jehan et Blonde* and *La Manekine*, Jakemes's *Châtelain de Couci*, and the anonymous *Joufroi de Poitiers*. Like twelfth-century non-Arthurian romance, they experiment with narrative forms and themes. As sentimental romance they mark one of the original features of thirteenth-century verse romance.

These romances were long considered "realistic" because of their apparently contemporary, French dramatis personae and settings. Lyric pieces inserted in several of them enhance the "realism" while serving to define the sentiments of the persons singing, the setting in which the songs are sung, or the plot they are related to. The first romance with lyric insertions is Jean Renart's *Roman de la rose* (*Guillaume de Dole*). Jean Renart was well aware of the originality of his adaptation. The example caught on. Lyric insertions appear in the *Roman de la violette*, the *Châtelain de Couci*, the *Châtelaine de Vergi*, as well as in the *Tristan en prose*, the *Cassidorus* branch of the Seven Sages prose cycle, Froissart's *Meliador*, and the allegorical *dit* that emerges in the thirteenth century.[18]

The insertion of lyric pieces evokes the *trouvère*, the northern French counterpart to the Occitan troubadour. Authors no longer seem to come from the clerical class. Rather, like the lives of troubadours described in Occitan *vidas* and *razos*,[19] narrative events illustrate the inserted songs. The *Châtelain de Couci* itself relates the fictional life of the *trouvère* of the same name.

These romances also adapt folktales and folktale motifs or plots to romance conventions. Much as in earlier adventure romances such as *Floire et Blancheflor* and *Ille et Galeron*, the separation of lovers permits the elaboration of a basic folktale plot including quest and reunion. Jean Renart's romances make the blemish in perfection—female beauty or birds of prey—the focus for narrative complication. In his *Roman de la rose*, the "rose" is a birthmark, a rose-colored blemish on the heroine's thigh; the *Escoufle* uses an ignoble bird, the *escoufle* (a variety of kite).

The *Escoufle* is a father-son romance like Chrétien's *Cligés*. It reports Richart de Montvilliers's crusading triumphs framed by his reception at the court of the Holy Roman Emperor. He enjoys such favor at court that the emperor promises the empire and the hand of Aelis, his daughter and sole heir, to Richart's son Guillaume. Richart's untimely death abruptly terminates his influence at court. Malevolent advisers prevail upon the emperor to take back his word. Meanwhile Guillaume and Aelis fall in love. They take flight together, but are separated when a kite—the *escoufle* of the title—seizes and carries away Aelis's ring. A number of years go by during which the two young people undergo numerous adventures in search of one another; they are finally reunited and marry, after which Guillaume wins the throne he had been promised.

In Jean Renart's *Rose*, Liénor, the maid with the blemish, is betrothed to the Holy Roman Emperor Conrad, through his friendship with her brother, Guillaume de Dole. The core of the plot is an adaptation of the folktale motif of the deceptive wager. The emperor's seneschal, jealous of Guillaume's preferment, contrives to prevent the marriage by pretending, through his inadvertent discovery of her secret blemish, that he seduced Liénor and that she cannot marry the emperor because she has lost her virginity. When the seneschal fails to recognize her at court, Liénor herself undoes his plot by proving that he never saw her or her blemish.

One feature of the *Rose* is highly original. The plot's three parts focus in turn on one of its three principal figures: the Emperor Conrad, Guillaume himself, and finally Liénor. The plot first evokes the playboy life of the emperor before he meets Guillaume. Then the narrative center shifts from Conrad to Guillaume, who triumphs in a great tournament and arranges the emperor's marriage with his sister, Liénor. In the last part, the seneschal falsely accuses Liénor and Liénor vindicates herself. This drift of the narrative from one major figure to another has been identified by Michel Zink as "sliding," or *glissement*, from one plot to another (Zink, *Roman rose*, 47–48, 66–68).

Jean Renart's romances manifest a freedom in mores, even a sensuality, not evident in most verse romance. The round of parties and other festivities that fill Conrad's life before he falls in love with Liénor, the intimacy of human contact even when there is no apparent sexual attraction, the free-spending economy based on celebration and pleasure seek-

ing—all evokes a utopian view of society hardly consonant with thirteenth-century reality (Zink, *Roman rose,* 17–44).

Gerbert de Montreuil wrote the *Roman de la violette* or *Gerard de Nevers*
in the tradition of the wager folktale. Corresponding to the rose on
Liénor's thigh is a birthmark on Euriaut's left breast that resembles a
violet. An unscrupulous wagerer learns of the birthmark and uses the
information to pretend that he has seduced Euriaut. But the deception is
ultimately unmasked.

Some non-Arthurian romances evince a world less "rosy" than Jean
Renart's, although they may retain the "happy ending" of his
romances. Philippe de Beaumanoir's *La Manekine* and Jean Maillart's
Comte d'Anjou, like the earlier *Apollonius de Tyr* and, indirectly, Marie de
France's "Lai des deux amants," deal with incest. Philippe de
Beaumanoir's *Jehan et Blonde* treats a forced marriage; it includes
mockery of the British accent in French.[20] Jakemes's *Châtelain de Couci
et dame de Fayel* concludes when the jealous husband serves the heart of
the dead castelain to his lady. In it we encounter the greyer tones of
the realism once used to describe these romances. That is, the ideal
world of the *roman rose* and *trouvère* lyric recedes before dramatic, even
tragic denouements. Beautiful tournaments become spectacles of violence and treachery. Marriages lead to unexpected infidelity, betrayal,
family interference, or incest.[21]

There is a striking "literary" quality to much thirteenth-century
romance. Michel Zink has identified this quality as a form of subjectivity
deriving from emphasis on the subject—the *moi*—of the specific
romance.[22] That is, the time and place of the narrative tends to coincide
with the time and place of the narrator or author, a coincidence that has
contributed to the designation "realist" for such romances. Moreover,
biographical features of the author's or narrator's own life may punctuate or counterpoint the narrative, or lyric pieces may be inserted for
which the romance provides a narrative commentary or explanation,
much as in the Occitan *vidas* and *razos* referred to above, which were
written to explain biographically the place of lyrics in the loves of the
troubadours who wrote them, their patrons, acquaintances, and loved
ones. Without actually inventing the modern individual, such subjectivity nonetheless introduces personal expression of emotion and experience, pointing both to the projection of subjective states in allegorical
romance and, later, to the sentimentality of some late medieval *nouvelles*
and novels.

Allegorical Romance

A major innovation in thirteenth-century romance was the extended use of allegory, especially in dream vision poetry. Romance used it in major works, notably the *Queste* and *Estoire* in the Vulgate cycle. But the *Roman de la rose* begun by Guillaume de Lorris and completed by Jean de Meun some 40 years later is the first thoroughly allegorical romance. Guillaume explicitly identifies the *Rose* as a dream vision in his prologue. He uses personifications, an idealized setting (*locus amoenus*), and stages in love from first sight of the beloved to potential consummation (*gradus amoris*), to elaborate his dream and vision of love.[23]

Guillaume still refers to his work in terms earlier romancers use: *conte*, *estoire*, and *roman*.[24] He says that the dream relates his own experience, transformed into the allegorical mode and generalized as an art of love. The God of Love's central discourse on love, including love's relation to courtesy and its trials and consolations, is followed by the Lover's encounters with the Rose and the personifications attributed to it.

The word *adventure* defines the encounters between the Lover and the woman he loves in the God of Love's "commandments" (*Rose*, l. 2255). The four adventures with which he illustrates the encounters are all unsatisfactory. Transformed into the Lover's allegorical quest of the Rose, the adventures are dream encounters. In the first adventure the Lover impetuously asks for the Rose, whereupon he is angrily and summarily dismissed. In the second he gains a kiss, but this too ends badly when doubts arise as to his intentions, and he is once again banished from the Rose. All the rose bushes are walled up in Jealousy's castle and guarded by four sentinals, Male bouche (Slander or Gossip), Dangier (Domination), Peur (Fear), and Honte (Shame).

The *Rose* is peopled by such personifications. They advance the plot from adventure to adventure. The personifications embody conventional attributes of lovers and ladies in *trouvère* lyric and earlier romances. The personified attributes define the qualities of an idealized figure and, consequently, of the ideal that the figure exemplifies. In the *Rose* two central images, the Lover and the Rose, epitomize lovers and their loved ones together with their respective attributes as detached personifications. These two complexes are brought into contact and interact throughout the rest of the narrative. For example, the Lover asks for a kiss, which Bel Accueil (Fair Welcome) grants at the instigation of Venus's firebrand of sexual desire. Other adventures are, as it were, internal, as when personified attributes like Peur and Honte debate various courses of action and, subsequently, Male bouche, scandalized, stirs up the Rose's guardians by denouncing the kiss to Jalousy.[25]

The personification of Dangier demonstrates how personification might play upon the semantic range of words. In the thirteenth century *dangier* did not yet mean "danger," as today, but rather "domination," power over someone or something; it is therefore related to words like *dominus*, *dame*, and *don* (*dom*). But domination may be exercised rightly or wrongly. Right domination is a noble prerogative; unjust domination is villainous. The description of Dangier as a peasant with a club rather than a baron with sword and shield underscores his villainy. When Bel Accueil is present, courtesy is manifest—Bel Accueil is the son of Courtesy—and Dangier falls asleep (Kelly, *Medieval Imagination*, 88–91).

Other figures are less complex. Reason remonstrates with the Lover, but is rejected and departs. Jealousy awakens Honte and Peur, who in turn awaken Dangier after the kiss. Jealousy herself may be variously interpreted—she may even manifest the beloved's fear that the Lover may not be sincere.

The allegorical mode problematizes the interpretation of the romance. By definition, allegory cannot have only a literal meaning. What is the other, allegorical meaning of the *Rose*? Is it the truth of a noble love shown forth through dreamlike settings, postures, and actions? Or is it a veiled critique of love that spoofs what is little more than lust? Or, finally, may we read it as a kind of Song of Songs, the biblical love story allegorized into love for God, the Virgin, and the Church?

The problem is compounded by the incomplete state of the work. Guillaume promises a gloss on the story, but there is no extant gloss unless by gloss he meant internal commentary. But there is Jean de Meun's continuation that adds some 18,000 lines to Guillaume's 4000. Jean adds to Guillaume's allegory lengthy discourses and dialogues not only on love but on an array of matters philosophical, moral, theological, scientific, and erotic which, as allegories, broaden and deepen the problematics of love.

In fact, Jean's continuation has little in common with romance. Instead of focusing on adventures, as Guillaume de Lorris still did, Jean elaborates his topics by extensive discourses and debates. To be sure, a war of the sexes continues, especially in the middle and at the end of the work. But the real meaning of the poem is developed in lengthy digressions that expand upon various ethical and moral issues the narrative exemplifies.

The *Rose* fits into a general movement away from the historical mode of romance toward the allegorical mode best represented in dream visions. Raoul de Houdenc had already experimented with allegorical visions. He used contexts of love and courtesy and of the afterlife in two short poems, the *Roman des eles* and the *Songe d'enfer*; these were followed in turn by Rutebeuf's vision of the path to salvation in the *Voie de paradis*. About the time Guillaume wrote his *Rose*, Huon de Mery wrote the *Tournoiement Antechrist*. This curious poem was influenced by both Raoul and Chrétien de Troyes. The framing image of the tournament, a psychomachia with personifications and Arthurian motifs, depicts a love that at first seems noble, but then drifts into carnality. To Rutebeuf such works are no longer *romans* but *dits*. The new designation is established by the end of the thirteenth century in Nicole de Margival's *Dit de la panthère d'amours*. At the turn of the fourteenth century, it represents a new kind of writing. Like the Rose in the *Roman de la rose*, the Panther— traditionally an allegory of Christ—is assigned the attributes of the beloved. It rather fits the *dit* of late medieval *poètes*.

The allegorical tradition contained the elements of the new genre of the *dit*, in which disparate material is arranged according to a model or plan that structures and explains its underlying significance. Authors of *dits* came to be called *poètes*. The poet in this tradition was learned in origin,[26] but the tradition itself developed from allegorizations of various sources, especially Ovid.

Chapter 5
Romance after 1300

Although the *dit* or dream vision dominates late medieval French literature, romance remains a viable genre, evincing new and interesting developments on its own as well as under the influence of the allegorical *dit* and the novella, the latter imported from Italy. Romance still rejects the harsh morality of the early and mid-thirteenth century in favor of marvels, fantasy, even humor, in adventures. This is not to say that late medieval romances are not interesting aesthetically and artistically. As in thirteenth-century prose romance, romances such as *Perceforest* and *Ysaÿe le triste* adapt earlier materials by rewriting, interpolation, or anticipation and continuation.

Concomitant with the cyclical extension of thirteenth-century prose romances are two contrasting developments. First, the focus changes from the single knight such as Lancelot, Tristan, Arthur, or Gauvain to whose story others attach themselves, like branches on a tree, to a collection of knights who epitomize what Taylor terms "collective heroism" ("Fourteenth," LCT 301). Each knight has a story parallel to others on the same level of nobility, as well as to the adventures of other knights on other social tiers. Second, emphasis passes from unique excellence defined by the accumulated accomplishments of an exemplary protagonist to the unique adventure that could, in fact, stand alone. The latter development breaks up the cycle, permitting isolation of sequences and episodes, as in the *Chevalier au papegau*, which relates a brief quest by young Arthur.

Such segmentation met two concurrent developments: the prosification of earlier verse romances, especially for the Burgundian court, and the appearance of the novella in France after translations of Boccaccio's *Decameron* popularized the new form. The novella develops one or more episodes from a conventional setting until a final surprise ending closes it humorously.[1] In the *Cent nouvelles nouvelles* the novella is a short story in prose, based on suspense and surprise in conventional farcical motifs: lust, drunkenness, robbery, stupidity, and the like. If the sentimental or moral potential of the plot is enhanced, the novella lengthens, transforming interest from the usually humorous denouement to the elaboration of character in novel or interesting ways. This may be observed by comparing the length of nouvelle 11 with 26, and the tonality of 8 and 26.[2] These developments enhanced the literary qualities and diversity of shorter tales more than did fabliaux. The shorter lay and romance evolve from farce to comedy and sentimentality. Internal consistency in plotting and characterization accompany the isolation of episodic sequences from interlaced prose cycles. The classical novel is beginning to emerge. We may observe its beginnings in some of the *Cent nouvelles nouvelles* (especially 26 and 99), *Jehan de Saintré*, *Floridan et Elvide*, *Paris et Vienne*, and *Jean de Paris*. These near-novels point toward Marguerite de Navarre's *Heptaméron* and the more distant *Princesse de Clèves*.

Amalgams and Compilations

Prose romance was not dead. Cycles were still evolving and reforming. *Ysaÿe le triste* prolongs the *Prose Tristan* by relating the careers of Ysaÿe, the son of Tristan and Iseut, and Ysaÿe's own son, Marques l'exilé. The longest and most original late prose romance is *Perceforest*, a fourteenth-century pseudohistory of Britain beginning with Alexander the Great's alleged stay there. This enormous compilation recycles Latin and romance traditions in a vast design. This last glorious image of chivalry amalgamates for grand display Christian, Arthurian, Roman, and French matters.

Perceforest fills the great historical stretch of British history from Alexander the Great's pre-Roman stay on the island to the immediate ancestors of Arthur, as chronicled in Geoffrey of Monmouth's *History* and the various versions of the *Brut* that derive from it. This contrived dynastic history of Britain alternates periods of glory with periods of decline during first Roman, then Danish invasions, as polytheism opposes a pre-Christian monotheism and villainy contrasts with courtliness. The narrative concludes with the Christianization of Britain in pre-Arthurian times.

But the anonymous narrator, lest he lose his audience in narrative prolixity, has adorned—*entrelardé* (Taylor, "Fourteenth," LCT, 283)—the dry annalistic sequence with amplifications that bring out the author's real intent and narrative art. Narrative patterns prefigure their Arthurian models, as in the founding of the Order of the Franc Palais that anticipates the Order of the Round Table. Genealogies identify distant ancestors of major Arthurian figures like Arthur, Lancelot, and Merlin.

Contemporary with *Perceforest* other scribes interweaved material from a variety of sources. David Aubert, a Burgundian scribe, adapted an amplified *Perceforest* in what is the longest extant manuscript version of the romance. Jehan Vaillant and Michot Gonnot meshed material from diverse Arthurian sources, and Gonnot did the same for the *Sept sages*. Even single manuscripts become uniquely important. Two of Michot Gonnot's manuscripts represent the range of scribal intervention in transmission of romance. Bibliothèque Nationale manuscript français 99 contains his copy of the *Prose Sept sages*, a faithful copy of this non-Arthurian cycle. But the Arthurian material in Bibliothèque Nationale manuscript français 112 offers Gonnot's original amalgam of material excerpted from various thirteenth-century cycles and conjoined in a unique new romance.[3]

Other as-yet unpublished manuscripts attest to the activity of anonymous or unidentified scribes in the recasting and retelling of traditional material (see Woledge, *Bibliographie*). Some twelfth- and thirteenth-century romances were rewritten in prose (*mises en prose*). These prosifications also reinterpreted their sources in order to make them conform to then-current ideals of chivalry and nobility. For example, those made for the Burgundian court attach greater importance to family and lineage than does Chrétien de Troyes: for example, the Burgundian *Erec and Enide* have children.[4]

René d'Anjou's *Livre du cuer d'amours espris* is a remarkable innovation in narrative mode and manuscript adornment and layout. It adapts the interlacing quest of Grail romances to a dream-vision world reminiscent of the *Roman de la rose*. Cuer (Heart) sets out with Desir (Desire) in quest of Doulce Mercy (Sweet Mercy). On the way he encounters numerous adventures adapted from Grail romances as well as a magic fountain in Broceliande like that in Chrétien's *Yvain*, malevolent dwarfs, and dangerous bridges and castles. These are interspersed with settings like the "forest de Longue Attente" (Forest of Long Wait) inspired by or analogous to those found in Charles d'Orléans's contemporary poems. The two questers are transported by boat to the Isle of the God of Love, after which the siege of Doulce Mercy begins. Cuer's failure to achieve his quest problematizes René's intention with the romance, in many ways a charming and even amusing tale (as when Cuer and Desir quarrel). Some manuscripts of the *Cuer* are magnificently illustrated, adding visual impact to the narrative in striking ways.

Single Works in Verse and Prose

Jean Froissart wrote a verse romance called *Meliador*,[5] most of which is extant. In it knights vie in a five-year quest for love and marriage. The romance is Arthurian insofar as the knights and ladies are ancestors of the knights of the Round Table. *Meliador* inserts lyrics into the plot, and chivalry and love are still mutually supportive. Moreover, it correlates current historical events, places, and figures with the fictional narrative, becoming thereby a virtual roman à clef; other late verse romances seem to have done so as well.[6]

There are very few verse romances after Froissart. Exceptions are Jean de Condé's narrative poems and Coudrette's verse *Melusine*. Jean de Condé explores the beneficial or harmful effects of love in traditional romance narrative. Coudrette's *Melusine*, based on Jean d'Arras's late fourteenth-century prose version, is almost an oddity, so unusual is it to find a prose work turned into verse at this late date. Both prose and verse redactions recount the legend of the mythical origins of the Lusignan family (an actual family) in the love between a human and a fay from the otherworld—a late medieval avatar of the conventional lay setting (Harf-Lancner, *Fées*, 79–198). Other prose romances, listed in the chronology, appear here and there, but like the *Roman du papegau* they are episodic rather than cyclic. Most are known today only by their titles; few have modern editions. They await study, analysis, and historical appreciation (see Woledge, *Bibliographie*, and *GRLMA* vol. 8, part 1).

Emergence of the Novel

The novella appears in the fifteenth century. It is subsequently adapted in ways that contribute to the emergence of the *roman* in its modern sense of "novel" in Antoine de la Sale's *Jehan de Saintré, Jean de Paris*, and other works (Morse, "Historical Fiction"). A full-fledged sentimental novel emerges in *Paris et Vienne*, adapted from Catalan. Pierre de Beauvau's *Roman de Troilus* turns Boccaccio's poem on Troilus and Cressida, *Il Filostrato*, into French prose.

Like its twelfth-century ancestor *Floire et Blancheflor*, which was still being read in prose versions in the late Middle Ages, the fifteenth-century *Paris et Vienne* combines the motif of parental opposition to young love with matters like degree of nobility, forced marriage, and the wanderings of the young lover typical of the earlier *romans roses*. Vienne's resourcefulness and ingenuity prevent a forced marriage. For example, she hides rotting chicken flesh under her armpits to convince potential husbands that she has terrible body odor. Despite this humorous episode, the romance is essentially a sentimental novel. The happy ending occurs after Paris, during his wanderings in Saracen lands, frees Vienne's father from prison—an analogue to the conclusion of the *Fille du comte de Pontieu*.

By contrast, Rasse de Brunhamel's *Floridan et Elvide* is a story of violent, drunken near-rape. This work reveals the seamy tastes during the the transition from romance to novel at the end of the Middle Ages. Incest, violence, and rape in narrative seem to have been especially popular at the end of the Middles Ages, as Michel Zink has shown (*GRLMA,* vol. 8, part 1, 214–16). In Antoine de la Sale's *Jehan de Saintré* the Dame des Belles Cousines, angry at her young protégé's signs of independence, cynically betrays him by cruelly flaunting a sexual affair with a young abbot of bourgeois background. Jehan de Saintré imposes in his turn cruel, violent punishment on them.

La Sale intended, it appears, to add *Paris et Vienne* to *Jehan de Saintré*, but influenced by Rasse de Brunhamel he substituted the latter's *Floridan et Elvide*. This tale of drunken violence and attempted rape prevented only by Elvide's suicide shows how far removed emergent novels are from the optimism of thirteenth-century *romans roses*. They are nearer to the grayer *Châtelaine de Vergi* or the *Châtelain de Couci*. Antoine de la Sale and Rasse de Brunhamel illustrate two tendencies of late medieval literature: fantastic idealism and perversion of idealism.

The Sixteenth Century

Many romances were printed and in this way passed on to the sixteenth and seventeenth centuries.[7] Most, especially prosifications from the thirteenth and fourteenth centuries, were printed virtually without change. These include the *Prose Lancelot-Graal*, the *Prose Tristan*, and later compilations like that of Rusticien de Pise, *Perlesvaus*, *Perceforest*, *Artus de Bretagne*, and *Ysaÿe le triste* in the Matter of Britain; *Alexandre* and *Troie* in the Matter of Rome; and prose versions of *Amis et Amile*, *Fierabras*, and *Renaud de Montauban* in the Matter of France. Many underwent at least some adaptation, as in the prosification of Chrétien's *Yvain* in Pierre Sala's *Chevalier au lion* and of his *Perceval* and its continuations in an anonymous prose redaction printed in 1530; still others were translated

into French for printing, as in a prose *Jaufre* and Herberet des Essarts's
and other versions of the Spanish romance *Amadis de Gaule*.

Renaissance humanists and young "demoiselles, dames et gentils-
hommes" (J. Frappier, "Romans," 181) fostered the survival of romances.
The humanists, while scorning the popularity of medieval romances,
looked to them for material with which an epic poet, imitating Ariosto
in Italy, might amalgamate "French" or Arthurian matter in a Homeric
epic as the Renaissance understood it. In his *Nouveau Tristan* (an abbreviated title), Jean Maugin tries to renovate Arthurian matter in prose
much as Ariosto had in Italian verse. Maugin anticipates the kinds of
adaptations Luigi Alemmanni would make in his verse *Gyrone il cortese*
and *Avarchide*, unsuccessful but interesting attempts to write in Italian,
but with French Arthuriana, the Homeric epic that François I and the
humanists desired. They, like François I, sought to evoke a glorious,
noble past, whence their preference for printings of translations and of
the older manuscripts rather than modernized adaptations. There was no
doubt a nostalgia for a past still idealized yet no longer realizable in the
new world of monarchy and the wars of religion.

A few authors stand out, notably Pierre Sala, not only for his modernization of the *Yvain*, mentioned above, but more so today for his
Tristan, a rather original episodic prose romance. This compilation of a
number of sources relates a specific period in the careers of Tristan and
Lancelot. It uses stock scenes and motifs rather liberally, like the quest,
the devil disguised as a seductive maiden, magic restoral of strength at
certain times of the day, disguises, clandestine meetings, and so on.
Finally, it combines a medieval scenario with Renaissance worldviews; if
the monks and hermits still have something of the austerity of their
counterparts in the *Queste*, the abbots, more attuned to this world, recall
the "abbé bon vivant" of *Jean de Saintré*.

Another work by Sala, *Les hardiesses de plusieurs roys et empereurs*, contains a number of Arthurian sections in a frame like that in the
Decameron and Marguerite de Navarre's *Heptaméron*. The cyclicity of
Arthurian prose romance is set aside in favor of the brief, self-contained
novella. In his *Tristan* and the *Hardiesses*, Sala is a precursor of the two
major kinds of seventeenth-century novel: the lengthy cycle, like
d'Urfé's *L'Astrée* and the novels of Madame de Scudéry, and the classical
novel like Madame de Lafayette's *Princesse de Clèves*.

Chapter 6
Sources of Romance

The sources of French romance have been debated since the early nineteenth century. There has not always been agreement as to what a source is, although the word usually implies the use of antecedent material in a new work. Generally speaking, all medieval romances allege the use of one or more antecedent sources.[1] Four factors are significant in the ways romancers and their contemporaries refer to sources: the patrons and public who commissioned or inspired the composition of the romance, the antecedent matter authors drew on for content, their art of invention or rewriting, and the influence of medieval historiography on the genre and art of romance.

Patrons, Patronage, and Audiences

Few artists could succeed in the Middle Ages without patronage. Patrons, audiences, and the social mores, conventions, and ideals they favored determined what writers wrote in order to be accepted or simply employed.[2] Chrétien is a useful illustration, since he explicitly states that the countess of Champagne was instrumental in the writing of the *Charrette* and that Philippe de Flandre provided him with the source—the "book"—for his *Conte du graal*.

Two factors are important in analyzing the patron as source of romance: commission or gift and influence.

Without commission no romance was written. This is a fundamental thesis of Bumke's study of patronage in medieval France and Germany. He adduces examples as proof for this contention: romances begun and abandoned, others left unfinished to be taken up again later under a new patron, as well as works written in the hope of reward (*Mäzene*, 13–21). One sees how commission and gift might be construed as a kind of service. But writing seen as service cautions us that the work must be made to suit the real or potential patron's predilections and tastes. Studies have appeared from time to time on specific courts and patrons, usually with a view to describing the court and its principal patrons as historical background to works written for it (Bezzola, *Origines*).

Drawing analogies between the modern author and the medieval romance writer is not a useful way to understand the relationship between patron and writer in the Middle Ages. A more apt comparison would be the modern architect and the medieval writer. Even today, if an architect is engaged to design and construct a building, work will proceed only for as long as financial and other material support is forthcoming and the specified design is followed; if agreed-upon specifications or payments are not met, construction stops. The same holds true for the medieval writer. Wace's *Rou* and Benoît de Sainte-Maure's *Chronique des ducs de Normandie* are both incomplete because Henry II allegedly terminated his patronage. Other incomplete romances may well be the result of similar loss of favor or support. For example, did Chrétien de Troyes fail to finish the *Conte du graal* because he himself died, or because his patron Philippe de Flandre died?

Beginning in the thirteenth century another kind of patronage emerged: the market. However, it accounts for copying more than composition. The tastes and desires of an anticipated public would be paramount considerations in choosing what romances to copy, what kind of anthologies to collect, or what parts to include in a compilation. Editorial preferences might also intervene. The famous "Guiot" collection of romances, Bibliothèque Nationale manuscript français 794, seems to have emerged from a Guiot atelier. Evidence from the manuscript tradition suggests that an "in-house" style often influenced the kind of revisions that could occur during several stages of copying and adapting on the scribal level. Scribes and their ateliers might speculate on the market, much as a housing developer might construct houses with a given clientele in mind.

The patron could be more than a donor; he or she could also be like a master who would instruct, correct, or reprimand a pupil or a loved one.[3] The patron as donor is well known. That he or she could also be a writer is evident from troubadour and *trouvère* lyric—notably, in French, Conon de Béthune, the Châtelain de Couci, and Wenceslas de Brabant whose lyrics Froissart inserted into *Meliador*. Thibaut de Champagne was himself a descendant of one of the earliest troubadours, Guilhem d'Aquitaine. Most early troubadours were of the high aristocracy, but this does not hold true for romancers. Almost none are of the nobility.

The audience identified and described in romance prologues usually did not know Latin or read widely in Latin literature. Indeed, it may have defined itself as opposed to audiences that understood Latin if we can generalize from the preference for French over Latin expressed by the author of *Partonopeu de Blois* (ll. 77–80, 91–94). The earliest romancers saw themselves as performing a special service by transmitting to those who could not read Latin the fruits of Latin literature. Benoît de Sainte-Maure says that he wrote in French so that those who did not understand Latin could know Dares through his French version (*Troie,* ll. 38–39). This statement conforms to the commonplace that romancers ought to communicate their knowledge to others.[4]

But not to everyone. Romancers do not write about or for the lower social orders (Badel, "Rhétorique," 85–86). This is not just the result of snobbery or a sense of blood superiority. It reflects faith in the noble mind,[5] which was often called *sens* or *san* in descriptions of noble persons.[6] Yet blood nobility was not forgotten, as is apparent in frequent references to kings and high nobility as patrons or audiences (Gallais, "Recherches," 337–38; Badel, "Rhétorique," 85).

The patroness was a special subclass among audiences, as twelfth-century verse romance in particular evidences. Eleanor of Aquitaine and her daughters Marie de Champagne and Aelis de Blois fit into this category, as do many other ladies in Eleanor's family and at other courts.[7] Romances and lays seem to have held a special attraction for women.[8] The beloved lady for whom a romance was written and to whom it was offered is also a potential patroness and benefactor. Some romances were even written as love service. Indeed, the narrators in *Partonopeu* and the *Bel inconnu* request approval from their lady before completing their works. The lady has become patron, so much so that the very conception and elaboration of the plot depend on her person and actions. It is difficult today to evaluate the historicity of such ladies. But the importance of the patron as such cannot be gainsaid. As Bumke declares, "Medieval art was commissioned art and must be understood as such" (*Mäzene,* 9).

The noble mind is very important to romancers. They illustrate it in their works, appeal to it in offering their writings, and applaud its authority and influence. Benoît de Sainte-Maure contrasts Eleanor of Aquitaine's virtue with Briseida's inconstancy (*Troie,* ll. 13429–94), a compliment that suggests that the forerunner of Chaucer's Criseyde may have been invented as the antithesis of a patroness. Chrétien bases his *Conte du graal* on a book given to him by Philippe de Flandre, a gift which he construes as an expression of the count's bounty and charity. The "matter" and "meaning" of the *Charrette* are ascribed to Marie de Champagne. Marie is the master artist who commissioned the composition of the *Charrette* by her cleric. Toward the end of the thirteenth-century several ladies give Adenet le Roi the *matière* of his *Cleomadés*.[9]

Eleanor as counter-model for Briseida illustrates the patron in both senses of the French word *patron*: patron, and pattern or model. The patron is exemplary. The patron's authority is also apparent, negatively, in assertions that the full truth cannot be openly stated because it would anger powerful persons. That the patron may intervene to correct a work is a literary commonplace found in a number of romances. Such authority does not apply to those excluded from the audience, or to those asked to remain silent because they are villains (in the moral sense), deceivers, or carping critics (Badel, "Rhétorique," 85–86).

Authors too could instruct. But what they had to say was what the audiences, and especially the patrons, wanted to hear. They provided the rhetoric, not original thought. Like Chrétien, they are instruments in the transmission of chivalry (*chevalerie*) and learning (*clergie*); they are not modern creative geniuses bent on expressing truths no one has heard before. Of course, they did try to tell stories no one had heard before: but originality in the modern sense of "creativity" was unknown in the Middle Ages. Only God could create.

No doubt, we shall never know what interaction actually occurred between romancers and their patrons, anymore than we can know about what went on between authors and their beloved. But we can perceive in the kinds of roles suggested by romance prologues and other interventions a model for composition. A patron commissions or even inspires, actively or passively, a romance. An artist uses the commission, as general or specific as it may be, to construe a romance. An artisan, whether the artist or another scribe, carries out the execution of the commission according to the artist's and the patron's plan. The model admits potentially very complex production—a veritable atelier of artisans, each completing a specific assignment.[10] It is, in the last analysis, the aristocratic mind that romances give expression to, address, and seek reward from.

Antecedent Sources, Reception, and Transmission

Romance relates the achievement of marvelous adventures. The adventures constitute the plot of the romance. Marvels are extraordinary and unique, at the very limits of the world, the mind, or the human. By knowing and achieving them, the knight acquires the extraordinary qualities of the marvel, imbuing his own character with the marvelous that unique achievement of an adventure bestows on the achiever. Romancers drew marvelous adventures from their sources.[11]

Romance marvels and the marvelous are usually defined in one of two ways in modern scholarship. Either they correspond to the supernatural, or what was once thought to be supernatural, or they refer to the kind of matter in which they occur: ancient marvels, Celtic marvels, or Christian marvels. These designations are not specific, nor do they fit medieval usage. the words *merveille*, *merveilleus*, and *merveiller* may refer to the experience of the reader, the source, or the goals of romance protagonists.

Romancers drew marvelous material for their stories from both Latin and vernacular sources. We designate sources Celtic, antique, or French, according to where the narrative is localized in time or geography. Celtic matter appears in Arthurian romances, the Tristan legend, and Breton lays—the Matter of Britain in general. Antique matter is found in Greco-Roman or Byzantine romances like the *Roman d'Eneas*, the *Roman de Troie*, the Alexander romances, as well as in Chrétien's *Cligés* and Gautier d'Arras's *Eracle*. French matter comes from folktale traditions and epics about French kings and knights, especially when these works—the *chansons de geste*—adopt romance features and techiques of composition.

The prologue to Jehan Bodel's epic, the *Chanson des Saisnes*, identifies these three kinds of matter: "De France et de Bretaigne et de Rome"[12] (that of France, Britain, and Rome). According to the *Saisnes*, each matter refers to a collection of stories or subjects associated with, in order, the French royal line, the British royal line, and the imperial Roman line represented in 1200 by the emperor of the Holy Roman Empire.

In fact, each of the three matters to which Jehan Bodel refers implies a tradition of writing and rewriting that relied on the use and adaptation of antecedent versions of the story being retold.[13] The source as preexistent text or oral tale is drawn upon in the composition of the new work. Sometimes it is possible to identify the precise sources an author used as well as secondary works that contributed to the realization of the new work, as in the cases of antique romances based on Vergil's *Aeneid* and Statius's *Thebais*.[14] In these cases, comparative study may yield very precise knowledge on the strategies and intentions of the medieval author.

But usually we do not know the actual sources of a given romance. Yet there is evidence that sources did exist. Rather than trying to draw a detailed picture of all the sources romancers used, as was common in critical scholarship before 1950, it is more useful to identify the kinds of sources the romancers speak about, what qualities and faults they perceive in them, and how they profess to rewrite them. For example, in the prologue to *Erec* Chrétien de Troyes contrasts his story with those told by jongleurs.

> D'Erec, le fil Lac, est li contes,
> Que devant rois et devant contes
> Depecier et corronpre suelent
> Cil qui de conter vivre vuelent.

(*Erec*, 19–22)

[The story is about Erec, son of Lac, which those who seek to tell stories before kings and counts are wont to tear apart and corrupt.]

Assuming these words refer to a reality Chrétien's audiences would have recognized—and there is no reason to suppose that they do not—we may glimpse in them the activities of storytellers practicing their trade for the noble and wealthy. But Chrétien faults their manner: they mutilate and corrupt the tale of Erec which he, by a "molt bele conjointure" (*Erec*, 14), makes acceptable. If nothing else, we may expect his *conjointure* to lack the faults he stigmatizes.

The identification of specific sources is a problem for several reasons. Important intermediary stages in the adaptation of a work may be lost today through the vicissitudes of time or the vagaries of oral and written traditions: not everything was recorded in writing, nor has everything written down survived. Medieval audiences would have understood many references and allusions that escape us today.[15] Moreover, as comparison with known sources reveals, romances often combined antecedent material into new wholes, and in the process modified them in important ways. A striking example is the *Roman d'Eneas*. Comparison with the *Aeneid* reveals significant deletions, such as the adventures during Aeneas's voyage from Troy to Carthage recounted in book 2 of Vergil's epic, as well as extensive adaptations, amplifications, and additions to accommodate the love story of Eneas and Lavinie, which is absent in Vergil's epic. Finally, manuscripts, including commentaries, scholia, scribal interventions in the sources, and intermediate versions of them may also enter into adaptations. Glosses were used in the adaptation of *Thèbes* and *Eneas*.[16]

Adaptation may occur not only in rewriting, but also in subsequent copying. Chrétien de Troyes warns his audiences against such "mendacious" tinkering (*Yvain*, ll. 6806–08). The history of a text must take into account not only its original version, insofar as this can be reconstructed, but also subsequent versions which the manuscript tradition illustrates.

Adaptation by both deliberate change and inadvertent error is common in both oral and written transmission. Roger Sherman Loomis has listed those changes that, in his view, influenced oral transmission of the Matter of Britain from Wales to the Continent (*Arthurian Tradition*, 38–58). Since they also occur in other matters and in written transmission, it is useful to summarize them here. They delineate in general terms major features associated with the oral and written transmission and rewriting of romances and romance matters.

There are references in romances and other texts to antecedent traditions or to incidents presumably known to the author and medieval publics, but not related in any extant romance. Such references occur in summaries, allusions, or catalogues of names. Variant versions of the same story, event, or person attest to diverse antecedents, as do variant versions of the same motif or episode, especially when a more archaic version survives in a later text. Variant versions may be rewritten in different ways, including conflation, which combines several versions of the same story, scene, or motif into a single new version, and contamination, which brings together two or more distinct stories, episodes, or motifs in a single new amalgam. These account for fusion of two or more characters in a single new one, or fission when a single character splits into two or more distinct personages. Transformation of proper nouns may result from misreading or mistranslation. In these ways adaptations may harmonize conflicts, inconsistencies, or misinterpretations that occur in oral or manuscript transmission. On the other hand, some mythological elements survive unexplained, whereas once-marvelous features may fade or become commonplace by repetition. Adaptation may also rationalize or modernize sources for contemporary medieval audiences by rewriting the realia of an older civilization in contemporary language and making actions conform to current mores, beliefs, and experiences.

Both oral and written lines of transmission are unstable. Romancers refer to this instability when they speak of selecting authoritative or reliable sources and of reconciling divergent accounts. Scholars often set aside such statements as spurious when they cannot identify actual sources today. However, oral versions that disappeared into the air as quickly as they were spoken could survive as an allusion comprehensible to an audience that remembered them. Written sources also disappear, as the fragmentary state of works as important as Thomas d'Angleterre's *Tristan* and the Post-Vulgate *Graal* demonstrate. Both authors and scribes intervened to delete from or expand on originals. For example, different manuscripts of Chrétien's *Erec* contain variant catalogues of guests at the wedding of Erec and Enide.

Changes also occur in manuscript traditions as authors or scribes seek to reconcile source material. Thomas d'Angleterre refers to cognates when he speaks of the different versions of the Tristan legend he knows; similarly, Marie de France begins her "Lai du chievrefoil" by referring to different versions she has heard and read. Aimon de Varennes details the transmission of his *Florimont* from a Greek folktale through a Latin first copy to the verse romance in French. The prose romances are veritable laboratory cases of manuscript transmission, adaptation, and confusion.

Adaptations in other languages may be important as well. For example, Ulrich von Zatzikhoven's Middle High German *Lanzelet* depicts Lancelot before Chrétien portrayed him as Guenevere's lover. An early version of the abduction of Guenevere that included Lancelot probably survives as well in Malory's fifteenth-century *Morte Darthur* (Loomis, *Arthurian Tradition*, 216–18).

In oral traditions the memory amalgamates a number of different tellings—much as, for example, any one individual's conception of the story of Little Red Riding Hood is a conflation of numerous tellings and retellings, readings and rereadings, since childhood. Conflation also occurs in manuscript transcription when a scribe dovetails disparate manuscripts in a new copy (Pickford, *Evolution*, 190–97).

Proper names are associated with a variety of figures and stories. For example, Briseida in Benoît's *Troie* combines features of several women in Dares and in the *Ilias latina*, an early Latin version of Homer's *Iliad*. Yvain multiplies in the *Lancelot-Graal* into at least five different persons. Perceval acquires names like "Perlesvaus" and "Parluifait" in *Perlesvaus*. Other more striking changes occur in the passage from one language to another, as Loomis has suggested in regard to Welsh names in French (*Arthurian Tradition*, 49–50).

Unresolved or unnoticed inconsistencies in the transmission of matter may derive from the actual author, as in the chronological discrepencies in *Yvain* (Woledge, *Commentaire* 2:64, to l. 4901, and 2:70, to ll. 5052–54). They may also be carried over from sources. Loomis has argued that the Welsh word *cors*, which could mean "horn" or "body" in French, may account for the metamorphosis of a Celtic horn of plenty (cornucopia) into a nourishment dispensing Grail (*Arthurian Tradition*, 172–75). Gauvain's traditional renewal of strength at noon (or sometimes at midnight), an attribute with its roots in Celtic mythology, is not rationalized but rather becomes a traditional feature of his character alongside his willingness to identify himself by name if asked (Gallais, *Imaginaire*, 1885–1906).

Rationalization is evident, however, when Chrétien compares the shame attached to the cart with that of the pillory and refers to a proverb current in his time linking the cart to misfortune (*Charrette*, ll. 321–44). Later the *Prose Lancelot* eliminates the cart as an object of shame by having Arthur, Guenevere, and a number of the Round Table knights ride in one (*Lancelot* sec. 40, pars. 8–21). Generally, modernization replaces the marvelous by the customary (Maddox, *Arthurian Romances*), like jousts and armor in antique romances and the Christianization of the Grail. The short *Gauvain* or *First Perceval Continuation* no doubt represents a Grail tradition that Chrétien first modernized—the Grail is a low-bottomed bowl made unique by its precious stones and the host it bears—and that Robert de Boron conflated with the cup or chalice of the Last Supper, a transformation that made obsolete the word's original meaning, "low-bottomed bowl," for the Grail thereafter was imagined as more like a vase than a flat vessel.

These factors explain the *depecier* (shredding) and *corronpre* (incomplete state) that Chrétien faults in his *Erec* sources while suggesting how he corrected them. Such statements are more helpful in evaluating specific features of romance invention from sources than reconstruction and comparison of hypothetical sources. The following considerations are paramount: first, virtually every romance alleges the use of a source or sources; second, most purport to adapt the sources; third, the truth and quality of the new version is proclaimed; fourth, fidelity to source was tempered by the art of romance and the desires of patrons.

Our view of the process of adaptation, from rereading an original to composition of a new work, is often hazy because of the complexity of manuscript traditions. Although some romances survive only in a single copy, others exist in multiple versions, suggesting independent adaptations. Chronology, new influences, precedence, and patronage complicate issues. Moreover, there is evidence that authors themselves sometimes wrote revised versions of their works, as the two manuscript versions of Gautier d'Arras's *Ille et Galeron* suggest. The distinction between the *Noncyclic Lancelot* and the cyclic version seems to stem from a new conception of chivalry and the knights that were to represent it (Kennedy, *Lancelot*, 49–110). Finally, there may be independent tellings of the same story, as in the "popular" and "aristocratic" versions of *Floire et*

Blancheflor. To understand these phenomena we must know something of the art of romance invention.

The Art of Romance Invention

A major difference between emergent romance and contemporary *chansons de geste* is the tradition out of which each grew. Epic surviving in the earliest *chansons de geste* adapts the oral tradition of *jongleurs* to written narrative.[17] Even when epic was written down, the style of oral improvisation survived and continued to be imitated. In late-eleventh- and early-twelfth-century France the written and oral traditions are represented by, respectively, a learned Latin, clerical tradition and a vernacular, oral French culture. The former was acquired in schools, the latter outside of them.

Both early romance and written *chansons de geste* presuppose a public accustomed to works written to be read aloud. The Alexander cycle uses the rhymed *laisse* typical of *chansons de geste*, even in additions written as late as the fourteenth-century *Paon* continuations. Even late manuscript illustrations of medieval authors show public readings. Yet evidence for private reading is not lacking (Petit, *Naissances*, 777–78). Chrétien's *Yvain* illustrates one stage in the movement toward private reading by describing a daughter reading to her parents (*Yvain*, ll. 5358–64). Prose romances could be listened to or read in private. No doubt, actual practice varied with circumstances, occasion, and audience literacy. To be sure, the oral tradition provided matter for the Latin tradition, just as the latter found its way into French, especially through the emergence and spread of romance. The epic tradition finally absorbed romance techniques and came to be identified with the works characteristic of that genre as *roman*.

An important feature of scholastic grammar and rhetoric was verse and prose composition based on imitation and adaptation of given images, motifs, and matters.[18] Instruction in grammar and rhetoric in the twelfth century and later exemplifies the kind of composition taught in medieval schools. Instruction fostered habits of invention in literary composition. Clerical authors of protoromance and early romance, Benoît de Sainte Maure, Chrétien de Troyes, Marie de France, and others, applied the literary models and paradigms of composition they studied and imitated in grammar, rhetoric, and Latin-language literature. These habits were transmitted to later generations of romancers who, as

Philippe de Beaumanoir avers, may not themselves have had specialized training in composition in the schools.[19]

The schools taught writers how to invent a new work by adapting a given subject matter or source. This was the path followed in the antique romances; it was soon applied to the matters of Britain and of France. Adaptation entailed choice, interpretation, rearrangement, and new emphases. A meaning—what Marie de France calls a *surplus de san* (*Lais*, "Prologue," l. 16)[20]—was elicited from extant sources for the new work by the author or the authority commissioning or requesting the romance. It influenced the representation of major figures and their actions as well as the choice and arrangement of material in the new work. Finally amplification or abbreviation of material and ornamental devices (tropes and figures) enhanced the desired meaning and reduced or eliminated whatever was considered to be extraneous or divergent material.

The art of invention learned through the story of grammar and, especially, rhetoric is too complex to detail here.[21] However, one must understand its major features in order to appreciate romance composition. Grammar and rhetoric developed as arts in ancient Greece and Rome. Certain Roman treatises were still studied in the Middle Ages, notably those written by Cicero, Horace, and Quintilian. Later grammarians and rhetoricians maintained the school tradition, especially Priscian, whom Marie de France refers to as an authority. Others wrote works whose influence on the Middle Ages is still imperfectly understood, for example, Macrobius, a writer from the late fourth and early fifth centuries referred to by Chrétien and Guillaume de Lorris as an authority. Literary composition is best represented in medieval treatises written by Matthew of Vendôme (ca. 1170) and Geoffrey of Vinsauf (early thirteenth century). Moreover, some writers ancient and medieval in the literary canon of the time were so authoritative that they served as exemplars of the art of writing; they were accordingly studied and imitated in school exercises that paved the way for the more gifted to write masterpieces. Vergil and Ovid were especially important for study and imitation. Similarly, the achievements of early romancers could be imitated and adapted by their successors.

The study of grammar and rhetoric suggests to most people today rote learning of grammatical paradigms and of ornamental tropes and figures. Although these were prominent features of grammar and rhetoric, they were not the principal goal of instruction. Grammar taught versification and prose style as well as the interpretation and imitation of literary masterpieces. It influenced the ways one romancer might imitate another while adapting recurrent subjects like the love potion of Tristan and Iseut, the love of Lancelot and Guenevere, or the Grail. Rhetoric is the art of persuasion. It involves the interpretation of matter as if it were evidence, and effective, convincing statement of that interpretation. I shall briefly review here the two aspects of rhetoric that are especially important for the art of romance: the three kinds of oratory and the phases of composition.

The three kinds of oratory are judicial, deliberative, and panegyric. Judicial oratory, which was used in legal debate in the presence of a judge or jury, was taught in the schools using fictitious examples, many of which were drawn from literature and mythology. The pupil was expected to make a case for or against, say, Brutus's assassination of Julius Caesar. This method paved the way for treating analogous issues in romance matters. Chrétien's *Erec* and *Charrette* are "problem romances."[22] The text argues, or at least problematizes, issues like whether Enide is right or wrong in urging her husband to participate more actively in tournaments[23] or whether Lancelot's adulterous love for Guenevere is a sin, a case of lèse-majesté, or an ideal.

Deliberative oratory comes to the fore in the antique romances during debates concerning appropriate action. For example, should Argos support Polinices's effort to force his brother Etiocles to relinquish the throne of Thebes for a year? It might also appear in inner monologues wherein lovers ask themselves whether they should declare their love, as when Lavine in *Eneas*, Alexandre and Soredamors in *Cligés*, or Laudine in *Yvain* analyze their feelings and decide among different courses of action. Such debates could well extend through various situations and episodes—a plot-line—and assume various modes of representation.

Panegyric oratory praises or blames persons, things, or actions. Its most obvious use in romances occurs when descriptions of romance protagonists[24] define and delineate context. It becomes the dominant rhetorical mode after the middle of the thirteenth century when romance tends to remove itself from problems or controversial issues in order to praise uniformly idealized knights and ladies.

The phases of composition are usually five: invention, disposition, ornamentation, memory, and delivery. *Invention* includes both the identification of source material and the excogitation of the author's construe of that material, that is, his or her interpretation of it. This leads to *disposition* or arrangement of the invented matter—most notably, in the problem whether the matter could be presented more effectively in normal chronological sequence or whether it would be better to rearrange it, as Chrétien does in *Yvain* by having Calogrenant relate his adventure at the magic fountain after later events at court. *Ornamentation* by the use of tropes and figures determines how the matter will be articulated. This may occur sentence by sentence, or in larger segments; in the latter case, ornamentation is usually termed amplification or abbreviation. It determines what aspect of a work will be emphasized and how, in the light of the author's understanding of the matter and the issues he or she raises in it. *Memory* and *delivery* have to do with the performance of the work; they do not directly influence the writing of romance, although they may have influenced oral performance, as when a romance was read or recited.

Memory is also important because of its relation to topical invention. Topical invention is the identification of those "places" in an author's matter where his or her conception of the work may be best expressed. Such places map out a mental picture of the work as the author subsequently puts it into words. Topical schemes may be static, as when persons and things are described or "colored" with specific traits they have in common with other examples of the same class—as, for example, whether a person is male or female, noble or serf, Christian or pagan; they can also determine how narrative is elaborated, as through the stages by which one for falls in love, or debates, or fights (Kelly, *Art*, 226–46).

In romance the most important phases are invention, disposition, amplification or abbreviation, and versification or prosification. The broad lines of composition are evident in interventions in which authors explain how they conceive and construe their works.[25] For example, Marie de France in the "Prologue" to her *Lais* states that she is applying the art she learned from Priscian not to Latin-language sources, but to the tales recorded in the several languages of Breton lays.

Invention was twofold: it entailed the finding of source matter suitable for retelling, whether written, as in the book Chrétien alleged he used for the *Conte du graal*, or oral, like the *jongleurs'* tales he scorns in the *Erec* prologue. They could also be both written and oral, as is suggested by Marie de France in the prologues to her individual lays or by Thomas d'Angleterre's and Beroul's references to different versions of the Tristan legend. Collecting these sources constituted a composite *matière* or "amalgam." The next step was to arrange the amalgam and then elaborate it as a *molt bele conjointure*, the very beautiful combination of material that for Chrétien distinguishes romance from mere story.

The new combination or *conjointure* includes a new interpretation of the sources. The interpretation is analogous to those of accusers and defendants in trial and debate. The assembled "facts" or evidence of a case—its *matière*—are interpreted for or against a verdict. The lawyer invents an argument, including a version of the evidence. Similarly, a given source needed to be interpreted according to the intention of an author, a patron, or a public. Interpretation could produce readings as different as that which glorifies the love of Lancelot and Guenevere in Chrétien's *Charrette* and that which condemns it in the *Queste del saint graal*. The former is a "courtly" reading, the latter a moral or Christian one. The contrast between the two readings is as great as that between the reaction of a saint like Alexis to his marriage bed: "cum fort pecét m'apresset"[26] (what great sin oppresses me), and that of Lancelot to Guenevere's bed: "puis vint au lit la reïne, / si l'aore et se li ancline, / car an nul cors saint ne croit tant" (*Charrette*, ll. 4651–53) (then he came to the queen's bed, adoring and bowing to it; for he has more faith in it than in any holy relique). Alexis's words conform to an idea of sainthood and express its morality; Lancelot's actions express his secular love and its standards.

Marie de Champagne asked Chrétien to write the *Charrette*. She also provided him with both *matière* and *san*, that is, source and meaning. Since her inspiration may well have prompted Chrétien to include the first instance of Lancelot and Guenevere as lovers in his romance, it suggests the originality of her conception and *conjointure* of the matter. The amalgam is the adulterous union; its truth is love as a source of prowess and worth.

The integration of a truth and a matter is a process of extraction, involution, and amplification. *Extraction* is the technique whereby the author elicits from an obscure or corrupt matter what he or she deems to be its inherent meaning. Marie de France describes this process in the "Prologue" to her *Lais* as "glossing" (ll. 9–16). The "glossing" Marie refers to was laborious. Chrétien distinguises between such glossing and invention in the *Charrette* prologue. Although he claims that Marie de Champagne's contribution is more effective in the composition of this romance than the "sans ne painne" (wit or effort)—glossing as writing— he brings to it, he nonetheless avers that his own effort is essential to effective, convincing storytelling. He achieves the *involution* of *matière* and *san*, that is, their narrative articulation and fusion. As a result the plot illustrates in an exemplary way the ideas or ideals the author incorporates into it.

Amplification expresses the truth or *san* of a romance narrative. It deploys a suitable mode of expression, like description, digression, comparison, contrast, and the other means of restating a proposition that traditional rhetoric taught as "ornamentation" by tropes and figures of thought and figures of diction. For example, Marie de France usually begins each of her lays with a description of one or more major characters. These descriptions are usually laudatory, emphasizing ideal features that the individual exemplifies. Guigemar is a perfect knight except that he does not love, and indeed seems incapable of loving at the beginning of the lay (*Lais*, "Guigemar," ll. 55–58). The defect is corrected when he falls in love. Each episode contributes to the moment of falling in love or, afterward, to demonstrating faithful love. Description in the beginning sets up an antithesis between Guigemar out of love and Guigemar in love. Such description may also reveal a defect. For example, Bisclavret has the distressing habit of turning into a werewolf once a week—a metamorphosis that provokes his wife's disgust (*Lais*, "Bisclavret," ll. 98–99).

Thomas d'Angleterre uses descriptive analogies in his *Tristan*. When Tristan is separated from Iseut the Queen, whom he loves, he tries to understand how she can continue to love him while fulfilling her conjugal duty toward her husband, Marc—and enjoy doing so, as Tristan jealously imagines. He therefore attempts to reconstruct the adulterous triangle he finds himself in with Iseut and Marc by a new triangle in which he takes her place. Since Iseut, whom he loves, is Marc's wife, Tristan decides to take a wife nearly as beautiful as she and one who also has the same name: he marries Iseut White Hands in Brittany. Tristan's experiment teaches him two things: first, he still loves Iseut as she, therefore, must love him; and, second, he derives no pleasure from his wife, just as Iseut derives none from her husband.

The use of rhetorical ornamentation is omnipresent in verse romance. Prose romance by and large eschews ornamental diction in favor of direct statement except in large compositional segments in which descriptions, the interlace of different plots, and contrasting truths at different stages in narrative progression evince on the narrative level configurations common in sentence ornamentation in verse romances. For example, there are different "truths" regarding Lancelot's love for Guenevere in the *Prose Lancelot*. Initially praised, as in Chrétien's romance, the love is later debunked and shown to be a defect in the prose romances—the exact opposite of the truth indicated above for Guigemar, whose only defect is that he does not love. But all these works illustrate the ways in which

different truths are worked into a received matter as glossing or interpretation: earlier authors were believed to have written obscure works so
that posterity might study and interpret them. Interpretation took the
form of a new work that was an adaptation of the earlier one. Romances
become thereby successive cases bearing on issues of importance to contemporary audiences.

Medieval Historiography

Estoire was a word commonly used to designate romance, even after
roman acquired its generic sense. Like Latin *historia* and modern French
histoire,[27] it can connote either "history" or "story"; often the distinction
between the two meanings is not obvious. Like *conte* (story) and *roman*,
estoire was used to refer to histories, romances from the Matter of Britain
and of Rome, and *chansons de geste*; Guillaume de Lorris even used it for
the *Roman de la rose* in the thirteenth century. It was, with *conte*, virtually
the only term used for thirteenth-century prose romances, perhaps in
order to distinguish them from verse *roman*, which to some appeared
more vain and mendacious. It also designated vernacular history.

Contemporary with the appearance of protoromance, vernacular history grew out of the traditions of medieval historiography. Like the art of
romance invention, medieval historiography construed history, or *estoire*,
as an amalgam of sources and topical amplifications. Medieval histories
in both Latin and French practiced such amalgamation in chronicles,
biographies, and hagiography. Romancers adopted or imitated these
compositional strategies. Indeed, some authors of protoromances also
wrote vernacular chronicles—for example, Wace and Benoît de Sainte-
Maure.

There were four principal kinds of medieval history: annals, chronicles, universal histories, and saints' lives.[28] These works collect a number of written and oral sources into chronological sequence in order to
report the lives of rulers or saints and the fates of nations. The twelfth
century was especially rich in Latin histories: in France and Britain
names like Orderic Vital and William of Malmesbury stand out.

The Anglo-Norman court of the Plantagenets in England and its continental conquests fostered historical writing in the twelfth century. It
also constituted the audience for which most protoromances were written (Bezzola, *Origines* 2:391–461, 3:3–311). However, historians seem to
have directly influenced the emergence and writing of romance through
only the most marvelous and "historically suspect" of them all: the *De*

excidio Troiae (On the destruction of Troy) of the pseudo-Dares (fifth century) and Geoffrey of Monmouth's *History of the Kings of Britain* (ca. 1136–37).

Dares was an alleged eyewitness to the Trojan War. He was believed to have fought on the Trojan side, recording in terse prose the major events as they occurred. His account begins with the Argonautic expedition during which Jason wins the Golden Fleece. Jason's voyage includes the first confrontation between Greeks and Trojans and the first destruction of the city. Dares then relates the abduction of Helen and the 10-year siege of Troy. When Dares stops at the sack of Troy, a Greek counterpart, the Latin pseudo-Dictys (ca. fourth century; there survive some earlier fragments in Greek) completes the account, narrating the capture of Troy and fate of the Greeks returning to their homeland.

Dares's and Dictys's reports were regarded as reliable historical documents on the faith of their alleged eyewitness authority, the best validation of a historical account for medieval historians (Lacroix, *Historien*, 45–49). Moreover, they interested European royalty because many dynasties traced their beginnings back to Troy. On the model of Aeneas' escape from Troy to the West, the British (and through them the English in the twelfth century), Germans, French, and others also discovered an escaped Trojan in their family tree (Fourrier, *Courant*, 392–94).

Among the historians to make this claim was Geoffrey of Monmouth. His *History* tells how a Trojan named Brutus, unable to establish himself in Greece or Italy, finally sailed to Gaul and thence to Britain (which is said to derive its name from him). There he established a dynasty that ruled the British Isles and conquered most of Europe, including Rome on two occasions; a third conquest aborts when Mordred revolts while Arthur is in Gaul preparing to march on Rome.

Dares and Geoffrey wrote chronicles. Chronicles focus on a particular nation like Troy or Britain. Geoffrey of Monmouth records an entire succession of British rulers leading up to Arthur's rise and fall. But he relies on legendary history more than eyewitnesses. Moreover, Geoffrey allowed for the play of marvels and adventures in human history, like most chronicles of his time (Lacroix, *Historien*, 75–79).

Marvelous adventures are also a staple in the fourth kind of medieval history, hagiography. Hagiography, or the saint's life, was a major, if ill-defined, genre from the earliest Christian times. Its credibility depended on the saintliness of the saint, a saintliness confirmed both by character and by marvelous or miraculous events. Like the ruler, the saint followed a path of conquest: conquest over the sinful Old Adam inside, and conquest over the enemies of the faith or Satan in the hostile external world.

The biography of both saint and ruler was therefore a marvelous story of conquest. To relate such conquest with sparse historical documentation, the author needed to call on the same resources in rhetoric that served romancers. For example, if a saint was known only to have died in martyrdom, the hagiographer had to reconstruct the life not from documents, but by invention: the person and acts in the saint's life were a case for the sanctity of the martyr's death. The same would obtain even if documentation was available, as in Guernes de Pont Sainte Maxence's remarkable *Thomas Becket*. Similarly, in chronicles military exploits could be reconstructed from a list of battles, provinces, or nations a ruler conquered, as Benoît does in adapting Dares in the *Troie* or Wace adapting Geoffrey of Monmouth in the *Brut*.

Patronage influenced the evaluation of historical evidence in chronicles. In fact, it imposed the evidence's *surplus de sen*, in Marie de France's sense. Although the eyewitness was deemed the most reliable source of data, the truth of the data required interpretation in the light of moral, political, or dynastic purpose perceived in, or read into, the data. A saint's life written for an audience of monks might well be intended to encourage imitation of that saint; the life of the same saint written with a lay audience in mind, however, might be written with the intention of encouraging lay people to pray to that saint in times of need (Kelly, *Art*, 206).

Similarly, the chronicles extolled a ruler's dynasty and historical mission. That is, they expressed a dynastic truth by illustrating its superiority. For a French public, a British monarch might be reduced to the status of vassal to the king of France. This is the context for Jehan Bodel's distinction among the Matters of Britain, France, and Rome. His *Saisnes*, written for a French public, asserts outright that French rulers, like Charlemagne, are superior to British rulers, like Arthur, because the French crown should come before all others. The relation between historian and patron was carried over to that between patron and romancer and even between the Matter of Britain and the Matter of France.

I may summarize the issues treated in this chapter by analyzing the prologue and epilogue to Chrétien's *Charrette*. Whatever the historical validity of the assertions they make about patron, author, and scribe, the model they articulate for the role of each is typical in medieval French romance.

> Puis que ma dame de Chanpaigne
> vialt que romans a feire anpraigne,
> je l'anprendrai molt volentiers
> come cil qui est suens antiers
> de quan qu'il puet el monde feire.

(Charrette, ll. 1–5)

[Since my lady of Champagne wants me to undertake to write a romance, I do so most willingly, entirely devoted as I am to serving her in every possible way.]

The patron appears in these lines with her commission and, more importantly, her specifications. The artist acquiesces, devoting his art willingly and totally to realizing the specified commission. Chrétien proclaims his patroness's role in writing the romance: "Mes tant dirai ge que mialz oevre / Ses comandemanz an ceste oevre / Que sans ne painne que g'i mete" (ll. 21–23) (But I'll say this much: her commission is more effective in producing this romance than any skill or effort on my part). The hierarchy of patronage is upheld: her idea, as *patron* or mental model, precedes and effects more than the romancer's art, that is, his mental and physical effort. Chrétien is expressing the common medieval notion that the idea of a work is both more real than and superior to its concrete realization in language or any other medium.

Chrétien now sets to work: "Del *Chevalier de la Charrete* / comance Crestïens son livre" (ll. 24–25) (Chrétien begins his book about the *Chevalier de la charrette*), reiterating the distinction between his patroness's contribution as source and his as executor.

> Matiere et san[29] li done et livre
> la contesse, et il s'antremet
> de penser, que gueres[30] n'i met
> fors sa painne et s'antancïon.

(ll. 26–29)

[The countess provides him with matter and meaning while he undertakes to think—for he adds scarcely anything more than his labor and his understanding.]

Marie's commission included *matière*, or the source material, and *san*, or signification—a context or sense of the narrative that finds expression in the combination, the *conjointure*, of Lancelot and Guenevere.[31] Chrétien recalls his effort and skill, making the sense of skill more explicit as his *antancïon* or mental application toward the realization of his patroness's wishes by his artistry (Kelly, *Sens*, 37–39).

The roles of Marie and Chrétien suggest three agents in the patron model: patron, architect, and artist or scribe. The patroness and author overlap when *matière* and *san* combine. On the level of *sans/antancïon* and *painne*, the artist applies the techniques of medieval invention and elaboration to the completion of the work.

The epilogue to the *Charrette* completes the picture. "Seignor, se j'avant an disoie, / ce seroit oltre la matire, / por ce au definer m'atire" (ll. 7098–100) (My lords, if I were to say anymore I would exceed the limits of my matter; therefore, I come to the conclusion). The matter which, we recall, was commissioned by Marie has limits the author refuses to exceed, and therefore "Ci faut li romans an travers" (l. 7101) (here the romance comes to a full stop).

But there is a surprise. The inscribed narrator is no longer Chrétien! "Godefroiz de Leigni, li clers, / a parfinee *La Charrete*" (ll. 7102–3) (Godefroy de Leigny, the clerk, has completed the *Charrette*). But, he assures us, he did so with Chrétien's approval and blessings:

> Mes nus hom blasme ne l'an mete
> se sor Crestïen a ovré,
> car ç'a il fet par le boen gré
> Crestïen, qui le comança.

(ll. 7104–7)

[But let no one blame him for working on Chrétien's text, because he did so with the approval of Chrétien who began it.]

Then he specifies the extent of his own contribution: "Tant en a fet des lors an ça / ou Lanceloz fu anmurez, / tant con li contes est durez" (ll. 7108–10) (He has written all of the story from the moment of Lancelot's imprisonment)—that is, the final thousand lines or so of the romance. Godefroy concludes by recalling the principle of *conjointure* as a harmonious and complete combination of *matiere* and *san*: "Tant an a fet, n'i vialt plus metre / ne moins, por le conte mal metre" (ll. 7111–12) (that much he wrote, but he will add no more nor omit anything lest he destroy the story's balance)—in the words of the *Erec* prologue, lest he tear it apart or leave lacunae. Godefroy fits into the model as artisan; like stonemasons who realize the plan of a general architectural design, he is a scribe writing for master and patroness.

Chapter 7
Special Topics

Medieval French romance presents a number of special features that are peculiar to medieval literature, that distinguish romance from the novel, or that problematize traditional and current critical theories and methodologies used to interpret or evaluate the genre. The student must be aware of these features when reading romance and criticism of it.

Textual Editing and Editions

Textual criticism is the art of preparing editions from manuscripts. Since almost no romance survives in holograph (except for some late scribal adaptations), editing such works is a kind of archeology: its aim is to recover the version that lay before the author when he or she finished it. The student must be acquainted with editorial procedures used to establish each edition in order to ascertain how editorial decisions interpreted the manuscript data, and what therefore the edited text may reasonably represent in relation to an author's original or originals and the different stages of transmission the surviving manuscripts represent.[1]

History of Textual Editing

The history of textual criticism for works in Old French, including romance, supports the statement by Foulet and Speer that "any edition is a conjecture; it also constitutes a critical interpretation of the text" (*Editing*, 38). Different editions satisfy different criteria and are prepared accordingly. Currently, two extremes, with intermediary species, characterize the preparation of editions. These extend from reconstruction of an original version from all extant manuscripts to the edition of a single "best" manuscript. The editions of Chrétien's romances illustrate the two. Wendelin Foerster's editions, based on all the manuscripts known to him, conform to Foerster's own conception of Chrétien's language and art. On the other hand, Mario Roques based his editions almost exclusively on Bibliothèque Nationale manuscript français 794 prepared by the scribe Guiot, which contains all of Chrétien's Arthurian romances. There has been considerable controversy as to the value and significance of these two editions, still the most widely used for the study of Chrétien de Troyes's romances.

Editions and Interpretation

Traditionally, editors have attempted to make editions that best represent the author's first version or versions. Yet there are problems associated with such attempts. Gautier d'Arras's *Ille et Galeron* illustrates the editing of what may have been two versions of the romance prepared by the same author. Other works evince a chain of authors and/or scribes. In order to reproduce adequately the reality of manuscript variance in the *Perceval Continuations*, William Roach edited not only the earliest manuscripts, but all the versions, including subsets, whenever these seemed to be of special interest. A similar procedure was followed in editing the complex cycle of Alexander poems, from Albéric de Pisançon to the late *Paon* interpolations and completions.

The Vulgate *Lancelot-Graal* cycle and the various cycles and other works branching from it raise complex issues regarding the history of a text. The noncyclic version identifies Perceval as the Grail hero, whereas the completed cyclic version replaces Perceval in this role with a new figure, Galaad (Kennedy, *Lancelot*, chap. 6 and pp. 271–73; see also *Lancelot*, ed. Micha, 7:462–76). The *Roman de la rose* survives in a number of manuscript versions that were rewritten after Jean de Meun's addition to Guillaume de Lorris. There are unique conclusions or adaptations that add to, interpret, revise, or abbreviate the original(s), or that introduce new allegorical readings.[2] Multiplicity of manuscripts complicates rather than simplifies the recovery of the author's original. Thus the modern reader must know what kinds of editions he or she is basing interpretation on and what version or versions may have been known and thus may have influenced *mouvance*, intertextuality, and reception.

Even small changes may effect overall revision of a plot or its meaning. A striking example is Guiot's intervention in the texts of Chrétien's romances and in the *Perceval Continuations* he included in what is known as Bibliothèque Nationale manuscript français 794. Although, on the one hand, his manuscript is considered the best representative of the works of Chrétien, it may still be unreliable because of Guiot's style of emendation. Guiot was a conscientious copyist, but he had his own tastes. They can be the source of controversy as to how the first author—in this instance, Chrétien de Troyes—wrote.[3] Since they concern for the most part minor modifications in a word, a grammatical feature, a rhyme, or some other detail, they may seem insignificant. Yet small changes may have a large cumulative effect (see note 3 above). As Pierre Gallais has noted: "c'est ainsi qu'on démolit un style ou une logique" (Gallais, *Imaginaire*, 139). Modern editions may demolish in similar ways.

Manuscriture and Illustration

Greater attention to the single manuscript has quickened interest in the manuscript as object and as vehicle of textual transmission. Rubrication, layout, illumination, and commentary or glossing, as well as the contents of the manuscript and the specific version of a text it transmits, may contribute to textual environment, influencing the reading and appreciation of the romance as part of a program or performance which the manuscript itself suggests by contents and layout (Huot, *Song*). The program of manuscript illustration and layout may tell us about its intended use and give clues as to the interpretation and reception of the works contained in it as well as to the roles of scribe, manuscript workshop, and patron in its production and dissemination. Because these characteristics of manuscript production distinguish it from the printed book (including the modern edition), scholars have coined the French word *manuscriture* to highlight the special features of manuscript production, especially those that distinguish the medieval work from its modern editions, or, more generally, from the modern printed book.[4] The important distinction to be made is between the intentions of the first author and his or her patron and those of each subsequent producer of a manuscript copy and the audience that received it. The latter may reflect a new purpose, in a specific milieu, rather than mirror the original intentions. Pierre Gallais has demonstrated how such adaptations in different manuscripts alter the *Gauvain Continuation* of Chrétien's *Perceval* (*Imaginaire*, 115–433).

However, although manuscripts may give clues as to how a romance was read and interpreted, one should not exaggerate the importance of this fact. Illustrations and layout may or may not tell something about the text. The hand that annotates or illustrates a given manuscript is usually anonymous; we rarely know the gender, social status, or purpose of the person adding these features to the text. The debate about the significance of manuscript programs and iconography in the some 300 manuscripts of the *Roman de la rose* for the interpretation of this problematic text illustrates the uncertainties of the use of manuscripts for textual interpretation.[5]

In general, the following factors must be weighed in evaluating *manuscriture*, including text, layout, and illustrations. First, the manuscript may reveal nothing about its contents, being the result of arbitrary decisions made by an unknown person or the work of scribes or illustrators who had no familiarity with what they were copying or illustrating, but who applied with little discrimination received techniques, models, motifs, and commonplace programs. Second, passing from manuscript to manuscript, one may discover divergent, even contradictory, readings of the same text. Third, scribes or others may deliberately modify a text or its illustrations and layouts, even introducing new or erroneous layouts or illustrations. Fourth, illustrators may add visually to the text, much as a scribe might introduce new material or make deletions.[6]

Genre

The Middle Ages had no theory of genre in any modern sense and does not seem to have reflected theoretically or even practically on genre distinctions. To speak of romance as a genre is thus anachronistic. Therefore, to identify romance as it was understood in the Middle Ages, either one must rely on statements by medieval authors about the works they wrote, which tend to be descriptive rather than definitive, or one must fall back on modern definitions derived from theory and reflection on genre. A useful compromise between the two approaches would be to seek criteria for modern identification of medieval genres from historical evidence. For romance, such evidence includes lexicography, authorial or narrator interventions, and the features of romance itself that emerge during its historical development.

Generic Boundaries

Today we commonly adopt medieval language when discussing romance, using designations such as romance (*roman*), narrative lay (*lai*), *chanson de geste*, chronicle, saint's life (*vie*), fabliau, and *dit*—designations that identify a corpus of works with identifiable common features. But usage of these terms in the Middle Ages was not consistent. These words were more like convenient tags rather than designations of perceived genres. Particular works take their place in a kind of spectrum in which generic boundaries are imprecise. Groupings include works like romanced epic that might fit more than one designation. The major kinds of narrative recognized today, as well as some discursive works bor-

dering on the formal treatise, may overlap with, borrow from, or influence works that we usually call romance. In his *Chanson des Saisnes*, a
chanson de geste, Jehan Bodel names three kinds of narrative *matières*:
French, Roman, and British. Yet we do not locate the *Saisnes* or, for
another example, the *Song of Roland*, among romances. Some argue that
the antique romances are not true romances because they do not contain
features of *conjointure* that distinguish romance proper after Chrétien de
Troyes. Other works contain romance features, but we do not call them
romances. *Saint-Brendan*, a saint's life, contains a voyage resembling a
quest and Celtic marvels. Wace's *Brut* is a chronicle, yet it is based on
Geoffrey of Monmouth's fantastic history and culminates with Arthur
and the Round Table. Fabliaux like the *Lai d'Aristote* and the *Vair palefroi*
contain courtly features. Allegories like the *Rose* and dream visions in *dits*
may be called *romans* at a time when this word referred almost universally to the kind of works we call romance. The *Lancelot-Graal* cycle, which
its authors call an *estoire* rather than a *roman*, interlaces the allegorical
mode and biblical or apocryphal typologies with Arthurian adventures.
Gautier d'Arras's *Eracle* includes a saint's life, crusading epic, and a
courtly love story. *Guillaume d'Angleterre* offers hagiography in the form
of adventure romance. The representation of women in the *Sept sages* in
verse and prose combines features of fabliaux and clerical misogynist literature. All these examples suggest a rather loose use of *roman* as
romance.

Nor has romance been defined in a satisfactory way by modern scholarship and criticism. In the most useful approach, Hans-Robert Jauss
accommodates historical variations in the emergence and evolution of
romance from the twelfth into the sixteenth century.[7] Romance constitutes itself as a genre diachronically and synchronically. Diachronically, it
emerges as each *roman* adds its features to the stock of features in the
works after Chrétien de Troyes usually designated by the word *roman*.
Synchronically, it accounts for contemporary diversity. Of course, it is
often uncertain whether authors or publics knew one another's work or
the work of predecessors, or the extent to which they knew them as we
know (or are ignorant of) them from extant manuscripts, or whether
they invented romances independently of one another. A good example
of this uncertainty is the nearly contemporary composition of Grail
romances by both Chrétien de Troyes and Robert de Boron. One wrote
before the other. Which came first? Did the later author know his predecessor? If so, one may reconstruct a sequence of versions of Grail

romances in which the later author responds to the earlier one. But how did he respond: by copying, by adapting, or by completely changing? If they were ignorant of one another's work, or knew of the other's work only by hearsay rather than directly, then the two romances are independent occurrences. In any case, both versions help us to define romance, as they would have determined how contemporary publics, in different milieux, comprehended the *roman* of their times.

Generic Interface of Romance and the Narrative Lay

A special problem is the relation between romance and the narrative lay. The obvious distinction between the two kinds of works is length. The lay is almost always shorter than 1000 lines; some contain scarcely more than 100 lines. However, Gautier d'Arras calls his *Ille et Galeron* a *lai*. To be sure, its plot contains themes and motifs found as well in Marie de France's "Eliduc," like the man with two wives and a Breton setting. Yet *Ille* contains over 6000 lines, whereas Marie de France's lay has only 1184. Other works usually defined as romances are as short as "Eliduc," notably the *Mule sans frein* (1136 lines) and the *Chevalier à l'épée* (1206 lines). Nor is every lay only "Breton" in *matière*. The authors designate as lay the *Lai de l'ombre*, the *Lai de l'oiselet*, the *Lai d'Aristote*, and the *Lai de Narcisus*, yet none are "Breton" or British. By similar criteria we could designate as lay *Philomena* and the *Châtelaine de Vergi*. Here too generic boundaries are hazy.

Orality

Romance is a written literature; it is not improvisational like early *chansons de geste*. On the other hand, although written, it was usually meant to be read aloud to an audience of one or more persons. This remains true until the end of the Middle Ages, although private reading became more common with the growth of literacy among the nobility and middle classes.[8]

A major distinction between improvisational orality and writing-based orality is that between live performance and monumentality. The oral tradition is based on *parole* as improvised utterance, whereas orality based on reading relies on utterance of the written *mot*. The latter is distinguished from the former by a stated intention to preserve the word as a monument—a kind of concrete memory. Thus, romances proclaim their desire to record in writing lest the memory of past deeds perish.

> Si escripture ne fust feite
> e puis par clers litte e retraite,
> mult fussent choses ublïees
> ki de viez tens sunt trespassees.

(Rou, part 3, ll. 7–10)

[If written works had not been produced, then read and recited by clerics, many past deeds would have been forgotten.]

The written word is therefore a generic marker for twelfth-century romance. It distinguishes *écriture* from *voix*; but it does not distinguish romance from other written narratives.

The Marvelous Adventure (*Aventure Merveilleuse*)

The awareness of *roman* as a distinct kind of writing surfaces in Chrétien de Troyes. His romances thus serve as a point of departure for the definition of the generic features of the word in Old French. Chrétien's romances focus on a marvelous adventure, that is, a seemingly fortuitous occurrence that calls for investigation by a knight who sets out to confront it. To seek the truth of an adventure is a marvelous and informing experience—"Je me merveil" in Old French can mean the same as "I wonder" in English.

> Forment desire l'aventure
> A savoir, qu'ele senefie;
> En son cuer pense et bien affie,
> Ja por poor nel leissera,
> Tant que de verite savra,
> Quel aventure est, qu'il va querre.

(Claris, ll. 24822–27)

[He is eager to know the meaning of the adventure. He determines in his heart that fear will not keep him from learning the truth about the adventure he seeks.]

The experience of the adventure is "marvelous." The marvelous in Old French is not merely the supernatural or fantastic. It is any extraordinary occurrence. A knight usually confronts the adventure and experiences its marvel. In doing so he in turn becomes marvelous. His qualities, as the achievement of the adventure demonstrates, are shown forth in the qualities or attributes that permit him to achieve the adven-

ture. Those to whom adventures come or occur are the dramatis personae of romance; their story is an *aventure merveilleuse* (Kelly, *Art*, 191–200).

The *aventure merveilleuse* may well contain episodic encounters along
the way that advance or impede progress toward the achievement of the
adventure. For example, in the *Charrette*, Lancelot sets out to rescue
Guenevere from abduction. During this quest he encounters a number
of adventures which, as stages in the quest, may further his progress by
providing lodging; may cause him shame, as when he rides in the cart;
may demonstrate his exceptional qualities by signs that he will achieve
the quest; or may impede his progress by mockery, combat, erotic temp-
tation, or physical obstacle. Furthermore, common features like
Lancelot's resistance to seduction or his ability to overcome all opponents underscore repeatedly the extraordinary quality of a love that gives
him the strength, courage, and will to overcome all obstacles. Romances
relate adventures leading to love, renown, or social and moral excellence.
In general, one may say that romance recounts a real or implicit grada-
tion of events leading to the achievement of, or failure to achieve (as in
many Grail romances), a specific goal. Achievement demonstrates the
superiority of an exemplary type.

Women often instigate adventures but seldom figure as the achiever
of adventure, except when they accompany a knight who is responsible
for them, like Enide in Erec's quest. The striking exceptions—female
knights in the *Eneas*, *Silence*, or *Claris et Laris*—are virile on the battle-
field, regardless of the persona they might represent in peacetime.

Temporal and Spatial Coordinates

Traditionally, for the Middle Ages a story contained four essential elements: protagonists, narrative, time, and place. The temporal and spatial coordinates of marvelous adventures could be realistic or
impressionistic.[9] Inconsistencies are not lacking since scientific chronology and cartography do not usually preoccupy romancers. Other factors
like the significance of place and time are more important. Medieval
mapmakers center the world on Jerusalem, regardless of the real geography they knew. Chrétien reports that Perceval wanders for five or six
years without encountering any adventure worth relating because he has
forgotten God; but on Good Friday he discovers God again, and the
time is for that reason significant because on that day Christ was cruci-
fied to offer the hope of salvation. The place is also important: Perceval
is near the dwelling of his uncle the hermit, who explains to him how he
may atone for past sins. Perceval's very confusion regarding time and

place mirrors his moral confusion; as he gains his bearings he is better equipped to direct his life along the right way.[10]

Other romances use subjective experience of time and space to show the state of mind of their protagonists. Elsewhere, accurate recording of time and place in one part of a romance, as in the *Lancelot Proper*, may give way to nonspecific coordinates, as in the *Queste*, where commonplace patterns of sin and redemption determine the protagonists' progress or lack thereof in the quest for the Grail.

Stock Characters and Characterization

The Middle Ages knew neither the individual nor the self as desirable, distinct entities with discrete sensibilities and unconscious desires.[11] Rather, the person is defined by moral standards, his or her place in the social order, age, sex, and so on. Thus, although narratives may be rich in diverse adventures and marvels, the protagonists tend to exemplify specific contexts representing an ideal view of life in the world. Prominent knights are distinguished only to the degree that they realize the prowess, love, or rectitude that qualifies knightly conduct, as for certain recurrent personages like Gauvain, Lancelot, Galaad, and other figures less well-known today. Unique excellence identifies the knight or lady who best realizes an ideal. The norm is the ideal, just as, in Christian morality, Adam and Eve before the Fall are the norm. By this standard, the most nearly "normal" knight in medieval romance is Galaad, the chaste virgin. There is no modern notion of individuality in the Middle Ages, only of physical, social, or moral deformity.

Adaptation

Adaptation is a major feature of romance composition (Vinaver, *Rise*, 16). Since the modern notion of original creation was foreign to the medieval mind—after all, only God could create—the artist was a humble imitator of such creation when he or she invented or "re-created" a given matter. But medieval poetics rejected in principle the new work that merely copied, paraphrased, or commented on an earlier work. The new work was expected to draw from earlier versions a new conception of the matter, implicit in earlier versions, but as yet unrealized in words. An obvious example is the adaptation of Chrétien's *Charrette* in the *Prose Lancelot*. Chrétien's romance does not treat Lancelot's love as a sin. The complete prose romance makes his sin explicit by fitting ideal love to the pattern of original sin. Guenevere replaces Eve, sex the forbidden fruit.

Adaptation precludes source study as practiced in early philology. Indeed, such source study was antithetical to the medieval art of adaptation. Traditional source scholarship sought to recover in extant texts traces of a lost or presumed source. This led to attempts to reconstruct lost sources, or lost parts of fragmentary works, as in Joseph Bédier's reconstruction of the lost parts of Thomas's *Tristan* based on works that derived from Thomas himself. Bédier's critical presuppositions have been called into question, with the result that his reconstruction is no longer considered reliable for the missing parts of the Old French romance.[12] A different approach was to determine what later authors borrowed from earlier works. Actual excerpting is found in some romances, although the new context for the excerpts usually alters their narrative significance.[13] But source scholarship is critically indiscriminate and historically inaccurate if mere replication of a phrase or group of words is presumed to be borrowing.

An equally suspect presupposition denies a source when none is extant today. Thus, although there can be no doubt that the authors of the antique romances used Vergil, Statius, or Ovid, the absence of such sources for the Matter of Britain has led many to argue that textual references to sources are meaningless and to assume the total originality of the extant works (see Gallais, "Recherches," 338–47).

In dealing with presumed or actual sources, one must above all identify the art of adaptation practiced by the romancers. Failure to do so led to errors like Bédier's. The medieval art of poetry and prose identifies three possibilities for adaptation. The adaptation may be identical to its source or sources, that is, a virtual restatement or paraphrase; it may be comparable; and it may be antithetical in its conception or plot. The only constant is that an antecedent work is adapted. The new author studies narrative strategies used in the antecedent source which he or she then redeploys by rewriting (Poirion, "Ecriture").

Three topics are paramount in romance adaptation: the language of the adaptation; intertextuality, a modern term that refers to the multifarious and complex features of medieval adaptation and reception; and manuscript format.

Language of Adaptation

French romance became a European genre through translations and adaptations into other languages, notably German, Dutch, Welsh, Italian, Occitan, the Hispanic languages, the Scandinavian languages, and English. Transmission of these romances outside the French-speaking world began with the family of Eleanor of Aquitaine.[14] Its members carried the literature of France to what were to become the major centers of vernacular literature in Europe for the rest of the Middle Ages. Their French imprint makes romances in other languages part of the history of medieval French romance.

The topic of adaptation of French romance has until recently been neglected unless the adaptation was written in another language. Middle High German versions of French romances have attracted the most attention, although other languages contain important works, for example, like Malory's *Morte Darthur* in England. However, adaptation also occurs in French itself, as in the prose adaptation of the *Charrette* referred to above.[15] French romance itself purports to use sources written in Latin and other languages. What is important is the new reading proposed by the adaptation, the new mores or audiences it addresses, and the strategies of composition the new work adopts and deploys. Comparison of extant sources and their adaptations may therefore illuminate both source and adaptation.[16]

For example, Hartmann von Aue adapted Chrétien's *Erec* into Middle High German, but with additions, motif reversals, and suppressions. The most striking change is his reevaluation of Erec. In the French version Erec pardons his wife for misjudging his chivalric worth and his love for her; in the German version, Erec asks her forgiveness for his mistreatment of her. As with the prose version of Chrétien's *Charrette*, Hartmann changed the loci of fault and innocence, and thus changed the context of the romance. Similar adaptations have been analyzed in the *Gauvain Continuation* of Chrétien's *Perceval* and the antique romances.[17] Studies of romances in other languages based on French originals have made valuable contributions to our knowledge of the art of romance adaptation.[18]

Some French romances survive only in foreign-language adaptations. Ulrich von Zatzikhoven's *Lanzelet* and Eilhart von Oberg's *Tristrant* both claim to use French-language romances as their sources. The *Lanzelet* represents the life and loves of Lancelot prior to his being linked with Guenevere in Chrétien's *Charrette*, whereas the *Tristrant*, an example of the *version commune* of the Tristan legend, is comparable to Beroul. *Moriz von Craûn* may also have adapted a lost tournament poem in French. Extensive Spanish and Portuguese fragments are all that survive of some parts of the Post-Vulgate *Graal* (Bogdanow, *Romance*).

Some claim that the two major romances in Occitan, *Jaufre* and *Flamenca*, are adaptations of French sources. *Jaufre* contains matter and motifs drawn from various romances in a new, perhaps parodic, plot analogous to those in thirteenth-century parodies of Arthur and the Round Table knights; Chrétien's influence has been suggested. On the other hand, *Flamenca* may have adapted a fabliau to the romance form.

(The Bibliography contains source works on romance in other languages, especially those that take into account French influence.)

Intertextuality

Adaptation has both a medieval and a modern face. The medieval face is that of the art of invention learned in rhetoric. The modern face is intertextuality.

Intertextuality is a useful term for the study of medieval adaptation.[19] For romance, the word has two historically demonstrable senses. First, it refers to the relation between two works in which at least one author is aware of and responding to the other. The author as reader reinterprets and rewrites what he or she has read. Second, it overlaps with the medieval notion of invention wherein a new version of an antecedent work is conceived and plotted out in the mind; the mental projection is then put into words.

Intertextuality in the first sense is a kind of rewriting. While studying the strategies deployed in an antecedent work or works and mining them for material, the new writer conceives of a new deployment in order to rewrite, recast, or correct the source. The strategy entails "plotting"—that is, setting forth of a plot and, prior to that, contriving an art by which to elaborate the new plot.[20] Dialogical, centrifugal, and centripetal intertextuality derive from the ways in which a source text is contrasted with, integrated into, or elaborated on in the new plot. Condensation and amplification are important techniques borrowed from the medieval art of poetry and prose.

Invention as rereading a text prior to rewriting it introduces a second kind of intertextuality, identified as such by Riffaterre (see note 20), but fundamentally medieval as a concept. This is the projection—the intertextual projection—of as yet unwritten works by which the author as reader invents, that is, "finds," a new version (cf. *trouvère*). One recognizes here the medieval conception of invention according to which thought about a given matter precedes adaptation and rewriting.

Intertextuality presupposes two kinds of readers. First, the actual author who construes a new work and writes it. This may include the intervention of a patron, as in the case of Marie de Champagne and Philippe de Flandre in the composition of, respectively, Chrétien's

Charrette and his *Conte du graal*. Second, the reader may be an audience, a public with its own baggage of intertextual references, thus implying complex reception ranging, in theory, from total ignorance of sources, analogues, and anterior traditions, to a rich mental storehouse of tales, motifs, and images that may surface in various, sometimes unexpected, ways, during the reading of a given text. Different manuscript versions of a text and its sources and epigones suggest an even more complex intertextuality. The scholar must define the terms of such intertextuality in interpretation.

The *Texte-Fragment*

Paul Zumthor has identified an aspect of intertextuality that is peculiar to *manuscriture*: the tendency to collect romance material in new combinations, especially when such combinations do not realize a new whole.[21] Adaptation need not be total. A number of related phenomena of scribal adaptation may occur in the transmission of a given romance as fragment. The following examples move from more to less coherent groupings of romances in manuscripts.

The Cycle.   Cyclic romance is a chain of romance branches or narrative sections identified by the original author or by subsequent authors who add new material to the beginning, end, or intervening parts of the narrative. The *Lancelot-Graal* describes itself as a narrative tree with trunk and branches. To the *Prose Lancelot* recounting the life and deeds of Lancelot and his family the *Estoire* and *Merlin* add a prehistory. The Post-Vulgate *Graal* adds events simultaneous with those in the *Prose Lancelot*. The *Prose Tristan*, *Guiron le courtois* (*Palamèdes*), and other compilations are added. In the fourteenth century the *Perceforest* adds a lengthy prehistory to the Vulgate cycle, including Troy, Alexander the Great, and Roman conquests. Another cycle, the *Prose Sept sages de Rome*, introduces Arthurian elements, especially in *Laurin*. An elaborate work emerges, cyclic in that it cycles or recycles events through different, more-or-less intertwining adventures.[22] All romances are thus explicit or implicit branches of a vast potential cycle.

The Continuation.   Romance continuations tend to be additive. For example, the four *Perceval Continuations* continue the quests of Perceval and Gauvain left incomplete in Chrétien's *Conte du graal*. Others are sequels (*suites*), genealogical in character (ancestral romance), as a son's deeds succeed those of his father. Hue de Rotelande's titular hero in *Ipomedon* is the father; it is followed by *Protheselaus* about his son. Both are construed as additions to the Old French *Thèbes*. The *Horn*, attributed to a certain Thomas, projects a romance about Horn's son, Aalof. Other continuations are looser, like the grafting of Chrétien's *Yvain* onto his *Charrette* to explain the absence of Gauvain at the time of Yvain's adventures.

The Compilation. Beginning in the thirteenth century, there emerges a tendency to compile romances or excerpts from romances in more-or-less coherent narrative wholes in manuscripts.[23] These compilations are usually unique to one or a few manuscripts, and may show greater or lesser degrees of scribal adaptation. Arthurian matter is the principal source of such compilations. The best-known compilers are Rusticien de Pise, Jehan le Vaillant, Michot Gonnot, and Thomas Salluste. Abroad, Malory's *Morte Darthur* compiles the French material it "Englishes."

The Anthology (*Recueil*). The collection of romances in a manuscript may follow a plan whereby discrete works are implicitly or explicitly interconnected or sequential. This occurs when, for example, antique romances are copied with chronicles so as to evoke a continuous line of descent from ancient to contemporary times. Collections of Arthurian romances achieve similar wholes implicitly interrelated. Varieties of the anthology include Perrot de Nesle's Bibliothèque Nationale manuscript français 375, which provides transitional passages from one romance to the other grouped in loosely chronological sequence; Bibliothèque Nationale manuscript français 1450, which inserts Chrétien's Arthurian corpus into Wace's *Brut* to explain what occurred during a period of peace in Arthur's reign; and Bibliothèque Nationale manuscript français 903 in which Jehan Malkaraume inserted the *Troie* into his translation of the Bible.[24]

Scribal Intervention. Scribes intervened in the transmission of manuscripts, either by correlating variant readings in the manuscripts they copied or by deliberately introducing changes in the copied texts. These may be as minor as grammatical or dialectical correction or modernization. But they may also extend to changes in episodes or the deliberate introduction of new material, like the so-called *Prose Erec* and *Alixandre l'Orphelin* insertions into the prose cycles. These interventions fit into the cyclic scheme and ethos of the prose romance to which they are added. Manuscript layout and illustration are also features of scribal intervention.

Scribal interventions may effect major rewriting. The intentional intervention adapts the original according to a new narrative standard or meaning; it thus conforms to the medieval notions of rewriting. The results may be successful or unsuccessful.[25]

Opening, Closure, Midpoint, and Open-endedness

The absence of holographs and the vagaries of manuscript reproduction raise problems that disappeared only with the printing press. Where does a given romance begin or end? What is one to make of incomplete episodes?[26] The fragmentary transmission of some romances (the Tristan poems, *Meliador*), the alleged incompleteness of others (*Bel inconnu*, Guillaume de Lorris's *Rose*), the relation among branches added later and by different authors (the complex redactional histories of the *Lancelot-Graal*, the Prose *Tristan*, and the *Prose Sept sages*), the uncertain nature of some combinations (Chrétien's and Godefroi de Leigni's parts of the *Charrette*, the connections between the *Charrette* and *Yvain*)—such problems raise the issue of narrative closure. The midpoint halfway between the beginning and end of a romance plot may be a highly significant moment either for narrative drama or for the meaning of the tale. The Middle Ages does not, always, seem to have sought unity or even coherence in any modern or classical senses, especially in romances like Beroul's *Tristan* or the *Gauvain Continuation*. The critic, as medievalist, must therefore endeavor to identify the art being used and the narrative strategies that art entails to appreciate the composition of the work. Thus he or she will measure the achievement of the text or manuscript by the standards of the art it illustrates.

Prosody and Prose Style

The medium of medieval romance is verse or prose.[27] Verse romances usually use octosyllabic rhyming couplets (*rimes plates*) with no fixed alternation between masculine and feminine rhymes; 10- and 12-syllable lines are uncommon, except in the Alexander romances, from which the French *alexandrin* designating the 12-syllable line derives its name.

Prosody and *Brisure du Couplet* (Couplet Breaking) in Verse Romance

The octosyllabic rhymed couplet predates protoromance, having been used in early saints' lives. When it appears in Wace and the *Thèbes*, the couplet tends to be used as a unit that is broken syntactically only at the end of an even-numbered line. The following example shows even numbers of lines that define sentence segments. Segments are separated by a space. The punctuation in the edition has been removed, to reflect what the reader of a manuscript might find.

> Por les nobles barons qu'il ot
> Don chascuns miaudre estre cuidot
> Chascuns se tenoit au meillor
> Ne nus ne savoit le peior
> Fist Artus la Reonde Table
> Dont Breton dient mainte fable
>
> Iluec seoient li vasal
> Tuit chevelmant et tuit egal
>
> A la table igalment seoient
> Et igalment servi estoient
>
> Nus d'aus ne se pooit vanter
> Qu'il seïst plus haut de son per
>
> Tuit estoient asis mayen
> Ne n'i avoit nul de forien.

(Brut, ll. 1207–20)

[For his noble barons Each of whom presumed himself to be better Nor could anyone identify the worst Arthur made the Round Table About which the Britons relate many a fable — There sat the vassals All like good knights and equal — They sat equally at the table And they were served alike — None of them could boast Of sitting higher than his peer — All were seated at mid level Nor was anyone excluded.[28]]

One sees how intonation and syntax detach each segment from those surrounding it into an even number of lines. The first segment itself may be further divided by intonation so as to emphasize the parenthetical character of the second couplet.

However, as romance developed, the couplet became more supple. Breaking at the uneven line became more common; in Chrétien's romances, it is the rule rather than the exception.

> Li graaus qui aloit devant
> De fin or esmeré estoit
>
> Precïeuses pierres avoit
> El graal de maintes manieres
> Des plus riches et des plus chieres
> Qui en mer ne en terre soient

> Totes autres pierres passoient
> Celes del graal sanz dotance
>
> Tout ensi com passa la lance
> Par devant le lit s'en passerent
> Et d'une chambre en autre entrerent
>
> Et li vallés les vit passer
> Ne n'osa mie demander
> Del graal cui l'en en servoit
> Que toz jors en son cuer avoit
> La parole au preudome sage
>
> Si criem que il n'i ait damage
> Por che que j'ai oï retraire
> Qu'ausi se puet on bien trop taire
> Com trop parler a la foiee
>
> Ou biens l'en viegne ou mals l'en chiee
> Ne sai le quel rien n'en demande

(Perceval, ll. 3232–53)

[The Grail which came first Was of fine, pure gold — There were precious stones Of many kinds in the Grail, Of the most precious and most dear In sea or on land — All other stones were surpassed by Those in the Grail, without doubt — As the Lance passed Before the bed they too passed And went from one chamber into another — And the valet saw them pass But did not dare ask About the Grail whom one served with it Because he ever bore in mind The words of the wise and worthy man — And I fear that harm will come to him on account of that Because I have heard tell That one can quite well be too quiet Just as one can on occasion talk too much — Whether good or evil befalls him, I don't know which, he asks nothing about it]

The complexity of sentence subordination, indicated within the segments by intonation and syntax, as well as the quality and character of an oral reading, suggests how varied the recounting of the narrative may be. Breaking couplets counterpoints intonation and rhyme alternation, thus diversifying narrative enunciation.

Other techniques were also available to the romancer. Stichomathy, for example, allows for rapid dialogue by even more daring breaks in verse. Although the technique antedates Chrétien,[29] some of the most remarkable examples are found in his romances. In the following passage, the lines are broken according to the speaker in order to show more clearly the variety of stichomathy in dialogue.

> . . . an ce voloir m'a mes cuers mis.
> —Et qui le cuer, biax dolz amis?
> —Dame, mi oel.
> —Et les ialz, qui?
> —La granz biautez que an vos vi.
> —Et la biautez qu'i a forfet?
> —Dame, tant que amer me fet.
> —Amer? Et cui?
> —Vos, dame chiere.
> —Moi?
> —Voire voir.
> —An quel meniere?
> —An tel que graindre estre ne puet . . .
>
> (*Yvain*, ll. 2019–27)

["My heart gave me this desire." "And who gave it to the heart, fair, sweet friend?" "My lady, my eyes did." "And who put the eyes to it?" "The great beauty I saw in you." "And what fault has the beauty in that?" "My lady, it made me love." "Love? Whom?" "You, dear lady." "Me?" "Oh! yes!" "In what way?" "In such a way that it cannot be greater."]

Parataxis and Hypotaxis in Verse and Prose

3Parataxis and hypotaxis designate two antithetical kinds of sentence structure. Parataxis juxtaposes successive propositions without indicating their relation to one another by coordinating parts of speech. Parataxis accumulates rather than articulates expression. It is common in *chansons de geste*.

> Dist Oliver: "Paien unt grant esfurz,
> De noz Franceis m'i semblet aveir mult poi.
> Cumpaign Rollant, kar sunez vostre corn!
> *Si* l'orrat Carles, *si* returnerat l'ost."
> Respunt Rollant: "Jo fereie que fols,
> En dulce France en perdreie mun los.
> Sempres ferrai de Durendal granz colps,
> Sanglent en ert li branz entresqu'a l'or.
> Felun paien mar i vindrent as porz.
> Jo vos plevis, tuz sunt jugez a mort."[30]

[Oliver said: "The pagans have a great army. We seem to have too few Franks. Companion Roland, sound your horn! *Then* Charles will hear it, *then* our army will return." Roland answers: "I would be a fool to do so. In sweet France I would lose my renown. I shall go on striking great blows with Durendal. Its blade will be bloody up to its golden hilt. What a misfortune the felonious pagans came to the mountain pass. I swear to you, all are destined to die."]

Parataxis is remarkable in some romances. For example, in Beroul's *Tristan*,

> Laisent le chien, tornent arire.
> Husdent aqeut une chariere,
> De la rote molt s'esbaudist;
> Du cri au chien li bois tentist.
> Tristran estoit el bois aval
> O la reïne et Governal;
> La noise oient, Tristran l'entent.
> "Par foi," fait il, "je oi Husdent."
> Trop se criement, sont esfroï.
> Tristran saut sus, son arc tendi.
> En un' espoise aval s'en traient;
> Crime ont du roi, *si* s'en esmaient,
> Dïent *qu'*il vient o le brachet.

(ll. 1527–39)

[They leave the dog, they turn back. Husdent enters on a cart-track. The road makes him happy. The woods resound with the dog's bark. Tristan was deep in the woods with the queen and Governal; they hear the noise, Tristan hears it. "In faith," he says, "I hear Husdent." They have great fear, they are frightened. Tristan jumps up, draws his bow. They draw back into a thicket; they are afraid of the king, *and* they are terrified. They say *that* he is coming with the dog.]

The almost total absence of conjunctions and the concomitant rapid-fire enunciation of simple clauses enhances the sense of terror as the dog quickly approaches with Marc. They fear the dog will betray their hiding place, exposing them to violent death.

Hypotaxis is the opposite of parataxis. It links successive propositions with one another by conjunctions, relative pronouns, prepositions, and other kinds of syntactic coordinators. It therefore articulates rather than accumulates. In the following example from Marie de France's

"Guigemar," we see more conjunctions, although they are less well defined than in modern French; furthermore the sentences, although not simple, are not complex either.[31]

> Sire, fet ele, vus amez!
> Gardez *que* trop ne vus celez!
> Amer poëz en iteu guise
> *Que* bien ert vostre amur assise.
> *Ki* ma dame vodreit amer
> Mut devreit bien de li penser.
> Ceste amur sereit covenable,
> *Si* vus amdui feussez estable:
> Vus estes bel *e* ele est bele!

(ll. 445–51)

[My lord, she says, you are in love! Make sure *that* you don't hide your feelings! You may love such *that* your love will be well placed. He *who* would love my lady should love her well. That love would be acceptable *if* you were both constant. You are handsome *and* she is beautiful!]

The following passage from Chrétien's *Cligés* shows how complex hypotaxis nuances efforts in early romance to express psychological problems.

> *Mes* de toz amanz est costume
> *Que* volantiers peissent lor ialz
> D'esgarder, *s*'il ne puent mialz,
> *Et* cuident, *por ce qu*'il lor plest
> *Ce dont* amors acroist et nest,
> *Qu*'aidier lor doie, *si* lor nuist;
> *Tot ausi con* cil plus se cuist,
> *Qui* au feu s'aproche et acoste,
> *Que* cil qui arrieres s'an oste.
> Adés croist l'amors *et si* monte;
> *Mes* li uns a de l'autre honte,
> *Si* se cuevre *et* çoile chascuns,
> *Si que* n'en pert flame ne funs
> Del charbon *qui* est soz la cendre,
> *Por ce* n'est pas la chalors mandre,
> *Einçois* dure la chalors plus
> Desoz la cendre que desus.

(ll. 584–600)

[*But* all lovers have the habit *that* they willingly feed their eyes by look-
ing, *if* they can't do better, *and* suppose, *because that* pleases them *by which*
love grows *and* is born, *that* it ought to help them, *yet* it harms them, *just
as* he or she is burned *who* draws near to a fire *or* sits next to it *more than*
one *who* pulls back from it. Love always grows *and* becomes greater. *But*
the one feels ashamed before the other, *and* both cover and hide their feelings *so that* neither flame nor smoke is visible from the coal *that* is under
the ashes. *For all that* the heat is not less, *rather* the heat lasts longer
under the ashes than on top of them.]

Thus the French language, made more supple by freer versification,
also developed more complex syntax, including greater subordination in
sentences and subtler articulation of expression by connectives. Hence,
the emphasis on word clusters that fit easily into the sharp metrical divisions in decasyllabic epic verse, with relatively few conjunctive features,
gave way in verse romance to progressively more sophisticated and
semantically rich sentence articulation.

When romance turned to prose in the thirteenth century, it retained
hypotaxis, but of a less complex kind than in verse.[32] The ubiquitous
use of connectives like *Car, si,* and *que* with various modifiers and the use
of relative pronouns in verse to correlate sentences is reduced to rather
straightforward conjunctions that connect rather than articulate sentences. The following passage on Galehaut's love for Lancelot is an
example:

MAIS ore laisse li contes a parler ici endroit de ses bontés et retorne a dire
ensi com il s'en vont entre lui et Lancelot et .IIII. escuier sans plus de com-
paignie ET chevalchent en tel maniere dolent et pensif, KAR il sont andui
molt corocié, Galehout *de ce qu'*il crient perdre son compaignon par le roi *de
cui* maisnie il est remés, ET Lancelos rest a malaisse de sa dame *que* il
esloigne si, ET molt li poise des mals *que* Galehout sueffre por lui: SI sont a
malaise li uns por l'autre *si* qu'il en perdent le boivre et le mengier; ET tant
entendent a penser *qu'*il enpirent molt de lor bialté et de lor force ET tant
s'entredotent par loial amistié *qui* entr'els deux est *qu'*alsint li uns d'eus
n'ose metre l'autre en parole de riens *dont* il soit a malaise, *altresint com* il
sentissent mesfet d'aucune chose li uns vers l'autre. —MAIS nule dolor ne
s'apareille *a ce que* Galehout sueffre, KAR il avoit mis en l'amor Lancelot tot
ce que hom i pooit metre, cuer et cors, et tote honor, *qui* miels valt. —Il li
avoit si doné son cors *qu'*il amast miels a veoir sa mort que la Lancelot; —il
li avoit si doné son cuer, *la ou* il ne pooit avoir joie sans lui. —ET por lui fist
il si grant amor *qu'*il cria merci le roi Artu, ET SI l'avoit il torné a desconfi-
ture ET aproché d'estre deserités. (*Lancelot*, sec. 2, pars. 1–2)

[BUT now the story leaves off at this point telling of his good qualities AND returns to telling *how* he, Lancelot, and the four squires leave without other accompaniment AND ride on grief-stricken and pensive, FOR both are sorely distressed, Galehaut *because* he fears losing his companion on account of the king *in whose* household he remained, AND Lancelot is also distraught on account of his lady *whom* he is going so far away from, AND he is greatly distressed because of the harm *that* Galehout suffers on his account: AND they are vexed for one another *to such an extent that* they stop drinking and eating; AND they are so absorbed in their thoughts *that* their beauty and strength suffer AND so much do they fear one another on account of the loyal friendship *which* they share *that* the one dares not speak to the other about anything *which* grieves him, *just as if* they felt guilty of some fault toward one another. —BUT no grief is *like that which* Galehaut suffers, FOR he had put into his love for Lancelot *everything that* a man could: heart and body and honor, *which* is worth more. He had given himself *such that* he would rather experience his own death than Lancelot's; —he had given him his heart *to such an extent* that he could know no joy without him. —AND for him he had manifested such great love *that* he asked for Arthur's mercy, AND YET he had brought him to defeat AND drawn him close to being entirely dispossessed.][33]

Tropical and Figural Embellishment

By the end of the twelfth century Latin versification included metrical verse based on feet defined by long and short syllables, rhythmic verse using feet defined by accented and unaccented syllables, and literary prose composition defined in various ways: semimetrical sentences, rhyming sentences, accent patterns for terminating sentences (*cursus*), and tropes and rhetorical figures. French, on the other hand, defined verse by syllable count and rhyme; there was as yet no prose art. The two literary languages shared only ornamental use of tropes and figures and rhyme. However, after the rather more ornamental embellishment that protoromance initiated, rather stiffly, and the achievements of masters like Chrétien, Thomas d'Angleterre, and Gautier d'Arras, verse romance drifted toward a plainer style. The prose romance that emerged in the early thirteenth century tended in the opposite direction, moving from a simple, hypotactic mode to more complex sentence structure in the late medieval period. This evolution may be observed by comparing works like the *Mort Artu*, *Perceforest*, and *Jehan de Saintré* (Ferrier, *Forerunners*).

Rhetorical embellishment is not mere artificial imposition of formal devices, including rhyme, on plain matter. Ornamentation by tropes and figures is intended to make narrative more pleasing to hear and to enunciate meaning more precisely and sensitively. Clerical training imbued pupils' minds with the habit of thinking metaphorically and figuratively (Vinaver, *Rise*, 16–22). When Chrétien used rhetorical devices for embellishment, he did not consciously choose a device; he found the mode or form of expression coming to him as naturally as a specific grammatical feature comes to the mind of one who has mastered a new language. For example, every time one chooses to use a French imperfect or simple past, one does not think: "I shall use an imperfect or simple past here!" Rather one uses the tense that best suits what one wishes to express. The same is true for figures and tropes.

Verse versus Prose and the Truth of Romance

The adoption of prose at the beginning of the thirteenth century appears to have been deliberate. About 1206 a certain Johannes turned a Latin chronicle into French prose rather than verse because, he asserts, versification—*rime*, which still meant verse and rhyme at the time, not (just) rhyme[34]—obliged the author to add extraneous material to the original.[35] Prose allows the truth to be expressed (ll. 23–24). But the French-language redaction is far from a faithful translation of the Latin original (see Walpole, *Johannes*, ll. 97–122). Wherein resides the truth of prose?

It is a romanced truth (Vinaver, *Rise*, 31–32). The real value of the *Pseudo-Turpin Chronicle* in French lies in the examples of honorable conduct the text proposes for inspiration and imitation. This conforms to another passage that justifies the use of prose.

> Issi vos an feré le conte
> Non pas rimé . . . ,
> Si con li livres Lancelot
> Ou il n'a de rime un seul mot,
> Por mielz dire la verité
> Et pour tretier sans fauseté;
> Quar anviz puet estre rimee
> Estoire ou n'ait ajostee
> Mançonge por fere la rime.[36]

[Now I'll tell you, but not in verse and rhyme . . . , the story—like the *Lancelot* which contains not a single word of verse or rhyme—in order to express the truth better and to treat my subject without falsification. For it is difficult to draft a story in verse and rhyme without introducing lies in order to complete the line and make it rhyme.]

The reference to the *Prose Lancelot* in the prologue suggests that the truth was not historical or factual but rather exemplary and topical. To express that truth unimpeded by the demands of versification, rhyme, and, perhaps, ornamentation requires prose. As in Jean Bodel's *Saisnes* prologue, the truth or falsity of certain matters depends on the truth the matter represents, a truth defined by the nobility of the dynasty the matter represents. Some verse romancers admit adding "lies" for purposes of versification, while others fault verse for its lies.[37] *Marques de Rome* in the Seven Sages cycle refers to its "derhymed prose" not to explain how an original verse work was recast in prose, but rather to point out that it is not in verse at all.[38] Prose became the mode in which the secular ideals of verse romance were criticized.

Social and Moral Ideals

In French romance four subjects define and influence character, milieux, and actions: *knighthood and chivalry* as these manifest themselves in warfare, single combat, tournaments and jousts, and feuds; *courtesy* as it defines relations among aristocrats, between aristocrats and other social orders, and between the sexes; *love and so-called courtly love* in marriage and in premarital and adulterous relations; and *Christian morality* as it abets, opposes, or seeks to influence and interpret the preceding subjects. All presume an aristocratic audience, although the makeup of even the aristocratic audience itself varied from court to court. Two factors loom large: the idealization or denigration of the principal characters and actions of romance narrative and the role of patrons in the definition and direction of authorial intent. I shall take these topics up in order.

But first a caveat: knighthood, chivalry, courtesy, and courtly love are not susceptible to general definition. As Maurice Keen puts it regarding chivalry, they are "elusive of definition, tonal rather than precise in [their] implications."[39] The tonality of different romances may differ or disagree when treating social and moral ideals. Romances and groups of romances represent, articulate, and modulate differently the tonalities of knighthood, chivalry, courtesy, and love, rather than simply define them.

Knighthood and Chivalry

Treatises were written during the Middle Ages on the practice of knighthood and chivalry.[40] Romances too provided models of conduct,

Quar qui romanz velt escouter
Et es biaus dis se velt mirer
Merveil est s'il ne s'en amende,
S'il est ensi qu'il i entende.[41]

[For it's a wonder if whoever likes to listen to romances and reflect on the
fine subjects they treat does not improve, provided he or she pays close
attention to them.]

Some even set forth rules. In Chrétien's *Conte du graal*, Perceval receives
three sets of partially overlapping rules from his mother, Gornemant de
Goort, and his uncle the hermit. By and large they are commonplace in
romance in defining "l'ordre de chevalerie / Qui doit estre sanz vilonnie"
(ll. 1637–38) (the order of chivalry, which should be free of villainy). In
brief, Perceval learns that the knight should:

1. Honor and assist ladies, maidens, and orphans in distress (ll.
   533–42, 1657–62, 6465–70)

2. Love maidens honorably, not importunately (ll. 543–56)

3. Know his companions (ll. 557–62)

4. Honor and seek out the acquaintance, counsel, and company of worthy men and women (ll. 563–66, 6460)

5. Attend mass regularly and pray for guidance (ll. 567–72, 1666–70,
   6440–59)

6. Grant mercy to defeated opponents (ll. 1640–47)

7. Moderate talking (ll. 1648–56)

8. Show due respect to men of the church (ll. 6461–64).

The *Prose Lancelot* offers even more elaborate instruction when the Lady
of the Lake teaches young Lancelot on his way to be dubbed what ritual he is to follow, what his conduct as knight should be, the meaning of
knighthood and chivalry, and the origins of nobility (*Lancelot*, sec. 21a,
pars. 6–22).[42] *Jehan de Saintré* contains disquisitions by which the
Dame des Belles Cousines educates her young protégé in matters of
knighthood, chivalry, love, and religion. They are a kind of mirror for
princes (Fürstenspiegel) wherein aspirants to knighthood might see
ways to improve themselves. The modern reader may use them to
delineate the moral and social standards by which the narrative is
meant to be evaluated.

Two medieval French terms loom large in knighthood and chivalry: *prouesse* and *compagnonnage*. *Prouesse* includes both martial prowess and the inner worth that prowess expresses. It makes the knight a *preudom* (Köhler, *Ideal*, 129–38). As the exercise of arms, prowess has three principal areas of activity in romance: single combat (jousts, duels, isolated combats between knights, as during quests), warfare between rulers or barons or on crusading expeditions, and tournaments. These activities, like dubbing itself, are rituals in an art of armed combat. The rituals vary with time and place, and thus from romance to romance. Of course, literary idealization obscured the reality of uncontrolled violence between enemies or opponents, where the conflict of good and evil is not at issue. For the knight, however, prowess in arms presupposed prowess as noble worth. Thus, the knight ideally fought in order to make right triumph and justice prevail, to exercise, and to distinguish himself as *preu* or worthy before his lord, lady, or God.

Compagnonnage, a special bond among knights, is also a kind of friendship. It may even emerge from rivalry, since it supposes a kind of equality in arms and chivalry and an affinity for the good life as knight.[43]

The knight as *chevalier* began as a *cavalier* or horseman. He was not always noble, nor was nobility always accessible to him. Jean Flori has shown how the high medieval notion of knight emerged in the twelfth century from the earlier distinction between horsemen and barons.[44] A new order of lord or king with noble vassals is epitomized by the Round Table, which in French romance still distinguishes between king and Round Table knights.[45] The emergence of the knight parallels the establishment of the distinction among the three orders of clergy, nobility, and people.[46] The two developments combine to define a civilization that unites clergy and knighthood. It passed, according to the commonplace *translatio studii et imperii*, from Greece and Rome to France. Romance is instrumental in articulating these ideals. Chrétien de Troyes, whose conception of dubbing is important in the history of chivalry,[47] expressed this ideal of civilization in *Cligés* as a civilization of *chevalerie* and *clergie*, just as *Athis et Prophilias* assigns complementary roles to Athens and Rome as seats of, respectively, *clergie* and *chevalerie*.

Courtesy

As chivalry regulates the martial activities of the knight while he is on horseback, as it were, courtesy regulates life at court. The narrative pat-

tern of most romance—from court the knight departs, to court he
returns—makes the court the locus of repose from which marvelous
adventures may call or which they may threaten. From Wace onward the
knight had a place at court, which imposed its own rituals and rules as
courtesy. For example, at the moment Rome threatens Arthur, Wace
introduces Gauvain to defend peacetime activities at court as properly
alternating with war (*Brut*, ll. 10767–72). He emphasizes two aspects of
courtesy in this passage: the proper peacetime activities for knights at
court and the special relations between knights and women, especially
amorous relations. For Gauvain, martial performance is compatible with
courtesy and love.

Courtesy was no more a precise code of conduct than was chivalry. It
reflects a state of mind translated into appropriate conduct and sentiments. Nonetheless, romances on occasion set some guidelines. The
injunctions to Perceval include elements of courtesy like deference to
women and the clergy. Guillaume de Lorris has the god of love deliver a
lengthy list of do's and don'ts on courtesy. Among his recommendations
to be courteous while avoiding whatever is base are instructions on polite
conversation, entertaining diversions, cleanliness, generosity, dress,
speech, and affability, especially toward women (*Rose*, ll. 2049–220).
Romances offer abundant examples of courtesy as opposed to villainy in
multifarious adventures and court scenes.[48] For the knight, courtesy
may be not only a social desideratum that redounds to his honor, it may
be a moral imperative that defines his very worth.

Many Old and Middle French words express the quality of courtesy in
noble men and women—from generosity (*largesse*) to youth (*jeunesse*),
from free birth (*franchise*) to prowess (*prouesse*) in arms and in human relations.[49] The choice and balance of these and other constituents of courtesy often determines the tonality of courtesy in a given romance.
However, two words often used to express the quality of courtesy in
noble men and women are especially noteworthy because of their prominence, and because they do not have quite the same meanings today as
they did in medieval romance. The two words are *umileté* and *simplece*.
"Humility" in this sense is the opposite of pride: "Humilités fait gens
molt gracieus, ne il n'a riens en homme ki tant soit haie comme
orguix"[50] (Humility makes one gracious, nor is there anything more
despised in men than pride). Perceval is told to rise in deference to priests
as a sign of humility (*Conte du graal*, l. 6464). Humility shows deference
out of respect for others, even underlings. The "humble" know what
actions are proper to themselves and to others in human relations. But

the notion does not suggest undue self-deprecation or submission. Such "humility" is a social, not a moral virtue.

Simplece defines the honesty with which deference is shown. Its opposite is duplicity, just as vain pride is the opposite of humility, by virtue of the fact that words and actions should be in harmony with mind and heart. Deference is sincere, and sincerity is the soul of courtesy. The word "simple" still has something of this force in modern French, where the person who is "simple . . . agit selon ses sentiments, avec une honnêteté naturelle et une droiture spontanée" (*Petit Robert*). Such courtesy is not simpleminded; it excludes vanity, arrogance, and flattery. Perceval's spontaneous gush of tears when he repents his sins shows his "simplicity" (*Perceval*, l. 6351). Spontaneous manifestations of hospitality and other forms of courtesy show simplicity as well. The unity of appearances and sentiment could be complicated by conflicts between levels of courtesy, as when Lancelot must choose between deference to court and deference to his love.

Love and "Courtly Love."

This brings us to the special problem of courtly love in romance.

The expression courtly love (*amour courtois*) appears to be no older than 1883. In an article on Chrétien's *Charrette*,[51] Gaston Paris characterized what he calls "courtly love" as secret, furtive, and adulterous; the courtly lover is jealous, ever fearful of losing his lady, who, in turn, is capricious, scornful, and demanding; to win her love, he must forever prove and improve himself so as to be worthy of her esteem, and she should inspire his efforts by rigorous demands; and there is a code of love. These traits define what has become the popular, widespread notion of courtly love today.

Since 1883 there have been numerous attempts either to explain courtly love or to explain it away by denying its validity for the interpretation of medieval literature. Medieval French did use expressions like *fin'amour*, *amour par amours*, and *bone amour* to refer to noble love. But in romances these terms refer to a variety of lovers, situations, emotions, and ideas. It is therefore obvious that the words did not always connote the same properties or qualities, nor were they viewed everywhere as good or evil. The same author could argue or exemplify seemingly contradictory kinds of *fin'amour*. For example, Chrétien de Troyes seems to idealize conjugal love, although he also illustrated a number of fundamental problems in aristocratic marriages and narrated the adultery of

Lancelot and Guenevere. Contrary to what Gaston Paris thought, medieval French romance by and large treats *fin'amour* as a love leading to and in marriage rather than as adultery.

Three factors characterize adultery in those romances that include it. First, whether justified or not, as when there is an old, jealous, or abusive husband, adultery occurs because there is no alternative available to the lovers. If the beloved is already married, especially when the spouse is a woman (cases of a husband's adultery in romance do not carry the same onus as a wife's adultery), there is no escape from the marriage, divorce being disallowed in the Middle Ages. Only by murder or natural death[52] could one expect to break out of a marriage; even flight did not annul it despite remarriage such as that in Marie de France's "Guigemar."

Second, evaluation of adulterous lovers depends on the evaluation of the other spouse in the triangle. For example, Guenevere's infidelity in the *Prose Lancelot* occurs after Arthur's. On the other hand, the Lady of Fayel in the *Châtelain de Couci* falls in love with the Châtelain despite her good marriage; the husband's jealousy when he discovers the liaison produces an intense desire for violent vengeance.

Third, the distinction Andreas Capellanus[53] makes between conjugal affection and extramarital love is socially comprehensible insofar as, in a medieval marriage, and certainly in many romance marriages, problems stem from the established position of the husband as head of the family. Noble marriages were arranged with little concern for compatibility or attachment. However, in love both partners have a choice and both strive for equality in excellence even if social circumstances impede the full attainment of their desires. Attraction, choice, and worthiness rest on a nobility of mind quite distinct from nobility of blood, which often dictated, for both young men and women, the choice of marriage partner by families; family choice could be made when children were quite young, before any possible knowlege of the physical, psychological, or moral person each spouse may become after puberty.

Love in marriage was therefore a far more novel notion in the Middle Ages than today. Epic and early chronicles mostly ignore it. After the marriage was consummated, adultery was the only other viable amorous relation with a person of the opposite sex.[54] In any case, adultery is not the most common relationship in romance. The prose romances treat adultery as immoral and sinful. The fascination with "courtly love" as adultery is therefore more modern than medieval.

Most romances focus on the choice, winning, and retention of a spouse. Choice based on real worth, proof of worth by means of a trial, and openness and even equality in conjugal relations are the major elements in courtship and marriage. Chrétien de Troyes is the first and perhaps the most important writer to base marriage on love. His first Arthurian romance, *Erec et Enide*, treats in its first part the attraction of two essentially equal persons that results in marriage.[55] That Erec meets, wins, and marries Enide without consulting his parents must have seemed extraordinary at the time. However, problems surface when Enide heeds the complaints of Erec's men, his and her inferiors, because he stops participating in tournaments (at the time participation in tournaments was a sin) rather than her own heart and mind regarding the quality and worth of her husband's love and lovemaking. Enide, heretofore wife and beloved (*femme* and *amie*) in Erec's mind, is then reduced to mere wife and thus becomes subject to her husband's authority. He later realizes that she still loves him, and their earlier love and equality is restored. As wife and *amie* Enide returns to Erec and to the joys of the marital bed; there is no more question of tournaments. The rediscovery of love and mutual understanding restores and glorifies the marriage in the crowning conclusion, when, after the death of Erec's father, King Lac, Erec and Enide accede to the throne before Arthur's court.

Christian Morality

Medieval romance celebrates secular ideals that sometimes run counter to religious or social morality. Adultery is sometimes portrayed as a positive act, for example, and warfare between Christians is often celebrated. But the Church condemned both adultery and bloodshed among Christians. The Church also condemned other acts that are commonplace motifs in romance, such as betrayal, tournaments, duels, warfare among Christians, and mistreatment of orphans, women, or religious persons. Accordingly, the emphasis on secular ideals in romance, no matter how glorified and fascinating they were, gave rise to criticism of romance's alleged vanity. The popularity of romance and the simultaneous ongoing criticism of romance suggest not only different audiences for different works, but also moral and social debate in audiences admiring both, say, Chrétien's *Charrette* and a saint's life. When, for example, an anonymous author enjoins a lady to set aside *Cligés* and *Perceval* in favor of saint's lives, we see her both reading Chrétien and being advised that his writings are vain and even sinful (in Mölk, sec. 75, ll. 19–36). The inclusion of *Perceval* in this condemnation suggests how stern criticism of romance could be, while the inclusion of *Cligés* undercuts claims that courtly literature was ironic or subversive criticism of secular ideals.[56]

Romance proves that sin was not always on the noble person's mind. Plots are usually decidedly this-worldly. The correlation of worth and sexuality was no doubt a strong force that could not go unnoticed, even in idealized, perhaps escapist, narratives. Of course, we know virtually nothing about love in the real but private world of romance audiences. However, since some romancers relate their writing to love service, comparing and contrasting their own experience with that of their fictional lovers, the idealization cannot have been entirely unrealistic. A negative response from both social and ecclesiastical authorities was to be expected.

The most effective criticism occurred in the romance mode itself. The first two branches of the Seven Sages cycle are harshly misogynist. More subtle are the *Lancelot-Graal* romance cycle and Jean de Meun's rewriting of Guillaume de Lorris's *Roman de la rose*. After the *Charrette* episode in the *Lancelot Proper*, the Lancelot narrative subtly undermines the originally beneficial harmony between love and prowess; Jean's *Rose* blatantly displays the folly he perceived beneath the courtly or noble veneer of much romance.

Extremely harsh moral condemnation in prose romance and the reevaluation of earlier models of chivalry may account for the emergence in the second half of the thirteenth century of a Hollywood kind of romance, that is, one in which nearly identical heroes and heroines parade fantastic achievements and display noble but undifferentiated loves without attention to the decline and debasement of aristocratic ideals in practice. Romance narrative turns away from the harsh morality of earlier thirteenth-century prose cycles (Van Coolput, *Aventures*).

The Representation of Exemplary Heroes and Heroines

Major characters in romance are represented in two ways: by descriptions (static) and by their actions (dynamic). The descriptions define their unique exemplarity, the actions their unique excellence (Kelly, *Art*, 231–40). Both are factors in defining the ethos—the context or *san*—of romance.

Description emphasizes exemplary attributes that articulate and evaluate character. On the narrative level, the attributes determine context. They are rarely defined as such but rather complement one another, producing a tonality based on character.[57] Romance evinces a movement from highly formalized, abstract descriptions of physical, social, and/or mental features to more dynamic descriptions wherein a defect is corrected in the course of the narrative. In Marie de France's "Guigemar," for example, the titular hero is described as handsome, well loved by his parents and all who know him, including prudent and worthy women. But he has no interest in love (ll. 57–58). This defect makes him hopelessly lost in everyone's eyes. The lay itself recounts the correction of the defect.

Exemplary romances foster conduct and form a mentality inclined to realize the kind of world the protagonists represent. Disagreement as to the right qualities of exemplary figures has much to do with adaptations of received material, as, for example, in the obvious reinterpretation of Chrétien's Lancelot in the Lancelot-Grail cycle or the late medieval Burgundian adaptations of twelfth-century romances.

The notion of the individual is so basic to modern conceptions of the person that it is difficult to imagine a time when neither the ideal nor the notion existed. From the medieval point of view, the individual as distinct, original, or uniquely different from the norm violates an order preestablished by God or by tradition and is essentially perverse, like the devil. The medieval notion of class fits into a worldview where the particular "individual" ideally seeks his or her place and roles in a hierarchy. What that place may be was subject to debate; the order was not. Ideally, the normal human being is man and woman as God created them, before the Fall. This accounts for the appeal and, in romance, the ultimate triumph of Galaad in the *Queste*. In this view, Galaad incarnates humanity as it was created, before the individualizing effects of sin intervened. But sin itself was ambiguous, insofar as it also marked the beginnings of inequality and, thus, of the rise of nobility itself.[58] Here are the grounds for the opposition between religious and secular moralities.

Knights and ladies stand out, not because of their individuality, but by their approximation to an ideal place in the order of things. In the *Queste* Galaad is as like to Adam before the Fall as fallen man can be; Perceval's sister occupies a similar position vis-à-vis Eve among women. This in turn defines the defects identified in knights further removed from Galaad's perfection, from Perceval and Boort to Lancelot and Gauvain. Similar hierarchies obtain within nonreligious contexts, as Guigemar shows.

The major contexts in romance are those identified by Dante for medieval vernacular lyric: prowess, love, and rectitude. In Wace and Geoffrey of Monmouth before him, the major virtue is prowess in arms, whereas later the quality of love tends to make martial prowess dependent on the quality of love, as in the *Charrette*. Rectitude (*droiture*) is essential to good knights in the *Queste* and in many parts of the *Prose Sept sages de Rome* cycle.

The Romance *Sitz im Leben*

The notion of the artist's individuality is also missing in the Middle Ages. Artists may be proud of their artistry, as Chrétien is in the *Erec* prologue. But two factors restrict that pride. First, the Middle Ages had no sense of artistic creation as such; second, the romancer wrote for a patron.

Since creation in any modern sense was not possible, the artist was expected to write a romance that would suit his or her patron; it might mirror regional and dynastic interests or reflect particular contemporary political and social issues much in the manner of a roman à clef. Recent studies have shown that analogies between certain features of a given romance narrative and the political, social, or other claims of potential patrons may not be coincidental. In these cases publics would perceive their own claims to sovereignty, power, or preferment glorified by the semifictional circumstances of a plot's characters and their ideals.

This does not mean that romance became political in any modern sense. It is, rather, idealistic in that it mirrors in a fictional past a state of affairs that would please the intended patrons of the work and illustrate their reality or desired reality. Thus, what Jauss has termed the romance *Sitz im Leben*—the specific milieu for which it is written—is important in narrative articulation of social or moral ideals, especially in dynastic and feudal matters.[59]

Traditional Philology and Modern Criticism

Since about 1950 the study of medieval romance has, like most medieval and indeed most modern literatures, been influenced by a variety of sometimes rapidly changing critical theories and methodologies. This seeming disarray reflects uncertainty regarding the character of "literature" and of desirable approaches to its interpretation. The changes have been beneficial for the study of romance in two ways. First, they have made romance perhaps more interesting to modern readers by refracting it through the lenses of a variety of modern critical approaches. Second, they have revealed the originality and interest of romance for current criticism. But there have been serious drawbacks too. As essentially unquestioned models of interpretation proliferate, some drawn from various sciences or disciplines, they are often applied by critics without expertise in the model science or discipline. There is also a curious, even alarming haste to abandon previous models for new ones as new methodologies or theories replace one another and vie for authority.[60] The study of medieval French romance will no doubt reflect this state of affairs if French critical thought and theories continue to dominate medieval scholarship as much as they have during most of the twentieth century.

Traditional Philology and the Study of Medieval Texts.

The major demarcation today is between traditional philology and new philologies. Both are modern.[61] The former prevailed in the twentieth century until after World War II, and is still authoritative. Building largely on methodologies defined in the nineteenth century, it has dominated all forms of study of romance from textual editing to interpretation. Since World War II numerous new approaches (an interesting phenomenon itself in the history of philology) have steadily emerged, gained momentum and scope, then declined. They include critical developments in, as well as new criticism opposed to or independent of, traditional philology.

Medievalists cannot do without certain features of traditional philology. One must be able to read Old French well; paleographical expertise is necessary to confront manuscript and oral tradition and to evaluate the editions that transmit romances to us today.

A middle way between anachronism and "presentism" will, in the long run, advance our appreciation of medieval texts and monuments as they were meant to be read or heard. Anachronism is fascination with the old that has no relation to the modern. "Presentism," a term I borrow from historians of science, is the imposition of present standards and critical values on the past. It is analogous to the medieval readings of Ovid. Medieval commentators—the so-called friar critics[62]—identified first the letter of Ovid's text, then applied the "modern" methods of Christian hermeneutics, rereading and rewriting Ovid as Christian allegorical poetry. A hermeneutic method is in place as long as its axioms are unquestioned. When a revolution in thought occurs, it may be replaced by a new method. Revolutions, or at least turnovers, have been frequent since 1950.

It is sometimes distressing that theories and methodologies proliferate or replace one another almost as soon as they are established. There is no doubt pleasure in discovering new interpretative approaches and fresh interpretations. But is it not a sign of cynicism to drop one in favor of another in the name of originality that is only novelty? Writings surviving from the Middle Ages may be interesting in themselves while also bringing to modern critical methodologies medieval data that they lack or ignore and that might oblige them to revise, correct, or even broaden their analyses. With very few exceptions, the Middle Ages has sparked little interest among modern critics, especially those influenced by French critical thought. The lack of interest goes back beyond Lanson and, in fact, beyond traditional philologists, who introduced medieval literature, and most notably romance, into the French *licence* curriculum after World War II. Recent efforts to correct this state seem more anxious to make medievalists aware of modern methods than to convince new critics that medieval literature has something of interest to offer and that, without it, their theories are untenable and their methods flawed.[63] Why indeed should modern critics make the considerable effort to read medieval romances if they add little or nothing new to their theories or methodologies?

The study of medieval romance requires a solid foundation in Old and Middle French, paleography, and textual editing. Attention to bibliography, an awareness of what kinds of criticism are available, and an understanding of how they are relevant to medieval romance are also essential. Medieval romance has its own art which can be recovered by historical criticism. That art can then be integrated into modern criticism after it has been set forth with reasonable certainty.

New Approaches in Traditional Philology

New approaches have also been making their mark in paleography and textual editing. Paleography is the study of manuscripts. As the Middle Ages passed from an oral to a print culture *manuscriture* became its mode of transmission. Romance itself survives in manuscripts. Reading manuscripts is therefore necessary for reading romances, as manuscripts are their only surviving "artifacts."

The reader of romances in manuscript encounters several phenomena unfamiliar to the reader of books. First, almost no romance is a holograph or autograph, that is, none was written by or with the approval of the author. Manuscripts are copies that reveal certain moments in the transmission of the text—moments that, as "performances" (Huot, *Song*, 3–4), may tell us about the uses it was put to, and therefore may teach us how it was read and understood in times and places different from those intended by its first author or patrons. This is crucial when manuscripts offer divergent versions of a given work, as in *Ille et Galeron* and the *Roman de la rose*, or, on a more extensive scale, the *Perceval Continuations* and the *Prose Lancelot*.

How, then, will the modern editor present the romance? Can an edition restore the version that emerged from the author's stylus or an important stage in its transmission? What is the critical significance of scribal intervention and rewriting? How important is the variant and in which contexts? Concern for the original version has dominated editorial practice up to this day, on the hypothesis that the earlier the version the "better" or more important it is—a survival of the demand for originality going back to the romantic movement's emphasis on original, creative genius. More recently, in despair at ever recovering that version, critics have focused on editing a "good" manuscript. This is the basis of Mario Roques's controversial CFMA editions of Chrétien de Troyes. Whatever the defects of these editions, even by Roques's own standards, his is in principle an effort to make available the manuscript that is "best" because closest to the original in time, dialect, fidelity, and context. All these issues involve editorial intervention, which, in the last analysis, depends on knowledge, taste, and interpretation.[64]

A truly critical edition provides all important readings culled from the available manuscripts and makes them available to the reader as variants. This was the goal of Wendelin Foerster's editions (*große Ausgaben*) of Chrétien and Elspeth Kennedy's of the *Noncyclic Lancelot*; it is still the goal of the new "Vinaver Chrétien" being prepared by a group of British and American scholars.[65] Another step in this direction is the publication of more than one manuscript, as in William Roach's *Perceval Continuations*. The use of computers will make such editing practical and economical.[66] It would be useful to have an edition of *Rose* manuscripts that differ radically from those that are the basis of all available editions.[67] The evidence of divergent manuscripts suggests the variety of ways in which a work is received. Medieval readings of the *Rose* hinge very much on whether contemporaries read the full version represented in current editions or whether they knew it through subsequent adaptations, abbreviations, or allegorizations.

Paleography includes study of manuscript illustration, format, and contexts, all of which fall within Sylvia Huot's notion of the manuscript as "performance." The "performance" is implicit: the romance was meant to be read, heard, and seen as the manuscript presents it. The modern reader may reconstruct to some extent a specific "performance" from a given manuscript. This is useful for study of reception.

Finally, the medieval propensity toward allegoresis may affect romance. Some romances are explicitly allegorical, like the *Roman de la rose*, the *Queste du saint graal*, and Huon de Mery's *Tornoiement Antecrist*. But how extensive was allegorical reading? For example, may we justifiably postulate a "courtly" allegory, as in Guillaume de Lorris's part of the *Rose* and in some parts of Huon's *Tornoiement*, or is this a veneer for ironic readings—even a "courtly obscenity"?[68] Some argue as much, denying the surface courtliness in favor of moral paradigms or images from the Christian faith.[69] In this way, Lancelot, the queen's lover, has been read as an allegory both of the Fall and of the Messiah. As Ovidian allegoresis demonstrates, the two allegories may be complementary rather than exclusive. Finally, readers may have understood romances in unique, albeit erroneous ways (Huot, "Medieval Readers").

Modern Philologies

Numerous interpretive approaches and methodologies—the "new philologies"—have been applied to medieval romance: semiotics, psychoanalytic theory, anthropology, sociology of literature, reception theory, and feminist criticism.

People living in the Middle Ages did not, of course, have a theory of individual psychology or psychoanalysis. Their notion of psychology was at best normative. It found expression in moral thought and evaluation. However, the insights of psychoanalysis can help us to appreciate the emotional impact romances once had, as in some configurations of father-son relations and of incest, not only in those romances that explicitly treat potential or real incest, like *Apollonius de Tyr*, *La Manekine*, or the *Comte d'Anjou*, but also in the romances containing configurations that fit Freudian models.[70] Similarly, patriarchal and matriarchal emphases in lineage reflect various ways by which medieval romancers evaluate the knights who are in quest of the Grail or who are associated with it (Schmid, *Familiengeschichten*).

Erich Köhler has been the principal proponent of a literary sociology. To him, four factors define the social function of a romance: (1) the historical circumstances in which it is written; (2) the intended audience as a social order or group, including the author's own awareness of his or her role vis-à-vis audience; (3) the personality and education of the author; and (4) the genre chosen.[71] These factors are detectable to varying degrees in specific romances; nonetheless, they offer a model for interpretation that accounts for the romance's place and significance in a particular historical and social constellation: its *Sitz im Leben*. The model does not dispense with artistic, aesthetic, or formal qualities in romance; on the contrary, it evaluates them as factors in the romance's historical significance.

Köhler's approach gives impetus to the study of romance alterity,[72] that is, features that distance it from modern expectations or presuppositions. He is sympathetic to that alterity, allowing for its eventual incorporation into a broader, yet deeper understanding of the amalgam of medieval and modern norms. The modes of reception in the Middle Ages, the expectations of medieval publics, are so different from ours as to falsify readings that rely only on modern modes of critical analysis.

The sociology of romance is related to feminist analyses of women in romance, including women in male roles like Camille in the *Eneas* and Silence in Heldris's *Silence*; misogyny; and women as authors, patrons, and audiences. In addition, critical reviews of scholarship show how conscious or unconscious male prejudices or male-oriented perspectives have warped interpretations.

Finally, romance scholarship is subject to waves of critical emphases, even fads, in current critical discourse outside medieval studies. Thus, in recent years topics like closure, the female reader, displacement, authority and subversion, the "politics" or "poetics" of various phenomena, and other topics have aroused attention. Some of these investigations, by their very ephemerality, rely more on speculation than concern for what is historically likely in medieval writing—for example, in attempts to show that romances that are incomplete in the manuscripts are in fact complete (Guillaume's *Rose*, the *Bel inconnu*), whereas others are incomplete (*Charrette*), or when multiple authorship is questioned (*Roman de la rose*). Without our knowledge of Flaubert's life could one not make a case that *Bouvard et Pécuchet* was finished? These ingenious studies assume that medieval romancers were deceptive or subversive and that the modern fascination with such deception or subversion—the "variant"—was shared from the twelfth to the fifteenth century.

This is not new. Just as Chrétien may, in feminist readings, be shown to undermine the authority of Marie de Champagne as the *Charrette* patron, so did earlier scholarship see him do so in the name of a so-called bourgeois idealization of marriage. These analyses fail to raise fundamental questions: was Marie de Champagne so obtuse as to notice nothing? What permitted a hired servant to get away with such a response to her request?[73]

At issue is historical probability. Modern interpretations of medieval writers must rest on the validity of projecting modern models or convictions onto romance without first demonstrating their plausibility at the time the romances were written. There are data for psychoanalytic, anthropological, feminist, and sociological readings of medieval romance. But since the Middle Ages did not know of or talk about, for example, the Oedipus complex or the Jungian archetype as such, any more than it read Karl Marx, we must carefully avoid unconsciously projecting issues of which medieval readers knew nothing into our readings of romance.

The fundamental question the reader of romance must ask is, Am I reading the romance to understand how it was received in its own time, or am I attempting to explain it in my own terms? The two questions are not incompatible, but they must be kept distinct.

Matilda Bruckner has argued that Chrétien's *Charrette* is not a fable that imposes a moral. It is a *cas*—a "case"—that raises issues audiences, medieval and modern, may respond to differently ("Interpreter's Dilemma"). Lancelot's adulterous love enables him to free Guenevere from captivity; the narrative is therefore about a certain kind of love. People today respond in various way to the data, as Bruckner shows. The same was doubtless true in the Middle Ages. Some may have gone along with the obvious reading, swayed by arguments like that attributed to the romance's patroness, Marie de Champagne: love outside marriage is essentially different from affection in marriage and has its own values. The *Prose Lancelot*'s rewriting of the *Charrette* is a different response. Others in Chrétien's and Marie's audiences may have responded to the romance as one maiden does to a poem in Froissart's *Meliador*: "Ceste parole n'est pas mienne, / Car onques n'amai par tel art"[74] (Those words are not mine, for I never loved in that way); others may have read according to personal conviction: "on le poet bien expondre / En quelque maniere c'on veut" (*Meliador*, ll. 30245–46) (one can interpret it any way one wishes). All these responses are possible. But that Chrétien makes Lancelot the lover of the queen, and a better knight because of it, cannot be gainsaid; it can only be appreciated.

A modern term that has retained currency for medievalists is intertextuality. It fits quite well many aspects of medieval textuality. Whether used for traditional or new philologies, it encompasses phenomena that medieval audiences and publics were familiar with. Of course, our only access to intertextuality is through surviving texts—all of them. Matilda Bruckner has provided a profound critical statement of intertextuality's importance and its demands on the critic: "The echoes between Chrétien and those that follow him must be heard generally against the sounding board of medieval tradition . . . , their individual voices must be located within the common language of romances, as it develops from the twelfth century onwards" ("Intertextuality," *LCT* vol. 1, p. 224). The first "philological" task is therefore to read all medieval romances, not just the great names and works in isolation.[75] In time, this will lead to better understanding of the romance tradition exemplified by the sum of its surviving manuscripts, and will preclude (to continue quoting Bruckner) our "confusing common participation in the romance genre with intertextual reference to Chrétien" alone or any other single author currently prominent.

Notes and References

Chronology

1. It is impossible to give a full bibliography. See in general Alfred Foulet and Mary Blakely Speer, *On Editing Old French Texts*, ECAMML 1 (Lawrence: Regents Press of Kansas, 1979), 88–89.

2. Aimé Petit, *Naissances du roman: Les techniques littéraires dans les romans antiques du XIIe siècle*, 2 vols. (Lille, France: Atelier National Reproduction des thèses/Paris: Champion-Slatkine, 1985), 497–98, 833.

3. On the different versions in verse and their dates, see Petit, *Naissances*, 1085–1187; cf. Udo Schöning, *Thebenroman-Eneasroman-Trojaroman: Studien zur Rezeption der Antike in der französischen Literatur des 12. Jahrhunderts*, BZRP 235 (Tübingen, Germany: Niemeyer, 1991), 52–57.

4. Attribution uncertain.

5. Listed in order of narrative chronology, not of composition.

6. On his adaptations, see Marc-René Jung, "Gui de Mori et Guillaume de Lorris," *VR* 27 (1968): 106–37.

7. Some parts survive only in Spanish and Portuguese. See Fanni Bogdanow, *The Romance of the Grail: A Study of the Structure and Genesis of a Thirteenth-Century Arthurian Prose Romance* (Manchester: Manchester University Press, New York: Barnes & Noble, 1966).

8. Compiled from the *Burgundian Florimont* and *Blancandin*; see René Stuip, "Entre mise en prose et texte original: le cas de l'*Histoire des seigneurs de Gavre*," in *Rhétorique et mise en prose au XVe siècle*, Actes du VIe Colloque International sur le moyen français, Milan 4–6 mai 1988, vol. 2, Contributi del "Centro studi sulla letteratura medio-francese e medio-inglese," 8 (Milan, Italy: Vita e Pensiero, 1991), pp. 211–28.

9. Linked by genealogy in the manuscripts to the fifteenth-century version of the *Fille du comte de Pontieu* and *Saladin*; the source of *Jehan d'Avennes* is the anonymous fourteenth-century *Dit du prunier*, ed. Pierre-Yves Badel, TLF 334 (Geneva: Droz, 1985).

Introduction

1. P. Volker, "Die Bedeutungsentwicklung des Wortes Roman," *ZRP* 10 (1886): 485–525; see also Paul Zumthor, *Essai de poétique médiévale* (Paris: Seuil, 1972), chap. 8.

2. Ed. Ivor Arnold, SATF (Paris: SATF, 1938–40), l. 3823.

3. *La vie de Saint Thomas Becket*, ed. Emmanuel Walberg, CFMA 77 (Paris: Champion, 1964), l. 6162.

4. Some manuscripts of *Cligés* have two lines with the sense of "romance"; see ed. Alexandre Micha, CFMA 84 (Paris: Champion, 1957), p. 208; all editions except Micha's include these lines.

5. Ed. Mario Roques, CFMA 86 (Paris: Champion, 1980), ll. 1–2.

6. Ed. Mario Roques, CFMA 80 (Paris: Champion, 1966), l. 14.

7. *Le bel inconnu*, ed. G. Perrie Williams, CFMA 38 (Paris: Champion, 1929), ll. 4–5.

8. Emmanuèle Baumgartner and Charles Mela, "La mise en roman," in *Précis de littérature française du moyen âge*, ed. Daniel Poirion (Paris: PUF, 1983), 90–91; Douglas Kelly, *The Art of Medieval French Romance* (Madison: University of Wisconsin Press, 1992).

9. Ed. Jean Rychner, CFMA 93 (Paris: Champion, 1968).

Chapter 1

1. See Jacqueline Cerquiglini, *GRLMA*, vol. 8, pt. 1, pp. 86–94.

2. Janet Ferrier, *Forerunners of the French Novel: An Essay on the Development of the "Nouvelle" in the Late Middle Ages* (Manchester, England: Manchester University Press, 1954); Michel Zink, *GRLMA*, vol. 8, pt. 1, pp. 197–218.

3. On oral traditions and romance, see Paul Zumthor, *La poésie et la voix dans la civilisation médiévale* (Paris: PUF, 1984); and his *La lettre et la voix: De la "littérature" médiévale* (Paris: Seuil, 1987); Evelyn B. Vitz, "Rethinking Old French Literature: The Orality of the Octosyllabic Couplet," *RR* 77 (1986): 308–21; and her "Orality, Literacy and the Early Tristan Material: Béroul, Thomas, Marie de France," *RR* 78 (1987): 299–310; and Joseph J. Duggan, "Performance and Transmission: Aural and Ocular Reception of the Twelfth- and Thirteenth-Century Vernacular Literature of France," *RPh* 43 (1989): 49–58.

4. On epic improvisation, see Jean Rychner, *La chanson de geste: Essai sur l'art épique des jongleurs*, PRF 53 (Geneva: Droz, Lille, France: Girard, 1955). On *jongleurs* in general, see Edmond Faral, *Les jongleurs en France au moyen âge*, BEHE 187 (Paris: Champion, 1987); and Constance Bullock-Davies, *Professional Interpreters of the Matter of Britain* (Cardiff: University of Wales Press, 1966).

5. See Pierre Gallais, "De la naissance du roman," *CCM* 14 (1971): 69–75.

6. For background, see Robert W. Hanning, *The Vision of History in Early Britain: From Gildas to Geoffrey of Monmouth* (New York: Columbia University Press, 1966).

7. Geiffrei Gaimar, *L'estoire des Engleis*, ed. Alexander Bell, ANTS 14–16 (Oxford, England: Blackwell, 1960).

8. William A. Kretzschmer, Jr., "Three Stories in Search of an Author: The Narrative Versions of Havelok," *Allegorica* 5, no. 2 (1980): 20–97.

9. A. R. Press, "The Precocious Courtesy of Geoffrey Gaimar," in *Court and Poet*, ed. G. S. Burgess (Liverpool, England: Cairns, 1981), 267–76.

10.   Beate Schmolke-Hasselmann, "The Round Table: Ideal, Fiction, Reality," *AL* 2 (1982): 41–75 (with bibliography).

11.   *Le roman de Rou*, ed. A. J. Holden, SATF (Paris: Picard, 1970–73), redaction 3, ll. 6377–98.

12.   On this interpolation, see Alexandre Micha, *La tradition manuscrite des romans de Chrétien de Troyes*, PRF 90 (Geneva: Droz, 1966), esp. 35–37; and Sylvia Huot, *From Song to Book: The Poetics of Writing in Old French Lyric and Lyrical Narrative Poetry* (Ithaca, N.Y.: Cornell University Press, 1987), 27–32.

13.   For what follows, see *The Medieval French Roman d'Alexandre*, vol. 2: *Version of Alexandre de Paris*, ed. Edward C. Armstrong et al., Emon 37 (Princeton: Princeton University Press, 1937), viii–xi.

14.   A German adaptation by Lamprecht (also incomplete) continues the story for about 1500 lines; see Alfred Foulet, ed., *The Medieval French "Roman d'Alexandre,"* vol. 3, Emon 38 (Princeton: Princeton University Press, 1949) 5–8, 42–60.

15.   In *Alexandre*, Emon 38, ll. 7–8 and translation. A different reading of this passage has recently been proposed; see Schöning, *Thebenroman*, 69–73. According to it, Alexander's career is proof of the vanity of this world.

16.   See especially his critique of Briseida, contrasted with praise of the lady who is possibly his patroness—probably Eleanor of Aquitaine—in *Le roman de Troie*, 6 vols., ed. Léopold Constans, SATF (Paris: Firmin-Didot, 1904–12), ll. 13438–91.

17.   See Jean Frappier, "Remarques sur la structure du lai: Essai de définition et de classement," in *La littérature narrative d'imagination: Des genres littéraires aux techniques d'expression*, Colloque de Strasbourg, 23–25 avril 1959 (Paris: PUF, 1961), 23–39; Richard Baum, "Eine neue Etymologie von frz. 'lai' und apr. 'lais.' Zugleich: Ein Plädoyer für die Zusammenarbeit von Sprach und Literatur Wissenschaft," *ZRP: Sonderband zum 100 jähriger Bestehen* (1977): 17–78.

18.   Cf. Peter Haidu, "Narrative Language in Some XIIth Century Romances," *YFS* 51 (1974): 133–46.

19.   Alfred Foulet and Karl D. Uitti, "The Prologue to the *Lais* of Marie de France: A Reconsideration," *RPh* 35 (1981): 242–49; Kelly, *Art*, 110–14.

20.   *Floire* is therefore analogous to the legend of Apollonius of Tyre, of which there are some early French fragments, and the early thirteenth-century *chantefable Aucassin et Nicolete*.

21.   *Ille et Galeron*, ed. Frederick A. G. Cowper, SATF (Paris: Picard, 1956), l. 929.

Chapter 2

1.   See Jean Frappier, "Structure et sens du Tristan: Version commune, version courtoise," *CCM* 6 (1963): 255–80, 441–54. The distinction is not universally recognized; see especially Erich Köhler, *Ideal und Wirklichkeit in der*

höfischen Epik: Studien zur Form der frühen Artus- und Graldichtung, 2d ed., BZRP 97 (Tübingen, Germany: Niemeyer, 1970), 153–56, 267–71, and Tony Hunt, "The Significance of Thomas's *Tristan*," *RMS* 7 (1981): 41–61. But compare Douglas Kelly, "*Fin amour* in Thomas's *Tristan*," in *Studies in Honor of Hans-Erich Keller: Medieval French and Occitan and Romance Linguistics* (Kalamazoo, Mich.: Medieval Institute Publications, 1993), pp. 153–76.

2. Because Beroul and Thomas survive only as fragments, derivative adaptations have been especially important in reconstructing the lost parts. The most important are Gottfried von Straßburg, the Scandinavian *Tristrams saga* and the *Folie d'Oxford* for Thomas's missing parts, and Eilhart von Oberg and the *Folie de Berne* for Beroul's lost sections.

3. See Merritt R. Blakeslee, *Love's Masks: Identity, Intertextuality, and Meaning in the Old French Tristan Poems*, AS 15 (Cambridge, England: D. S. Brewer, 1989), 4–11.

4. Thomas d'Angleterre, *Les fragments du Roman de Tristan*, ed. Bartina H. Wind, TLF 92 (Geneva: Droz and Paris: Minard, 1960), Douce, ll. 841–46; Marie de France, *Lais*, ed. Jean Rychner, CFMA 93 (Paris: Champion, 1968), "Chievrefoil," ll. 5–6; Beroul, *The Romance of Tristran*, ed. A. Ewert (Oxford, England: Blackwell, 1939), ll. 1264–70, 1789–90. On Eilhart, see Danielle Buschinger, *Le "Tristrant" d'Eilhart von Oberg*, 2 vols. (Lille, France: Service de Reproduction des Thèses, 1974).

5. Eugène Vinaver, *A la recherche d'une poétique médiévale* (Paris: Nizet, 1970), 87–100.

6. Alberto Vàrvaro, *Il "Roman de Tristan" di Beroul*, Università de Pisa, Studi di filologia moderna, n.s. 3 (Turin, Italy: Bottega d'Erasmo, 1963); Vinaver, *A la recherche*, 79–100.

7. Douglas Kelly, "*En uni dire* (*Tristan* Douce 839) and the Composition of Thomas's *Tristan*," *MP* 66 (1969): 9–17.

8. Not everyone agrees with this conjecture; see Roger Dragonetti, *La vie de la lettre au moyen âge* (Paris: Seuil, 1980), 13–17; David Hult, "La double autorité du *Chevalier de la charrete*," in *Théories et pratiques de l'écriture au moyen âge*, Actes du Colloque Palais du Luxembourg-Sénat, 5 et 6 mars 1987, Littérales 4, ed. Emmanuèle Baumgartner and Christiane Marchello-Nizia (Paris: Nanterre/St. Cloud: ENS de Fontenay, 1988), 41–56.

9. Hubert Weber, *Chrestien und die Tristandichtung*, EurH 32 (Bern, Switzerland: H. Lang, Frankfurt am Main, Germany: P. Lang, 1976). But compare Renée L. Curtis, "The Validity of Fénice's Criticism of Tristan and Iseut in Chrétien's *Cligés*," *BBSIA* 41 (1989): 293–300.

10. See Wilhelm Kellermann, *Aufbaustil und Weltbild Chrestiens von Troyes im Percevalroman*, BZRP 88 (Halle, Germany: Niemeyer, 1936), 11–13.

11. See Barbara Nelson Sargent-Baur, "The Missing Prologue of Chrétien's *Chevalier au lion*," *French Studies* 41 (1987): 385–94.

12. Donald Maddox, *The Arthurian Romances of Chrétien de Troyes: Once and Future Fictions*, CSML 12 (Cambridge, England: Cambridge University Press, 1991).

13. Keith Busby, *Gauvain in Old French Literature*, Degré second, 2 (Amsterdam: Rodopi, 1980), and "Diverging Traditions in Some of the Later Old French Verse Romances," *LCT* 2, 93–109; and Beate Schmolke-Hasselmann, *Der arthurische Versroman von Chrestien bis Froissart: zur Geschichte einer Gattung*, BZRP 177 (Tübingen, Germany: Niemeyer, 1980), 86–115.

14. See *Le chevalier à l'épée*, in *Two Old French Romances*, ed. R. C. Johnston and D.D.R. Owen (Edinburgh: Scottish Academic Press, 1972), ll. 12–28.

15. Recent critics have suggested that the author intended the narrative to stop where it does and that therefore the *Bel inconnu* only *appears* to be incomplete; see, for example, Alice M. Colby-Hall, "Frustration and Fulfillment: The Double Ending of the *Bel Inconnu*," *YFS* 67 (1984): 120–34; and Jeri S. Guthrie, "The *Je(u)* in *Le Bel Inconnu*: Auto-Referentiality and Pseudo-Autobiography," *RR* 75 (1984): 147–61.

16. On the Grail in general, see Roger Sherman Loomis, *The Grail from Celtic Myth to Christian Symbol* (Cardiff: University of Wales Press/New York: Columbia University Press, 1963); and Charles Méla, *La reine et le graal: La "conjointure" dans les romans du graal de Chrétien de Troyes au "Livre de Lancelot"* (Paris: Seuil, 1984).

17. See examples in Carl Theodor Gossen, "Zur etymologischen Deutung des Grals," *VR* 18 (1959), esp. 181–84.

18. Other objects in Chrétien's Grail procession do not have the significance of the Grail and Lance, nor do they figure prominently in subsequent Grail romances.

19. *Perceval ou le Conte du graal*, 2d ed., ed. William Roach, TLF 71 (Geneva: Droz/Paris: Minard, 1959), ll. 3593–94; compare ll. 6392–433.

20. This is the most obvious interpretation of the *Charrette* prologue; see Matilda T. Bruckner, "An Interpreter's Dilemma: Why Are There So Many Interpretations of Chrétien's *Chevalier de la charrette?*," *RPh* 40 (1986): 178.

21. Robert de Boron, *Le roman de l'Estoire dou graal*, ed. William A. Nitze, CFMA 57 (Paris: Champion, 1927), ll. 2658–78.

22. There are allusions to this book elsewhere; it was allegedly written in Latin. No independent evidence for its existence survives. See Richard O'Gorman, "The Prose Version of Robert de Boron's *Joseph d'Arimathie*," *RPh* 23 (1970): 452–54.

23. See *Dictionnaire d'archéologie chrétienne et de liturgie* (Paris: Letouzey, 1925), s.v. "Calice"; the paten on pp. 1641–42 resembles Chrétien's Grail, the wooden chalice on p. 1638 Robert's Grail.

24. Paul Zumthor, "L'écriture et la voix: Le roman d'Eracle," in *The Craft of Fiction: Essays in Medieval Poetics*, ed. Leigh A. Arrathoon (Rochester,

Mich.: Solaris, 1984), 161–209; Friedrich Wolfzettel, "La recherche de l'universel: Pour une lecture nouvelle des romans de Gautier d'Arras," *CCM* 33 (1990): 113–31.

25.   Gautier d'Arras, *Eracle*, ed. Guy Raynaud de Lage, CFMA 102 (Paris: Champion, 1976), ll. 2903–5.

26.   Typical readings include Roberta L. Krueger, "The Author's Voice: Narrators, Audiences, and the Problem of Interpretation," *LCT* 1, 122–25; and William Calin, "The Exaltation and Undermining of Romance: *Ipomedon*," *LCT* 2, 111–24.

27.   *Partonopeu de Blois*, 2 vols., ed. Joseph Gildea and Leon Smith (Villanova, Pa.: Villanova University Press, 1967–70); Continuation, ll. 1463–66.

28.   Anthime Fourrier, *Le courant réaliste dans le roman courtois en France au moyen âge*. Vol. 1: *Les débuts (XIIᵉ siècle)* (Paris: Nizet, 1960), 441–42; Laurence Harf-Lancner, *Les fées au moyen âge. Morgane et Mélusine: La naissance des fées*, NBMA 8 (Paris: Champion, 1984), 323–28.

29.   Aimon de Varennes, *Florimont*, ed. Alfons Hilka, GRL 48 (Göttingen, Germany: Niemeyer, 1932), l. 9213.

30.   Douglas Kelly, "The Composition of Aimon de Varennes' *Florimont*," *RPh* 23 (1970): 283–86.

31.   *Amadas et Ydoine*, ed. John R. Reinhard, CFMA 51 (Paris: Champion, 1974), ll. 7985–89.

Chapter 3

1.   However, verse was not impossible per se. The so-called *Lanceloetcompilatie*, a Middle Dutch compilation based on French prose romances, including the *Prose Lancelot*, contains about 87,000 lines in the extant fragment.

2.   See Elspeth Kennedy, "The Scribe as Editor," *Mélanges Jean Frappier*, PRF 112 (Geneva: Droz, 1970), 523–31.

3.   Richard O'Gorman, "The Prose Version,": 449–61.

4.   Rupert T. Pickens, "'Mais de çou ne parle pas Crestiens de Troies . . .': A Re-Examination of the Didot-*Perceval*," *Romania* 105 (1984): 492–510; John L. Grigsby, "The Remnants of Chrétien's Æsthetics in the Early *Perceval* Continuations and the Incipient Triumph of Writing," *RPh* 41 (1988): 379–93; and Francesco Zambon, *Robert de Boron e i segreti del Graal* (Florence, Italy: Olschki, 1984).

5.   Elspeth Kennedy, *Lancelot and the Grail: A Study of the Prose "Lancelot"* (Oxford: Clarendon Press, 1986).

6.   See Norris J. Lacy, "*Perlesvaus* and the *Perceval* Palimpsest," *PQ* 69 (1990): 263–71.

7.   In fact, Perlesvaus is given several other names in the romance: Perceval, Parluifet, Buens Chevaliers. See Elisabeth Schmid, *Familiengeschichten*

und Heilsmythologie: Die Verwandschaftsstrukturen in den französischen und deutschen Gralromanen des 12. und 13. Jahrhunderts, BZRP 211 (Tübingen, Germany: Niemeyer, 1986), 146–54.

8. Thomas E. Kelly, *Le haut livre du graal: Perlesvaus. A Structural Study*, HICL 145 (Geneva: Droz, 1974), 24–31.

9. Richard Barber, "Is Mordred Buried at Glastonbury? Arthurian Tradition at Glastonbury in the Middle Ages," *AL* 4 (1985): 37–69.

10. See Alexandre Micha, *Essais sur le cycle du Lancelot-Graal*, PRF 179 (Geneva: Droz, 1987), 85–88.

11. On the careful chronology of the *Prose Lancelot*, see Ferdinand Lot, *Etude sur le Lancelot en prose*, BEHE 226 (Paris: Champion, 1954), 29–64; Micha, *Essais*, 94–142.

12. On terminology, see Lot, *Etude*, 17–28, and Carol Chase, "Sur la théorie de l'entrelacement: Ordre et désordre dans le *Lancelot en prose*," *MP* 80 (1983): 227–41.

13. *Lancelot*, 9 vols., TLF 288, ed. Alexandre Micha (Paris: Droz, 1978–83), sec. 71a, par. 48; *Lancelot do Lac: The Non-Cyclic Old French Prose Romance*, 2 vols., ed. Elspeth Kennedy (Oxford, England: Clarendon Press, 1980), p. 571, ll. 24–31.

14. *La queste del saint graal*, ed. Albert Pauphilet, CFMA 33 (Paris: Champion, 1980), p. 271, ll. 10–11.

15. See, for example, *Lancelot* sec. 106 par. 9 (others in notes), and *Queste* pp. 251, ll. 22–30, and 265, ll. 15–33.

16. Jean Frappier, *Etude sur la Mort le roi Artu, roman du XIIIᵉ siècle: Dernière partie du Lancelot en prose*, 2d ed., PRF 70 (Geneva: Droz, 1968), 63–73, 120–30, 449–50.

17. Fanni Bogdanow, "The *double esprit* of the Prose *Lancelot*," in *Courtly Romance: A Collection of Essays*, ed. Guy R. Mermier and Edelgard E. Du Bruck (Detroit: Fifteenth-Century Symposium, 1984), 1–22.

18. *Lancelot do Lac*, p. 1, ll. 7–8.

19. See Alexandre Micha, "Les manuscrits du *Lancelot en prose*," *Romania* 81 (1960): 145–87, 85 (1964): 293–318, 478–517; 86 (1965): 330–59.

20. Renée L. Curtis, *Tristan Studies* (Munich, Germany: Fink, 1969); Emmanuèle Baumgartner, *Le "Tristan en prose": essai d'interprétation d'un roman médiéval*, PRF 133 (Geneva: Droz, 1975), 88–98.

21. *Le roman de Tristan en prose*, ed. Marie-Luce Chênerie and Thierry Delcourt, TLF 387 (Geneva: Droz, 1990), sec. 105.

22. The studies of Dinadan are numerous; see Colette-Anne Van Coolput, *Aventures querant et le sens du monde: Aspects de la réception productive des premiers romans du graal cycliques dans le "Tristan en prose,"* MLov 1.14 (Leuven, Belgium: Leuven University Press, 1986), 156n129 for a bibliography.

23. Roger Lathuillère, *Guiron le courtois: Etude de la tradition manuscrite et analyse critique*, PRF 86 (Geneva: Droz, 1966), 23–30.

24. *Histoire de Philippe-Auguste*, ll. 99–107, in *Französische Literarästhetik*

des 12. und 13. Jahrhunderts: Prologe—Exkurse—Epiloge, Sammlung romanischer Übungstexte 54, ed. Ulrich Mölk (Tübingen, Germany: M. Niemeyer, 1969), sec. 103.

    25.   See Mary B. Speer, "Cassidorus: The Fallen Hero," *RPh* 27 (1974): 479–87.

Chapter 4

    1.   The prime example is the *Perceval Continuations*; see Gallais, *L'imaginaire d'un romancier français de la fin du XIIᵉ siècle* (Atlanta, Ga.: Rodopi, 1988) vol. 1.

    2.   On these romances, see Michel Zink, *Roman rose et rose rouge: Le Roman de la rose ou de Guillaume de Dole de Jean Renart* (Paris: Nizet, 1979); Zink, "Une mutation de la conscience littéraire: Le langage romanesque à travers des exemples français du XIIᵉ siècle," *CCM* 24 (1981): 23–25; Fernando Carmona, *El roman lírico medieval* (Barcelona, Spain: Promociones y Publicaciones, 1988).

    3.   *Claris et Laris*, ed. Johann Alton, BLVS 169 (Tübingen, Germany: Laupp, 1884), ll. 79–88.

    4.   Schmolke-Hasselmann, *Versroman*; Susan Crane, *Insular Romances: Politics, Faith, and Culture in Anglo-Norman and Middle English Literature* (Berkeley and Los Angeles: University of California Press, 1986).

    5.   Emmanuèle Baumgartner, "'L'absente de tous bouquets . . . ,'" in *Etudes sur le Roman de la rose*, ed. Jean Dufournet, Unichamp 4 (Paris: Champion, 1984), 37–42.

    6.   Reto R. Bezzola, *Les origines et la formation de la littérature courtoise en Occident (500–1200)*, 3 vols. (Paris: Champion, 1944–63), 3:68–70, 79–81.

    7.   Peter Rickard, *Britain in Medieval French Literature, 1100–1500* (Cambridge, England: Cambridge University Press, 1956), 107–13; Bezzola, *Origines*, 3:306–11.

    8.   On this seamy story, see Michelle Szkilnik, "Les deux pères de Caradoc," *BBSIA* 40 (1988): 268–86.

    9.   The long redaction of the First Branch contains another visit.

    10.   Corin F. V. Corley, *The Second Continuation of the Old French Perceval: A Critical and Lexicographical Study*, MHRADS 24 (London: Modern Humanities Research Association, 1987).

    11.   Gerbert de Montreuil, *La continuation de Perceval*, ed. Mary Williams and Marguerite Oswald, CFMA 28, 50, 101 (Paris: Champion, 1922–75), ll. 3375–4832, 12381–14077.

    12.   For these interpolations, see *Der Percevalroman von Christian von Troyes*, ed. Alfons Hilka (Halle, Germany: Niemeyer, 1932), 457–80, 790–91.

    13.   Recent studies of this phenomenon include Michelle A. Freeman, "*Fergus*: Parody and the Arthurian Tradition," *FrF* 8 (1983): 197–215; D.D.R. Owen, "The Craft of Guillaume le Clerc's *Fergus*," in *The Craft of Fiction: Essays in Medieval Poetics*, ed. Leigh A. Arrathoon (Rochester, Mich.: Solaris, 1984),

47–81; and Kathryn Gravdal, *Vilain and Courtois: Transgressive Parody in French Literature of the Twelfth and Thirteenth Centuries* (Lincoln: University of Nebraska Press, 1989), 20–50.

14. Norris J. Lacy, "The Character of Gauvain in *Hunbaut*," *BBSIA* 38 (1986): 298–305.

15. Douglas Kelly, "Multiple Quests in French Verse Romance: *Mervelles de Rigomer* and *Claris et Laris*," *ECr* 9 (1969): 257–66.

16. Beginning with *Guillaume de Dole*. See *GRLMA*, vol. 4, part 1, pp. 410–12, 447–48, 477–78; vol. 6, part 1, 278–79.

17. See Bernard Guidot, *Recherches sur la chanson de geste au XIIIe siècle d'après certaines œuvres du cycle de Guillaume d'Orange*, 2 vols. (Aix-en-Provence, France: Publications de l'Université de Provence, 1986), esp. 279–36.

18. See Huot, *Song*, esp. 106–34, and "Voice and Instruments in Medieval French Secular Music: On the Use of Literary Texts as Evidence for Performance Practice," *Musica Disciplina* 43 (1989): 63–113.

19. This is analogous to the emergence in Provençal of *vidas* and *razos* purporting to recount the biographical origins of lyric poems; see Elizabeth Wilson Poe, *From Poetry to Prose in Old Provençal: The Emergence of the "Vidas," the "Razos," and the "Razos de trobar"* (Birmingham, Ala: Summa, 1984).

20. Elisabeth Schulze-Busacker, "French Conceptions of Foreigners and Foreign Languages in the Twelfth and Thirteenth Centuries," *RPh* 41 (1987): 24–47.

21. François Suard, "Le *Roman du Castelain de Couci* et l'esthétique romanesque à la fin du XIIIe siècle," in *Farai chansoneta novele: Hommage à Jean–Charles Payen* (Caen, France: Université de Caen, 1989), 355–67.

22. Michel Zink, *Subjectivité littéraire: Autour du siècle de saint Louis* (Paris: PUF, 1985).

23. Lionel J. Friedman, "*Gradus amoris*," *RPh* 19 (1965): 167–77.

24. Guillaume de Lorris and Jean de Meun, *Le roman de la rose*, ed. Félix Lecoy, CFMA 92, 95, 98 (Paris: Champion, 1965–70), ll. 37, 984, 2058, 3487.

25. Heather M. Arden, *The Romance of the Rose*, TWAS 791 (Boston: Twayne, 1987), chap. 5.

26. Douglas Kelly, "Assimilation et montage dans l'amplification descriptive: La démarche du poète dans le Dit du XIVe siècle," in *Mittelalterbilder aus neuer Perspektive: Diskussionanstöße zu amour courtois, Subjektivität in der Dichtung und Strategien des Erzählens*, Kolloquium Würzburg 1984, ed. Ernstpeter Ruhe and Rudolf Behrens, BRP 14 (Munich, Germany: Fink, 1985) 289–302.

Chapter 5

1. Janet Ferrier, *Forerunners*; Roger Dubuis, *Les "Cent Nouvelles nouvelles" et la tradition de la nouvelle en France au moyen âge* (Grenoble, France: Presses universitaires de Grenoble, 1973).

2. *Les Cent nouvelles nouvelles*, ed. Franklin P. Sweetser, TLF 127 (Geneva: Droz, 1966).

3. Cedric Edward Pickford, *L'évolution du roman arthurien en prose vers la fin du moyen âge d'après le manuscrit 112 du fonds français de la Bibliothèque Nationale* (Paris: Nizet, 1960); François Suard, *Guillaume d'Orange: Etude du roman en prose*, BXV 44 (Paris: Champion, 1979).

4. Martha Wallen, "Significant Variations in the Burgundian Prose Version of *Erec et Enide*," *MAE* 51 (1982): 187–96; Willy Van Hoecke, "La littérature française d'inspiration arthurienne dans les anciens Pays-Bas," in *Arturus rex*, 2 vols. (Leuven, Belgium: Leuven University Press, 1987), 1:229–42. Compare Charity C. Willard, "A Fifteenth-Century Burgundian Version of the *Roman de Florimont*," *M&H* n.s. 2 (1971): 21–46; and Ruth Morse, "Historical Fiction in Fifteenth-Century Burgundy," *MLR* 75 (1980): 48–64.

5. See Peter F. Dembowski, *Jean Froissart and His "Meliador": Context, Craft, and Sense*, ECAMML 2 (Lexington, Ky: French Forum, 1983).

6. See A. H. Diverres, "Froissart's Travels in England and Wales," *FCS* 15 (1989): 107–22; Schmolke-Hasselmann, *Versroman*, 228–32; and Dembowski, *Jean Froissart*, chap. 1 (with bibliography).

7. See Georges Doutrepont, *Les mises en prose des épopées et des romans chevaleresques du XIVe au XVIe siècle* (1939; reprint, Geneva: Slatkine, 1969); Jean Frappier, "Les romans de la Table Ronde et les lettres au XVIe siècle," *RPh*, 19 (1965–66): 178–84; Cedric E. Pickford, "Les éditions imprimées de romans arthuriens en prose antérieures à 1600," *BBSIA* 13 (1961): 99–109, including 103–04 on non-Arthurian printings. There are modern reprints of some incunabula; see Bibliography.

Chapter 6

1. Pierre Gallais, "Recherches sur la mentalité des romanciers français du moyen âge," *CCM* 13 (1970): 338–47; Douglas Kelly, *Art*, chap. 3.

2. Bezzola, *Origines*; Gallais, "Recherches," 333–38; Joachim Bumke, *Mäzene im Mittelalter: Gönner und Auftraggeber der höfischen Literatur in Deutschland, 1150–1300* (Munich, Germany: Beck, 1979) (includes French examples).

3. For these types, see my *Art*, 125, 217–25.

4. Pierre-Yves Badel, "Rhétorique et polémique dans les prologues de romans du moyen âge," *Lit* 20 (1975): 83–84.

5. The Middle Ages knew the distinction between blood nobility and nobility of mind; see Köhler, *Ideal*, 129–38.

6. See Kelly, *Art*, 106–25; compare Alice M. Colby, *The Portrait in Twelfth-Century French Literature: An Example of the Stylistic Originality of Chrétien de Troyes*, HICL 61 (Geneva: Droz, 1965), 118.

7. Rita Lejeune, "Rôle littéraire d'Aliénor d'Aquitaine et de sa famille," *CN* 14 (1954): 5–57, "Rôle littéraire de la famille d'Aliénor d'Aquitaine," *CCM*

1 (1958): 319–37, and "La femme dans les littératures française et occitane du XIᵉ au XIIIᵉ siècle," *CCM* 20 (1977): 204–08.

8. Denis Piramus, *Vie de saint Edmund*, in Ulrich Mölk, sec. 74, ll. 46–48.

9. Ed. Albert Henri, in Adenet le roi, *Œuvres* (Brussels: Editions de l'Université de Bruxelles, 1971), 6.1–2, ll. 19–52, 18529–40.

10. Compare Frappier, *Etude*, 142–46; see also my "Le patron et l'auteur dans l'invention romanesque," in *Théories et pratiques de l'écriture au moyen âge*, Actes du Colloque du Palais du Luxembourg-Sénat, 5 et 6 mars 1987, ed. Emmanuèle Baumgartner and Christiane Marchello-Nizia, Littérales 4 (Paris: Nanterre/St. Cloud: ENS Fontenay, 1988), 25–39.

11. Jean Fourquet, "Le rapport entre l'œuvre et la source chez Chrétien de Troyes et le problème des sources bretonnes," *RPh* 9 (1956): 298–312.

12. Ed. Annette Brasseur, TLF 369 (Geneva: Droz, 1989), l. 7.

13. See Daniel Poirion, "Ecriture et ré–écriture au moyen âge," *Lit* 41 (1981): 109–18.

14. L. G. Donovan, *Recherches sur "Le roman de Thèbes"* (Paris: CDU & SEDES, 1975), passim; Petit, *Naissances*, 19–326.

15. Roger Sherman Loomis, *Arthurian Tradition and Chrétien de Troyes* (New York: Columbia University Press, 1949), 39–40.

16. Arianna Punzi, "I volgarizzamenti della *Tebaide* nella cultura romanza ed in quella irlandese," *CN* 50 (1990): 7–43; Raymond J. Cormier, "Qui détient le rameau d'or devant Charon (*Enéide*, VI.405–407)," *Rheinisches Museum für Philologie*, n.s. 131 (1988): 151–56; Cormier, "An Example of Twelfth-Century *Adaptatio*: The *Roman d'Eneas* Author's Use of Glossed *Aeneid* Manuscripts," *Revue d'histoire des textes* 19 (1989): 277–89.

17. Jean Rychner, *La chanson de geste: Essai sur l'art épique des jongleurs*, PRF 53 (Geneva: Droz/Lille, France: Girard, 1955); Joseph J. Duggan, *The Song of Roland: Formulaic Style and Poetic Craft*, Publications of the Center for Medieval and Renaissance Studies UCLA 6 (Berkeley and Los Angeles: University of California Press, 1973).

18. Edmond Faral, *Les arts poétiques du XIIᵉ et du XIIIᵉ siècle* (Paris: Champion, 1924); Douglas Kelly, *The Arts of Poetry and Prose* (Turnhout, Belgium: Brepols, 1991). Compare Hunt, *Chrétien*, chap. 6.

19. *La Manekine*, ll. 30–33, in Philippe de Remi, sire de Beaumanoir, *Œuvres poétiques*, ed. Hermann Suchier, SATF (Paris: Firmin-Didot, 1884).

20. See Alfred Foulet and Karl D. Uitti, "Prologue."

21. For an introduction, see James J. Murphy, *Rhetoric in the Middle Ages: A History of Rhetorical Theory from Saint Augustine to the Renaissance* (Berkeley and Los Angeles: University of California Press, 1974). Also see Ernst Robert Curtius, *European Literature and the Latin Middle Ages*, trans. Willard R. Trask (New York: Pantheon, 1953); and James J. Murphy, *Medieval Eloquence: Studies in the Theory and Practice of Medieval Rhetoric* (Berkeley and Los Angeles: University of California Press, 1978). For a bibliography, see James J. Murphy,

Medieval Rhetoric: A Select Bibliography, 2d ed. (Toronto: University of Toronto Press, 1989).

22. See Bruckner "Interpreter's Dilemma"; cf. Vinaver, *The Rise of Romance* (Oxford: Clarendon Press, 1971), chap. 2–3.

23. For the interpretations of this problem, see René Ménage, "*Erec et Enide*: Quelques pièces du dossier," *Marche romaine* 30, nos.3–4 (1980): 203–21.

24. See Alice Colby, *Portrait*; and Douglas Kelly, "The Art of Description," *LCT* 1, 191–221.

25. For examples of authorial interventions, see Mölk, *Literarästhetik*. To his bibliography add Tony Hunt, "The Rhetorical Background to the Arthurian Prologue: Tradition and the Old French Vernacular Prologues," *FMLA* 6 (1970): 1–23, and "Tradition and Originality in the Prologues of Chrestien de Troyes," *FMLA* 8 (1972): 320–44; Badel, "Rhétorique"; and Kelly, *Art* (with additional bibliography).

26. *La vie de saint Alexis*, ed. Christopher Storey, TLF 148 (Geneva: Droz/Paris: Minard, 1968), l. 59.

27. See Karl Keuck, *Historia: Geschichte des Wortes und seiner Bedeutungen in der Antike und in den romanischen Sprachen* (Emsdetten, Germany: Lechte, 1934). On the ambiguity of historical fiction in the late Middle Ages, see Ruth Morse, "Historical Fiction."

28. See Benoît Lacroix, in *L'historien au moyen âge*, Conférence Albert-le-Grand 1966 (Montreal: Institut d'Etudes Médiévales, Paris: Vrin, 1971), 34–45; Bernard Guenée, "Histoires, annales, chroniques: Essai sur les genres historiques au moyen âge," *Annales: Economies, sociétés, civilisations* 28 (1973): 997–1016; and Daniel Poirion, ed., *La chronique et l'histoire au moyen âge*, Cultures et civilisations médiévales 2 (Paris: Presses de l'Université de Paris-Sorbonne, 1982).

29. On the spelling *san* for "meaning" as distinguised from *sans* as the author's mind at work on it in l. 23, a distinction apparent as well in Marie de France's Prologue to her *Lais*, see Foulet and Uitti, "Prologue," Kelly, *Art*, 106–14.

30. *Rien,* "nothing," is the reading in the other manuscripts; see, for example, the *Chevalier de la charrete (Lancelot)*, ed. Alfred Foulet and Karl D. Uitti (Paris: Bordas, 1989), l. 28.

31. The idea is striking, since *conjointure* also means "sexual union."

Chapter 7

1. Alfred Foulet and Mary Blakeley Speer, *On Editing*, 1–39.

2. Sylvia Huot, *The Romance of the Rose and Its Medieval Readers: Interpretation, Reception, Transmission*, CSML 16 (Cambridge: Cambridge University Press, 1993).

3. See David F. Hult, "Lancelot's Two Steps: A Problem in Textual Criticism," *Speculum* 61 (1986): 836–58, and his "Steps Forward and Steps

Backward: More on Chrétien's *Lancelot*," *Speculum* 64 (1989): 307–16; Karl D. Uitti with Alfred Foulet, "On Editing Chrétien de Troyes: Lancelot's Two Steps and Their Context," *Speculum* 63 (1988): 271–92.

    4. Poirion, "Ecriture," 117; cf. Paul Zumthor, *Poésie*, 51–52.

    5. Sylvia Huot, "Medieval Readers of the *Roman de la rose*: The Evidence of Marginal Notations," *RPh* 43 (1990): 400–420.

    6. Alison Stones's "Arthurian Art since Loomis" (*Arturus rex*, 2:21–78), includes an extensive bibliography. Items of interest not listed there include Sandra L. Hindman, "The Roles of Author and Artist in the Procedure of Illustrating Late Medieval Texts," *Text and Image: Acta* 10 (1983):28–61, and her "King Arthur, His Knights, and the French Aristocracy of Picardy," in *Contexts: Style and Values in Medieval Art and Literature*, ed. Daniel Poirion and Nancy Freeman Regalado, YFS Special Issue (New Haven, Conn.: Yale University Press, 1991), 114–33; Huot, *Song*; Angelica Rieger, "Neues über Chrétiens Illustratoren: Bild und Text in der ältesten Überlieferung von *Perceval-le-vieil* (*T*)," *BBSIA* 41 (1989): 301–11; Jacqueline Cerquiglini, "Histoire, image: Accord et discord des sens à la fin du Moyen Age," *Lit* 78 (1989): 116–23; Lori Walters, "The Creation of a 'Super Romance': Paris, Bibliothèque Nationale, fonds français, MS 1433," *AY* 1 (1991): 3–25 (includes 13 plates); and Véronique Roland, "Folio liminaire et réception du texte: Les manuscrits parisiens du *Merlin en prose*," *BBSIA* 43 (1991): 257–69. A useful survey of issues is *The Manuscripts of Chrétien de Troyes*, ed. M. Alison Stones, Terry Nixon, Lori J. Walters, and Keith Busby, 2 vols. (Atlanta, Ga.: Rodopi, 1993).

    7. Hans-Robert Jauss, *GRLMA* 1:107–39, and his "The Alterity and Modernity of Medieval Literature," *NLH* 10 (1979): 208–11; see as well Paul Zumthor's comments, *NLH* 10 (1979): 373–75.

    8. Paul Saenger, "Literacy, Western European," in *Dictionary of the Middle Ages* (New York: Scribner's, 1986), 7:597–602 (with bibliography).

    9. See Lot, *Etude*, 29–64; Philippe Ménard, "Le temps et la durée dans les romans de Chrétien de Troyes," *Moyen âge* 73 (1967): 375–401. See in general *Le temps et la durée dans la littérature au moyen âge et à la Renaissance*, Actes du Colloque organisé par le Centre de Recherche sur la Littérature du Moyen Age et de la Renaissance à l'Université de Reims (novembre 1984) (Paris: Nizet, 1986); and *Le nombre du temps: En hommage à Paul Zumthor*, NBMA 12 (Paris: Champion, 1988).

    10. Rupert T. Pickens, *The Welsh Knight: Paradoxicality in Chrétien's "Conte du graal,"* FrFM 6 (Lexington, Ky: French Forum, 1977).

    11. This topic is much debated. Contrast Robert W. Hanning, *The Individual in Twelfth-Century Romance* (New Haven, Conn.: Yale University Press, 1977) and Kelly, *Art*, 231–40.

    12. Alberto Vàrvaro, "La teoria dell'archetipo tristaniano," *Romania* 88 (1967): 13–58.

    13. Keith Busby, "*Cristal et Clarie*: A Novel Romance?," in *Convention*

and Innovation in Literature, ed. Theo D'haen, Rainer Grübel, and Helmut Lethen, UPAL 24 (Philadelphia: Benjamins, 1989), 77–103.

14. Rita Lejeune, "Rôle d'Aliénor," and "Rôle de la famille."

15. The Chronology identifies instances of adaptation by grouping identifiable adaptations with the earliest example.

16. This is also true for analogues, that is, those cases where an actual source dependency is not likely. It also illustrates the importance of studying adaptations of French romance into other languages.

17. Gallais, *Imaginaire*; Petit, *Naissances*; Donovan, *Recherches*; Schöning, *Thebenroman*.

18. Recent examples include Karen Pratt, *Meister Otte's Eraclius as an Adaptation of Eracle by Gautier d'Arras*, GAG 392 (Göppingen, Germany: Kümmerle, 1987); and Karin Trimborn, *Syntaktisch-stilistische Untersuchungen zu Chrétiens "Yvain" und Hartmanns "Iwein,"* Philologische Studien und Quellen 103 (Berlin: Schmidt, 1985).

19. *Intertextualités médiévales*, ed. Daniel Poirion, in *Lit* 41.

20. On what follows, see Michael Riffaterre, "L'intertexte inconnu," *Lit* 41 (1981): 4–7; Matilda Tomaryn Bruckner, "Intertextuality," *LCT* 1, 223–65; and Friedrich Wolfzettel, "Zum Stand und Problem der Intertextualitätsforschung im Mittelalter (aus romanistischer Sicht)," in *Artusroman und Intertextualität*, ed. F. Wolfzettel (Gießen: Schmitz, 1990), 1–17.

21. Paul Zumthor, "Le texte-fragment," *Langue française* 40 (1978): 75–82.

22. Mary B. Speer, "Recycling the Seven Sages of Rome," *ZRP* 99 (1983): 288–303.

23. See Huot, *Song*; and Walters, "Creation."

24. Huot, *Song*, chap. 1; Ian Short, "L'avènement du texte vernaculaire: La mise en recueil," in *Théories et pratiques de l'écriture au moyen âge*, ed. Emmanuèle Baumgartner and Christiane Marchello-Nizia, Actes du Colloque Palais du Luxembourg-Sénat 5 et 6 mars 1987, Littérales 4 (Paris: Nanterre/St. Cloud: ENS Fontenoy, 1988), 11–23.

25. Compare Kennedy, "Scribe," and Gallais, *Imaginaire*; see Baumgartner, *La harpe et l'épée: Tradition et renouvellement dans le "Tristan en prose"* (Paris: SEDES, 1990), 25–61.

26. Vinaver, *Rise*. See the notes in Micha's *Lancelot* to cross-references that have no referent, that is, they are erroneous: 2: 240, 291 (but cf. 9:331), 4: 362, 6: 55, 56; only partially accurate: 5: 120, 140. Others are correct, for example, 5: 57, 104, 149.

27. There is no general study of Old or Middle French verse or prose. But consult Jean Frappier, "La brisure du couplet dans *Erec et Enide*," *Romania* 86 (1965): 1–21, *Etude sur Yvain ou le Chevalier au lion de Chrétien de Troyes* (Paris: SEDES, 1969), 245–72, and *Chrétien de Troyes et le mythe du graal: Etude sur Perceval ou le Conte du graal* (Paris: SEDES, 1972), 257–72; Gallais, *Imaginaire*,

435–634. On prose, see Jens Rasmussen, *La prose narrative du XV* siècle: Etude esthétique et stylistique* (Copenhagen: Munksgaard, 1958).

28. In translations a capital letter marks a new line; — marks a *brisure*.

29. *Eneas*, ed. J.-J. Salverda de Grave, CFMA 44, 62 (Paris: Champion, 1925–29), ll. 1932–58, 8489–8568.

30. *La chanson de Roland*, ed. F. Whitehead (Oxford, England: Blackwell, 1942), ll. 1049–58. Italics mark conjunctions.

31. Notice as well the infrequency of couplet breaking.

32. Perhaps because a reading public was replacing a listening public. Relatively simpler sentence stucture in thirteenth-century prose accommodated less-proficient readers who could more easily follow complex sentences when they heard them than when they read them.

33. Capitals mark conjunctions, italics subordinating conjunctions, dashes sentence divisions.

34. Paul Zumthor, *Langue, texte, énigme* (Paris: Seuil, 1975), 125–43; Kelly, *Arts*, 169 and n.375.

35. *The Old French Johannes Translation of the "Pseudo-Turpin Chronicle,"* ed. Ronald N. Walpole (Berkeley and Los Angeles: University of California Press, 1976), Prologue ll. 10–12 (p. 130).

36. Mölk, *Literarästhetik*, sec. 80, ll. 99–107.

37. Heldris de Cornuälle, *Le roman de Silence*, ed. Lewis Thorpe (Cambridge, England: Heffer, 1972), ll. 1663–69; Mölk, *Literarästhetik*, sec. 80.

38. Mary B. Speer and Alfred Foulet, "Is *Marques de Rome* a Derhymed Romance?," *Romania* 101 (1980): 336–65; compare Joan Tasker Grimbert, "Testimony and 'Truth' in *Joseph d'Arimathie*," *RPh* 44 (1991): 379–401.

39. Maurice Keen, *Chivalry* (New Haven, Conn.: Yale University Press, 1984), 2. See also Robert W. Hanning, "The Social Significance of Twelfth-Century Chivalric Romance," *M&H*, n.s.3 (1972): 3–29; Josef Fleckenstein, ed., *Das ritterliche Turnier im Mittelalter: Beiträge zu einer vergleichenden Formen- und Verhaltensgeschichte des Rittertums*, VMPG 80 (Göttingen, Germany: Vandenhoeck & Ruprecht, 1985), and *Curialitas: Studien zu Grundfragen der höfisch-ritterlichen Kultur*, VMPG 100 (Göttingen, Germany: Vandenhoeck & Ruprecht, 1990).

40. For clarity, I use the two terms as follows: knighthood refers to the acts appropriate to the knight, chivalry to the manner in which he executes those acts.

41. *Floriant et Florete*, ed. Harry F. Williams, MPLL 23 (Ann Arbor: University of Michigan/London: Geoffrey Cumberlege and Oxford University Press, 1947), ll. 6243–46.

42. Jean Frappier, "L'institution de Lancelot dans le *Lancelot en prose*," in *Amour courtois et Table Ronde* (Geneva: Droz, 1973), 169–79. See also Jean d'Arras, *Mélusine*, ed. Louis Stouff, Publications de l'Université de Dijon 5 (Dijon, France: Bernigaud et Privat, 1932), 84–88.

43. Kelly, *Sens and conjointure in the "Chevalier de la charrette,"* Studies in French Literature 2 (The Hague: Mouton, 1966), 42–43.

44. Jean Flori, *L'essor de la chevalerie XIe–XIIe siècles,* Travaux d'histoire éthico-politique 46 (Geneva: Droz, 1986); W. H. Jackson, ed., *Knighthood in Medieval Literature* (Woodbridge, England: Brewer, 1981); and Marie-Luce Chênerie, *Le chevalier errant dans les romans arthuriens en vers des XIIe et XIIIe siècles,* PRF 172 (Geneva: Droz, 1986).

45. Schmolke-Hasselmann, "Round Table."

46. Georges Duby, *Les trois ordres ou l'imaginaire du féodalisme* (Paris: Gallimard, 1978).

47. Jean Flori, "Pour une histoire de la chevalerie: L'adoubement dans les romans de Chrétien de Troyes," *Romania* 100 (1979): 21–53; Barbara Nelson Sargent-Baur, "Promotion to Knighthood in the Romances of Chrétien de Troyes," *RPh* 37 (1984): 393–408.

48. See Matilda T. Bruckner, *Narrative Invention in Twelfth-Century French Romances: The Convention of Hospitality (1160–1200),* FrFM 17 (Lexington, Ky.: French Forum, 1980); and Katalin Halász, *Structures narratives chez Chrétien de Troyes,* SRUD 7 (Debrecen, Hungary: Kossuth Lajos Tudományegyetem, 1980).

49. Nelly Andrieux-Reix's *Ancien français: Fiches de vocabulaire* (Paris: PUF, 1987) is a useful reference for the meanings of these words in Old French; it includes a bibliography.

50. Richard de Fornival, "The *Consaus d'amours*," ed. William M. McLeod, *Studies in Philology* 32 (1935): 12 (par. 19).

51. Gaston Paris, "Etudes sur les romans de la Table Ronde: Lancelot du Lac," *Romania* 13 (1883): 518–19. According to the OED, 1972 supplement, the word entered English in 1896; *amour courtois* appeared in English first in 1906.

52. Examples of all are found in Marie de France's *Lais,* in order: "Equitan," "Bisclavret," and "Milun." On aristocratic ideas about the inviolability of the womb, see Georges Duby, *Medieval Marriage: Two Models from Twelfth-Century France* (Baltimore: Johns Hopkins University Press, 1978). Lancelot would marry Guenevere if it were possible; see *Lancelot,* sec. 4, pars. 4–5.

53. There is considerable debate about the intentions of Andreas's *De amore:* is it a serious disquisition on love, a satire, or a moral condemnation? For our purposes, Andreas's distinction may be taken as representative, whatever he may have intended in his book. See in general Rüdiger Schnell, *Causa amoris: Liebeskonzeption und Liebesdarstellung in der mittelalterlichen Literatur,* Bibliotheca Germanica 27 (Bern, Switzerland: Francke, 1985).

54. Women condemn homosexuality in romances, but do not mention lesbianism.

55. Enide's poverty makes her a female counterpart to the younger sons, or *jeunes,* disinherited by primogeniture and therefore compelled to seek a good marriage elsewhere; see Duby, *Trois ordtes* on the *jeunes* in romance; but see also

Philippe Ménard, "Le chevalier errant dans la littérature arthurienne: recherches sur les raisons du départ et de l'errance," in *Voyage, quête, pèlerinage dans la littérature et la civilisation médiévales*, Senefiance 2 (Aix-en-Provence, France: CUER-MA/Paris: Champion, 1976), 289–311.

56. D. W. Roberson, Jr., *A Preface to Chaucer: Studies in Medieval Perspectives* (Princeton, N.J.: Princeton University Press, 1962).

57. Rupprecht Rohr, *Matière, sens, conjointure: Methodologische Einführung in die französische und provenzalische Literatur des Mittelalters* (Darmstadt, Germany: WB, 1978), chap. 4.

58. See Keen, *Chivalry*, chap. 8–9.

59. See Jauss, "Alterity," 209; also see *GRLMA*, vol. 1.

60. Paul Zumthor, *Parler du moyen âge* (Paris: Minuit, 1980), 25; R. Howard Bloch, "New Philology and Old French," *Speculum*, 65 (1990): 38, esp. n.1.

61. Romance philology has been marked by revolutions in methodologies since its beginnings in nineteenth-century Germany; see H. J. Gumbrecht, "Un souffle d'Allemagne ayant passé: Friedrich Diez, Gaston Paris, and the Genesis of National Philologies," *RPh* 40 (1986): 1–37; Vinaver, *Recherche*, 15–47.

62. Judson Boyce Allen, *The Friar as Critic: Literary Attitudes in the Later Middle Ages* (Nashville, Tenn.: Vanderbilt University Press, 1971).

63. See the following special issues on New Philology: *Speculum* 65 (1990); *Comparative Literature Studies* 27 (1990).

64. See Karl D. Uitti, "Preface," and Alfred Foulet, "On Grid-Editing Chrétien de Troyes," *ECr* 27 (1987): 5–23, for interesting discussion.

65. *BBSIA* 44 (1992): 274; Keith Busby's edition of the *Perceval* has appeared (Tübingen, Germany: Niemeyer, 1993).

66. Karl D. Uitti, "Poetico-Literary Dimensions and the Critical Editing of Medieval Texts: The Example of Old French," in *What Is Literature? France, 1100–1600*, ECAMML 7 (Lexington, Ky: French Forum, 1993), 143–79.

67. Sylvia Huot, "Medieval Readers"; on other versions, see Karl August Ott, *Der Rosenroman* (Darmstadt, Germany: WB, 1980), 18–23.

68. Irony is a variety of allegory. See Dennis H. Green, *Irony in the Medieval Romance* (Cambridge: Cambridge University Press, 1979). On "courtly obscenity," see Leonard W. Johnson, *Poets as Players: Theme and Variation in Late Medieval French Poetry* (Stanford, Calif.: Stanford University Press, 1990), 283–86.

69. See Robertson, Jr., *Preface*; Jacques Ribard, *Chrétien de Troyes: Le Chevalier de la charrette. Essai d'interprétation symbolique* (Paris: Nizet, 1972), and *Le moyen âge: Littérature et symbolisme* (Paris: Champion, 1984); and Anna Valeria Borsari, *Lancillotto liberato: Una ricerca intorno al "fin amant" e all'eroe liberatore*, Università di Bologna: Pubblicazioni della Facoltà di Magistero, n.s. 12 (Florence, Italy: Nuova Italia, 1983).

70. See the bibliography in Friedrich Wolfzettel, "Mediävistik und

Psychanalyse: Eine Bestandsaufnahme," in *Mittelalterbilder aus neuer Perspektive: Diskussionsanstöße zu amour courtois, Subjektivität in der Dichtung und Strategien des Erzählens*, BRPM 14 (Munich, Germany: Fink, 1985), 210–39; see also Jean-Charles Huchet, *Littérature médiévale et psychanalyse: Pour une clinique littéraire* (Paris: PUF, 1990).

71. Erich Köhler, "Einige Thesen zur Literatursoziologie," *GRM*, n.s. 24 (1974): 258; see as well *GRLMA* vol. 4, part 1: 82–103.

72. Jauss, "Alterity," 181–229.

73. For instances of narrators rejecting misogyny because of a patroness, see *Amadas et Ydoine*, ed. John R. Reinhard, CFMA 51 (Paris: Champion, 1974), ll. 7037–97; *Troie*, ll. 13438–94.

74. Ed. Auguste Longnon, SATF, 3 vols. (Paris: 1895–99), ll. 20353–54.

75. See Margarete Newells, "From Narrative Style to Dramatic Style in *Les Moralités*," in *Contexts: Style and Values in Medieval Art and Literature*, ed. Daniel Poirion and Nancy Freeman Regalado, YFS Special Issue (New Haven, Conn.: Yale University Press, 1991), 255–56.

Glossary

Abbreviation: shortening or deemphasizing a subject not essential or important in narrative.

Adaptation: the art of rewriting a source so as to produce a new or original version of it.

Adventure romance: romance that emphasizes number and variety of adventures rather than character portrayal or narrative meaning.

Adventure: an event, no matter how long or how brief, that occurs, or seems to occur, unexpectedly or without explanation.

Ages of man or of life: the various stages in the life of a person from infancy to old age; the number of stages varies, usually from three to seven.

Alexandrine or dodecasyllable: a line of French verse 12 syllables long; the term *alexandrin* originated with the romances on Alexander the Great that commonly use this verse.

Allegoresis: the science or art of eliciting a meaning from a text that is different from its literal meaning and may not have been intended by the first author.

Allegory: 1. an extended metaphor; 2. a text with both a literal meaning and one or more different meanings.

Alterity: features of medieval writing that are different from, foreign to, or strange for modern expectations.

Amalgam: a heterogeneous collection of narrative material.

Amplification: lengthening or emphasizing a subject essential or important in narrative.

Analogues: two narratives that are alike.

Ancestral romance: romance or romances that sequentially relate the deeds of a family, usually proceeding from father to son in successive works.

Ancient: a deceased writer, usually, but not always, identified with a Greek or Roman writer.

Anglo-Norman: French dialect spoken in the British Isles, as distinguished from Norman French and other French dialects spoken on the Continent.

Antancïon: the intention of an author, which usually supposes in romance a mental picture of the work to be written.

Antique romance (*roman antique* or *roman d'antiquité*): romances based on Greek, Roman, or Byzantine subject matters.

Assonance: a form of rhyme consisting of the same vowel sound but different consonant sounds.

Branch: a large narrative segment that is joined to and part of a larger whole made up of one or more other branches.

Breaking (*brisure du couplet*): a strong break in syntax after the first line in a couplet.

Chanson de geste: French epic narrative, usually written in *laisses* and relating the deeds of great warriors; the earliest examples reflect the art of oral improvisation.

Chastity test: in romance, a marvelous test of a person's chastity.

Chronicle: historical account, usually in chronological order, of events in a given reign or realm.

Cleric (*clerc*): a member of the clergy who often functioned as a writer in an aristocratic household.

Compagnonnage: the ideal relation between companions in arms, especially knights.

Compilation: a collection of works in a single manuscript.

Conjointure: a combination of diverse source materials, especially different versions of a story, such that the resulting romance is complete and whole.

Continuation: addition to the end or some other part of a given romance, usually when it appears to be incomplete.

Couplet: two lines of verse that rhyme.

Courtly love (*fin'amour*): noble love, whose characteristic features depend on the way it is described or interpreted in any given work.

Cycle: a sequence of related romances, usually dominated by a large historical design or perspective and treating more than one subject matter.

Decasyllable: a line of French verse 10 syllables long.

Disposition: the arrangement of the parts of a work.

Dit: late medieval dream vision or allegorical narrative.

Dodecasyllable. See **Alexandrine**.

Drift or sliding (*glissement*): passage in a single work from one central character or kind of event to a different character or kind of event, or the gradual replacement of the one by the other.

Encasement: the placing of one narrative segment inside another.

Epigone: an author who imitates an often more distinguished or famous predecessor, or, by extension, a work that is such an imitation.

Errance: wandering in search of an adventure in a romance; differs from a quest in lacking a specific goal.

Extraction: the art of eliciting or drawing from a source a plot, meaning, or significance hidden or presumed hidden or implicit in that source.

Fabliau: a farcical narrative.

Figure of thought or speech: deflection from plain speech, either by a distinctive manner of expression (figure of thought), or by artful arrangement of the language itself (figure of speech).

Genealogy: a family tree that identifies all members of a family over a specific period of time, or all members of importance in the family; the use of the principle in romance narrative.

Geste: 1. deeds; 2. a family.

Gloss (glossing): the interpretation of details in a text; the gloss may be either imbedded in the text itself or be written in the margins (marginal gloss) or between the lines of the text (interlinear gloss) in the manuscript.

Hagiography: saint's life.

Hermeneutics: methodology of textual interpretation.

Historiography: the art of writing history.

Holograph (autograph): a manuscript handwritten by the original author.

Horizon of expectation: what an audience expects from a new work based on its knowledge of similar works in the past.

Hypotaxis: language or narrative that makes abundant use of connectives.

Improvisation: the art of rendering narrative extemporaneously, whether in prose, verse, or music.

Insertion, lyric: lyric pieces that are inserted into a narrative by the narrator and that contribute to narrative progression, explanation, or amplification.

Interlace (*entrelacement*): combination of different narratives or narrative segments interconnected by relating first one, then another, in alternation.

Interpolation: the insertion of one text into another.

Intertextuality: the perceived relation between one text and another, or between a text and a potential text.

Intonation: pitch, or the rise and fall of voice peculiar to a given language.

Invention: the art of identifying a subject matter, explaining a narrative, and developing it according to a certain intention (*antancïon*).

Involution: the art whereby meaning is worked into a given narrative.

Issue: a matter of debate about which various opinions are argued.

Jongleur: a performing artist who relates or improvises narrative.

Laisse: a group of verses with a variable number of lines, each verse of which is usually of the same length and ends with a common assonance or rhyme.

Lay (*lai*): a short romance, usually consisting of less than 1000 lines and describing only one or two main adventures.

Manuscriture: a modern coinage that designates the special features of manuscript writing and the manuscript as literary artifact.

Marvelous: anything extraordinary in narrative, including, but not limited to, supernatural occurrences.

Matter (*matière*): 1. a source; 2. a narrative concerned with Rome, Britain, or France; 3. the contents of a work.

Mescheance: an unfortunate adventure, usually meaningless or inexplicable.

Monorhyme: two or more lines of verse ending with the same rhyme.

Multiplication of quests: the tendency to increase the number of quests in a narrative, especially quests occurring simultaneously, and to relate all or many of them.

Novella (*nouvelle*): a short story in the late Middle Ages.

Occitan: the medieval romance language, also called Provençal, that was spoken in southern France from the Alps to the Atlantic; it also refers to works written in that language.

Octosyllable: a line of French verse eight syllables long.

Orality: 1. oral improvisation of a work; 2. reading a written work aloud, especially for audiences unable or unwilling to read privately.

Oratory: formal declamation.

Ornamentation: the way by which speech is enhanced, usually by tropes and figures of thought and speech.

Otherworld: a world separate from the usual world of romance protagonists, usually a supernatural, extraordinary, or wild setting.

Paleography: the science of reading and editing manuscripts.

Parataxis: speech or narrative lacking connectives.

Patronage: support of an artist by a patron or patroness, as well as the latter's influence on the work written.

Philology: the science of literary interpretation and appreciation.

Poète: in Old and Middle French, an author who writes allegories.

Post-Vulgate cycle: a term commonly used to refer to the various manuscripts and manuscript fragments that once were part of the *Roman du graal*, written after the *Lancelot-Graal* or Vulgate cycle, but related to narrative events in it.

Prelude: a beginning added to an extant work.

Prosification (*mise en prose*): writing in prose, or rewriting a verse work in prose.

Prosody: the science of verse writing and prose style.

Protoromance: narratives that contribute to the emergence of French romance, most of which were written before Chrétien de Troyes.

Prowess (*prouesse*): high valor, either in arms or as an expression of noble qualities.

Quest: movement toward a set goal as a narrative motif.

Reception: the manner in which an author or audience receives and interprets a given work.

Recreantise: failure to do one's duty; especially by a knight who neglects customary, appropriate knightly activities.

Redaction: a version of a work.

Rhetoric: the art of writing or speaking well so as to carry conviction and to sway or move audiences.

Roman rose: sentimental romance.

Romance (*roman*): the narrative that emerged in the second half of the twelfth century, and that acquired identifiable generic features with Chrétien de Troyes; romances relate marvelous adventures.

Rubrication: headings or other markings in a manuscript, usually written in red ink, that identify or introduce sections or illustrations.

San: 1. narrative meaning; 2. the mind of the author that expresses meaning in narrative.

Scribe: one who writes or copies a manuscript.

Sitz im Leben: the milieu in which a work is written or found.

Stichomathy: rapid exchange among speakers over several lines of verse, with frequent internal breaks so as to pass back and forth from speaker to speaker.

Surplus de san: an expression coined by Marie de France that refers to the meaning deemed hidden in a source and which the new author elicits or extracts from it and expresses by rewriting the source.

Textual criticism: the science of preparing a modern edition based on medieval manuscripts.

Topical invention: the identification of "places" (*topoi*) in a matter in which an author can insert his or her conception of the work.

Translatio imperii and *translatio studii*: medieval notion according to which power (*imperium*) and learning (*studium*) pass from one people or civilization to another.

Trope: figurative speech that uses words in other than their literal sense, as in metaphor, allegory, and metonymy.

Trouvère (troubadour): in the broadest sense, an author who invents a work; usually, the term refers to lyric poets in French (trouvère) or Occitan (troubadour).

Typology: a conception of history according to which an event or events in one time assume the form of, and thus "prefigure" and announce, an event or events in another time.

Variant: 1. different readings of the same passage in different manuscripts; 2. among narratives, different versions of the same story.

Vers: 1. narrative segment; 2. line of verse.

Vulgate cycle: a name commonly used to refer to the entire *Lancelot-Graal* cycle, so called because the cycle became the most widespread and influential version of the Arthurian and Grail romances.

Wager tale: traditional plot based on a wager, usually a wager as to a woman's chastity or fidelity.

Bibliography

Primary Sources

Items are listed by author if known, or by title. For further documentation, including bibliography, references are given to the two standard texts, *Grundriß der romanischen Literaturen des Mittelalters* (*GRLMA*) and Brian Woledge's *Bibliographie des romans et nouvelles en prose française antérieurs à 1500* (Wol).

Editions and Translations

Modern Editions and Translations
This bibliography includes recent translations into English and modern French only.[1]

Abladane. Edited by L.-F. Flutre. In *Romania* 92 (1971): 458–506. (See Wol item 1.)

Abuzé en court. Edited by Roger Dubuis. TLF 199. Geneva: Droz, 1973. (See Wol item 2.)

Adenet le roi. *Cleomadés*. In Adenet le Roi, *Œuvres*, 5 vols., edited by Albert Henry, vol. 5, parts 1 and 2. TrB 46. Brussels: Editions de l'Université de Bruxelles, 1971. (See *GRLMA* vol. 4, item 4, and vol. 8, item 55300; Wol item 117.)

Aimon de Varennes. *Florimont*. Edited by Alfons Hilka. GRL 48. Göttingen, Germany: Niemeyer, 1932. (See *GRLMA* vol. 4, item 8, and vol. 8, item 31680; Wol items 58–61.)

Albéric de Pisançon. *Alexandre*. Edited by Alfred Foulet. In vol. 3, *The Medieval French "Roman d'Alexandre,"* 37–60. Emon 38. Princeton: Princeton University Press, 1949. (See *GRLMA* vol. 4, item 12.)

Alexandre. Text of the Arsenal and Venice Version. Edited by Milan S. La Du. In vol. 1, *The Medieval French "Roman d'Alexandre."* Emon 36. Princeton: Princeton University Press, 1937. (See *GRLMA* vol. 4, item 28.)

Alexandre de Bernay. *Athis et Prophilias*. Edited by Alfons Hilka. GRL 29, 40. Dresden, Germany: GRL/Halle, Germany: Niemeyer, 1912–16. (See *GRLMA* vol. 4, item 16.)

Alexandre décasyllabique. Edited by Alfred Foulet. In vol. 3, *The Medieval French "Roman d'Alexandre,"* 61–100. Emon 38. Princeton: Princeton University Press, 1949. (See *GRLMA* vol. 4, item 28.)

Alexandre de Paris. *Roman d'Alexandre*. Edited by E. C. Armstrong et al. In vol. 2, *The Medieval French "Roman d'Alexandre."* Emon 37. Princeton: Princeton University Press, 1937. (See *GRLMA* vol. 4, item 20.)

Alexandre du Pont. *Mahomet*. Edited by Y. G. Lepage. BFR 16. Paris: Klincksieck, 1977.

Alexandre en prose. Edited by Alfons Hilka. Halle, Germany: Niemeyer, 1920. (See *GRLMA* vol. 4, item 32, and vol. 8, items 58100, 58120, 58140; Wol items 4–8.)

Alixandre empereur de Constentinoble et Cliges son filz. In *Cliges*, edited by Wendelin Foerster, 281–338. Halle, Germany: Niemeyer, 1884. (See Wol item 43.)

Alixandre l'orphelin. Edited by Cedric E. Pickford. Manchester, England: Manchester University Press, 1951. (See *GRLMA* vol. 8, item 10940; Wol item 9.)

Amadas et Ydoine. Edited by John R. Reinhard. CFMA 51. Paris: Champion, 1974. (See *GRLMA* Vol. 4, item 36.)
Amadas et Ydoine. Translated into French by Jean-Claude Aubailly. TCFMA 36. Paris: Champion, 1986.

Anglo-Norman Brut (Royal 13.A.xxi). Edited by Alexander Bell. ANTS 21–22. Oxford, England: Blackwell, 1969.

Antoine de la Sale. *Jehan de Saintré*. Edited by Jean Misrahi and Charles A. Knudson. TLF 117. Geneva: Droz, 1967. (See *GRLMA* vol. 8, item 32100; Wol item 16.)
———. *Paradis de la reine Sibylle*. Edited by Fernand Desonay. Paris: Droz, 1930. (See *GRLMA* vol. 8, item 32160.)
———. *Paradis de la reine Sibylle*. In *La salade*. In vol. 1, *Œuvres complètes*, 63–130, edited by Fernand Desonay. BUL 68. Paris: Droz, 1937.
———. *Le paradis de la reine Sibylle*. Translated into French by Francine Mora. Moyen âge. Paris: Stock, 1983.

Apollonius de Tyr. Edited by C. B. Lewis. RF 34. (See *GRLMA* vol. 8, item 44; Wol item 17.)

Apollonius de Tyr (15th-century version). Edited and translated into French by Michel Zink. Collection 10/18, 1483. Paris: EGE, 1982. (See *GRLMA* vol. 8, item 24520.)

Le livre d'Artus. Edited by H. Oskar Sommer. In vol. 7, *The Vulgate Version of the Arthurian Romances.* Washington, D.C.: Carnegie Institution, 1913. (See *GRLMA* vol. 4, item 328; Wol item 96.)

Atre périlleux. Edited by Brian Woledge. CFMA 76. Paris: Champion, 1936. (See *GRLMA* vol. 4, item 52.)

Aucassin et Nicolete. 3d ed. Edited by Mario Roques. CFMA 43. Paris: Champion, 1955.

Aucassin et Nicolette. Translated into French by Gustave Cohen. TCFMA 2. Paris: Champion, 1977.

Aucassin et Nicolette. Edited and translated into French by Jean Dufournet. Paris: Flammarion, 1984.

Balain. See *Graal, Roman du.*

Beauvau, Louis or Pierre.[2] *Troilus.* In *Nouvelles françoises du XIVe siècle*, edited by L. Moland and C. D'Héricault, 115–304. Paris: Jannet, 1858. (See *GRLMA* vol. 8, item 33400; Wol item 119.)

Belle Heleine de Constantinople. Edited by A. H. Krappe. In *Romania* 63 (1937): 314–24. (See *GRLMA* vol. 4, item 68, vol. 8, item 24600; Wol items 21–22.)

Benoît de Sainte-Maure. *Troie.* 6 vols. Edited by Léopold Constans. SATF. Paris: Firmin Didot, 1904–12. (See *GRLMA* vol. 4, item 70.)

———. *Troie.* Translated into French by Emmanuèle Baumgartner. Collection 10/18: Bibliothèque médiévale. Paris: Union Générale d'Editions, 1987.

Berinus. 2 vols. Edited by Robert Bossuat. SATF. Paris: SATF, 1931–33. (See *GRLMA* vol. 8, item 11500; Wol item 23.)

Beroul. *Tristran.* 2 vols. Edited by A. Ewert. Oxford: Blackwell, 1939–70. (See *GRLMA* vol. 4, item 72.[3])

———. *Tristan.* Edited by Ernest Muret; 4th edition revised by L. M. Defourques. CFMA 12. Paris: Champion, 1947.

———. *Tristan et Iseult.* Translated into French by Pierre Jonin. TCFMA 19. Paris: Champion, 1980.

————. *Tristran.* Edited and translated into English by Norris J. Lacy. GMLL 36A. New York: Garland, 1988.

————. *Tristran et Iseut.* Edited and translated into French by Herman Braet and Guy Raynaud de Lage. Ktemata 10–11. Louvain: Peeters, 1989.

————. *Tristan.* Edited by Stewart Gregory. Atlanta, Ga.: Rodopi, 1992.

Besançon Venjance Alixandre. Edited by Edward Billings Ham. In *Five Versions of the Venjance Alixandre,* 79–82. Emon 34. Princeton: Princeton University Press, 1935. (See *GRLMA* vol. 4, item 304.)

Blancandin et l'Orgueilleuse d'amour. Edited by Franklin P. Sweetser. TLF 112. Geneva: Droz/Paris: Minard, 1964. (See *GRLMA* vol. 4, item 76; Wol items 25–26.)

Blandin de Cornouaille. Edited by C. H. M. van der Horst. PIFOU 4. The Hague: Mouton, 1974.

Bliocadran. Edited by Lenora D. Wolfgang. BZRP 150. Tübingen: Niemeyer, 1976.

Bretel, Jacques. *Tournoi de Chauvency.* Edited by Maurice Delbouille. BUL 49. Liège, Belgium: Vaillant-Carmanne/Paris: Droz, 1932. (See *GRLMA* vol. 4, item 284, vol. 6, item 6324.)

Brun de la Montagne. Edited by Paul Meyer. SATF. Paris: Firmin Didot, 1875. (See *GRLMA* vol. 8, item 11700.)

Butors, Bauduin. *Fils du roi Constant.* Edited by Lewis Thorpe. In *Nottingham Mediaeval Studies* 12 (1968): 3–20; 13 (1969): 49–64; 14 (1970): 41–63. (See *GRLMA* vol. 4, item 64; Wol item 19.)

Cardenois. Edited by Marcello Cocco. Testi e saggi di letterature moderne: Testi 6. Bologna, Italy: Pàtron, 1975. (See Wol item 98.)

Cent nouvelles nouvelles. Edited by Franklin P. Sweetser. TLF 127. Geneva: Droz/Paris: Minard, 1966. (See *GRLMA* vol. 8, item 11760; Wol item 30.)

"The One Hundred New Tales": "Les cent nouvelles nouvelles." Translated into English by Judith Bruskin Diner. GLML 30B. New York: Garland, 1989.

Champier, Symphorien. *Palanus* (by Guillaume Ramèze?). Edited by Alfred de Terrebasse. Lyon, France: L. Perrin, 1833. (See *GRLMA* vol. 8, item 58580; Wol item 111.)

Chastelaine de Vergi. Edited by F. Whitehead. Manchester, England: Manchester University Press, 1944, 1951.

Chastelaine de Vergi: édition critique du ms. B. N. f. fr. 375, avec introduction, notes, glossaire et index, suivie de l'édition diplomatique de tous les manuscrits connus du XIIIᵉ et du XIVᵉ siècle. Edited by René Ernst Victor Stuip. PIFOU 5. The Hague: Mouton, 1970.

Chastelaine de Vergi. Edited and translated into French by René Stuip. Collection 10/18: Bibliothèque médiévale. Paris: Union Générale d'Editions, 1985.

Châtelaine de Vergi en prose. Edited by the Barone di Saint-Pierre. In *Novella e poesie francesi inedite o rarissime del secolo XIV*, 1–41. Florence, Italy: G. Cicelli, 1888. (Wol item 35.)

Chevalier à l'épée. In *Two Old French Romances. Part 1: "Le chevalier à l'épée" and "La mule sans frein."* Edited by R. C. Johnston and D. D. R. Owen. Edinburgh: Scottish Academic Press, 1972. (See *GRLMA* vol. 4, item 96.)

Chevalier du papegau. Edited by Ferdinand Heuckenkamp. Halle, Germany: Niemeyer, 1896. (See *GRLMA* vol. 8, item 11960; Wol 40.)

"The Knight of the Parrot" (Chevalier du papegau). Translated into English by Thomas E. Vesce. GLML 55B. New York: Garland, 1986.

Chevaliers as deus espees. Edited by Wendelin Foerster. Halle, Germany: Niemeyer, 1877. (See *GRLMA* vol. 4, item 100.)

Chrétien. *Guillaume d'Angleterre.* Edited by A. J. Holden. TLF 360. Geneva: Droz, 1988. (See *GRLMA* vol. 4, item 104.)

———. *Guillaume d'Angleterre.* Edited by Maurice Wilmotte. CFMA 55. Paris: Champion, 1927.

———. *Guillaume d'Angleterre.* Translated into French by Jean Trotin. TCFMA 18. Paris: Champion, 1974.

Chrétien de Troyes.[4]

———. *Chevalier au lion (Yvain).* Edited by Mario Roques. CFMA 89. Paris: Champion, 1982. (See *GRLMA* vol. 4, item 120; Wol item 190[5])

———. *Chevalier au lion (Yvain).* Translated into French by Claude Buridan and Jean Trotin. TCFMA 5 (Paris: Champion, 1991).

———.*Yvain (Le chevalier au lion).* Edited by Wendelin Foerster and T. B. W. Reid. Manchester, England: Manchester University Press, 1942.

———. *The Knight with the Lion, or Yvain (Le chevalier au lion).* Edited and translated by William W. Kibler. GLML 48B. New York: Garland, 1985.

———. *Der Löwenritter (Yvain).* In vol. 2, *Christian von Troyes: Sämtliche erhaltene Werke*, edited by Wendelin Foerster. Halle, Germany: Niemeyer, 1887.[6]

————. *Chevalier de la charrete*. Edited by Mario Roques. CFMA 86. Paris: Champion, 1970. (See *GRLMA* vol. 4, item 116.)

————. *Chevalier de la charrette*. Translated into French by Jean Frappier. TCFMA 4. Paris: Champion, 1980.

————. *Lancelot or the Knight of the Cart (Le Chevalier de la charrete)*. Edited and translated into English by William W. Kibler. GLML 1A. New York: Garland, 1981.

————. *Chevalier de la charrette (Lancelot)*. Edited and translated into French by Alfred Foulet and Karl D. Uitti. Classiques Garnier. Paris: Bordas, 1989.

————. *Chevalier de la charrette (Lancelot)*. Edited and translated into French by Charles Méla. Lettres gothiques. Paris: Livre de poche, 1992.

————. *Der Karrenritter (Lancelot)*. In vol. 4, *Christian von Troyes: Sämtliche erhaltene Werke*, edited by Wendelin Foerster. Halle, Germany: Niemeyer, 1887.

————. *Cligés*. Edited by Alexandre Micha. CFMA 84. Paris: Champion, 1957. (See *GRLMA* vol. 4, item 112; Wol item 43.)

————. *Cligès*. Translated into French by Alexandre Micha. TCFMA 3. Paris: Champion, 1980.

————. *Cliges*. In vol. 1, *Christian von Troyes: Sämtliche erhaltene Werke*, edited by Wendelin Foerster. Halle, Germany: Niemeyer, 1884.

————. *Erec et Enide*. Edited by Mario Roques. CFMA 80. Paris: Champion, 1966. (See *GRLMA* vol. 4, item 108; Wol item 51.)

————. *Erec et Enide*. Edited and translated into modern French by Carleton W. Carroll. GLML 25A. New York: Garland, 1987.

————. *Erec und Enide*. In vol. 3, *Christian von Troyes: Sämtliche erhaltene Werke*, edited by Wendelin Foerster. Halle, Germany: Niemeyer, 1890.

————. *Perceval ou le conte du graal*. Edited by Keith Busby. Tübingen, Germany: Niemeyer, 1993. (See *GRLMA* vol. 4, item 124.)

————. *Perceval ou le conte du graal*. 2d ed. Edited by William Roach. TLF 71. Geneva: Droz/Paris: Minard, 1959.

————.*Conte du graal (Perceval)*. Edited by Félix Lecoy. CFMA 101, 103. Paris: Champion, 1973–75.

————. *Conte du graal (Perceval)*. Translated into French by Jacques Ribard. TCFMA 29. Paris: Champion, 1979.

————. *The Story of the Grail or Perceval (Li contes del graal)*. Edited by Rupert T. Pickens and translated into English by William W. Kibler. GLML 62A. New York: Garland, 1990.

————. *Conte du graal (Perceval)*. Edited and translated into French by Charles Méla. Lettres gothiques. Paris: Livre de poche, 1990.

————. *Der Percevalroman*. In vol. 5, *Christian von Troyes: Sämtliche erhaltene Werke*, edited by Alfons Hilka. Halle, Germany: Niemeyer, 1932.

There have been numerous translations, many of which are included in recent editions. Other recent English translations into prose include:

———. *Arthurian Romances*. Translated by D.D.R. Owen. London: Dent-Everyman, 1987.

———. *Complete Romances*. Translated by David Staines. Bloomington: Indiana University Press, 1990. (Includes *Guillaume d'Angleterre*.)

———. *Arthurian Romances*. Translated by William W. Kibler and Carleton W. Carroll. London: Penguin, 1991.

Good free-verse translations, all made by Ruth Harwood Cline, include: *Lancelot or the Knight of the Cart*. Athens: University of Georgia Press, 1990; *Perceval or, the Story of the Grail*. New York: Pergamon, 1983; and *Yvain or, the Knight with the Lion*. Athens: University of Georgia Press, 1975.

Chrétien li Gois. *Philomena*. Edited by C. de Boer. Paris: P. Geuthner, 1909.

———. *Philomena*. In *Three Ovidian Tales of Love*, edited and translated into English by Raymond Cormier, 181–281. GLML 26A. New York: Garland, 1986.

Claris et Laris. Edited by Johann Alton. BLVS 169. Tübingen, Germany: H. Laupp, 1884. (See *GRLMA* vol. 4, item 128.)

Cleriadus et Meliadice. Edited by Gaston Zink. TLF 328. Paris: Droz, 1984. (See *GRLMA* vol. 8, item 12140; Wol item 42.)

Comte d'Artois. Edited by Jean-Charles Seigneuret. TLF 124. Geneva: Droz/Paris: Minard, 1966. (See *GRLMA* vol. 8, item 24700; Wol item 44.)

Comte de Poitiers. Edited by Bertil Malmberg. Etudes romanes de Lund 1. Lund, Sweden: Gleerup/Copenhagen, Denmark: Munksgaard, 1940. (See *GRLMA* vol. 4, item 132.)

Condé, Jean de. *Opera*. Vol. 1: *I manoscritti d'Italia*. Edited by Simonetta Mazzoni Peruzzi. ATSL 94. *Dis dou chevalier a le mance*, 175–231; *Dis dou levrier*, 381–441; *Dis dou blanc chevalier*, 476–533. Florence, Italy: Olschki, 1990.

———. In *Dits et contes*, ed. Auguste Scheler. 3 vols. *Dis dou chevalier a le mance*, vol. 2: 167–242; *Lays dou Blanc Chevalier*, vol. 2: 1–48; *Dis dou levrier*, vol. 2: 303–53. Brussels: Devaux, 1866–67.

Conseil. Edited by Albert Barth. In *RF* 31 (1912): 799–872.

Cor. Edited by C. T. Erickson. ANTS 24. Oxford, England: Blackwell, 1973.

Coudrette. *Roman de Mélusine ou Histoire de Lusignan*. Edited by Eleanor Roach. BFR B18. Paris: Klincksieck, 1982. (See *GRLMA* vol. 8, item 58260.)

Cristal et Clarie. Edited by Hermann Breuer. GRL 36. Dresden, Germany: Niemeyer, 1915. (See *GRLMA* vol. 4, item 148.)

Dame a la lycorne et du biau chevalier au lyon, Roman de la. Edited by Friedrich Gennrich. GRL 18. Dresden, Germany: Niemeyer, 1908. (See *GRLMA* vol. 8, item 14620.)

Des grantz geanz. Edited by Georgine E. Brereton. MAE Monographs 2. Oxford, England: Blackwell, 1937. (See *GRLMA* vol. 8, item 14360.)

Desiré. See Lays, Anonymous.

Didot "Perceval" according to the Manuscripts of Modena and Paris. Edited by William Roach. Philadelphia: University of Pennsylvania Press, 1941. (See *GRLMA* vol. 4, item 376; Wol item 113.)
Romance of Perceval in Prose: A Translation of the E Manuscript. Translated into English by Dell Skeels. University of Washington Publications in Language and Literature 15. Seattle: University of Washington Press, 1961.

Doon. See Lays, Anonymous.

Douin de Lavesne. *Trubert*. Edited by Guy Raynaud de Lage. TLF 210. Geneva: Droz, 1974.

Durmart le Galois. 2 vols. Edited by Joseph Gildea. Villanova, Pa.: Villanova Press, 1965–66. (See *GRLMA* vol. 4, item 160.)

Edipus. Edited by A. Veinant. Paris: L. Potier, 1858. (See Wol item 165.)

Eledus et Serene. Edited by John Revell Reinhard. University of Texas Studies. Austin: University of Texas Press, 1923.

Elucidation: A Prologue to the Conte del graal. Edited by Albert Wilder Thompson. New York: Institute of French Studies, 1931.

Empereur Constant: Edition critique des versions en vers et en prose, avec une étude lin-guistique et littéraire. Edited by James Coveney. PSTE 126. Paris: Belles Lettres, 1955. (See Wol item 45.)

Eneas. 2 vols. Edited by J. J. Salverda de Grave. CFMA 44, 62. Paris:
    Champion, 1925–29. (See *GRLMA* vol. 4, item 164; Wol items 48–50)
Eneas. Translated into French by Martine Thiry Stassin. TCFMA 33. Paris:
    Champion, 1985.

Enfances Gauvain. Edited by Paul Meyer. In *Romania* 39 (1910): 1–32. (See
    GRLMA vol. 4, item 168.)

Epervier. Edited by Gaston Paris. In *Romania* 7 (1878): 1–21.

Erec (Burgundian prose version). In *Erec et Enide*, edited by Wendelin Foerster,
    251–74. Halle, Germany: Niemeyer, 1870. (See Wol item 51.)

Erec, Prose. See *Graal, Roman du*.

Espine. See Lays, Anonymous.

Eustache. *Fuerre de Gadres*. Edited by E. C. Armstrong and Alfred Foulet. Emon
    39. Princeton: Princeton University Press, 1942. (See *GRLMA* vol. 4
    item 176.)

Fille du comte de Pontieu: Versions du XIIIe et du XVe siècle. Edited by C. Brunel.
    SATF. Paris: Champion, 1923. (See Wol items 54–55 and *Jehan d'Avennes*
    below.)

Flamenca. 2 vols. Edited by Elrich Gschwind. RH 86AB. Bern, Switzerland:
    Francke, 1976. (See *GRLMA* vol. 4, item 180.)
Flamenca. Edited and translated into English by Merton J. Hubert and Marion
    Eugene Porter. Princeton: Princeton University Press, 1962.
Flamenca. Edited and translated into French by Jean-Charles Huchet.
    Collection 10/18: Bibliothèque Médiévale. Paris: Union Générale
    d'Editions, 1988.

Floire et Blancheflor ("version aristocratique"). Edited by Jean-Luc Leclanché.
    CFMA 105. Paris: Champion, 1980. (See *GRLMA* vol. 4, item 184.)
Floire et Blanchefleur ("version aristocratique"). Translated into French by Jean-
    Luc Leclanché. TCFMA 34. Paris: Champion, 1986.
Floire et Blancheflor ("version aristocratique"). 2d ed. Edited by Margaret M.
    Pelan. PSTE 7. Paris: Belles Lettres, 1956.
Floire et Blancheflor: Seconde version. Edition du ms. 19152 du fonds français ("version
    populaire"). Edited by Margaret M. Pelan. Association des Publications
    près les Universités de Strasbourg. Paris: Ophrys, 1975. (See *GRLMA*
    vol. 4, item 188.)

Floire et Blancheflor. Edited by Felicitas Krüger. Romanische Studien 45. Berlin: Ebering, 1938. Version aristocratique, 3–144; version populaire, 145–239.

Florence de Rome. 2 vols. Edited by A. Wallensköld. SATF. Paris: Firmin-Didot, 1907–09. (See *GRLMA* vol. 4, item 192; Wol item 56.)

Floriant et Florete (verse version). Edited by Harry F. Williams. MPLL 23. Ann Arbor: University of Michigan Press, 1947. (See *GRLMA* vol. 4, item 196.)

Floriant et Florete ou Le chevalier qui la nef maine (prose version). Edited by Claude M. L. Lévy. Ottawa, Canada: Editions de l'Université d'Ottawa, 1983. (See *GRLMA* vol. 8, item 24560; Wol item 57.)

Folie Lancelot. See *Graal, Roman du.*

Folie Tristan de Berne. 2d ed. Edited by Ernest Hoepffner. PSTE 3. Paris: Belles Lettres, 1949.

Folie Tristan d'Oxford. 2d ed. Edited by Ernest Hoepffner. PSTE 8. Paris: Belles Lettres, 1943.

Fouke le fitz Waryn. Edited by E. J. Hathaway, P. T. Ricketts, C. A. Robson, and A. D. Wilshere. ANTS 26–28. Oxford, England: Blackwell, 1975. (See *GRLMA* vol. 8, item 17500; Wol item 62.)

Froissart, Jean. *Meliador.* 3 vols. Edited by Auguste Longnon. SATF. Paris: Firmin Didot, 1895–99. (See *GRLMA* vol. 8, item 45380.)

Gautier d'Arras
Eracle. Edited by Guy Raynaud de Lage. CFMA 102. Paris: Champion, 1976. (See *GRLMA* vol. 4, item 200.)
Ille et Galeron (ms. *W*). Edited by Frederick A. G. Cowper. SATF. Paris: Picard, 1956. (See *GRLMA* vol. 4, item 204.)
Ille et Galeron (ms. *P*). Edited by Yves Lefèvre. CFMA 109. Paris: Champion/Geneva: Slatkine, 1988.

Gautier d'Aupais. Edited by Edmond Faral. CFMA 20. Paris: Champion, 1919.

Gautier de Tournay. *Gille de Chyn.* Edited by Edwin B. Place. Northwestern University Studies in the Humanities 7. Evanston, Ill.: Northwestern University, 1941.

Gencien, Pierre. *Tournoiement as dames*. Edited by Mario Palaez. In *Studj romanzi* 14 (1917): 5–68.

Gerard de Nevers: Prose Version of the "Roman de la violette." Edited by L.F.H. Lowe. Emon 22. Princeton: Princeton University Press, 1928. (See *GRLMA* vol. 8, item 41180; Wol item 66.)

Gerbert de Montreuil. *Le roman de la violette ou de Gerart de Nevers*. Edited by Douglas Labaree Buffum. SATF. Paris: Champion, 1928. (See *GRLMA* vol. 4, item 216.)
————. See also *Perceval Continuations*.

Gilion de Trasignyes et dame Marie, sa femme. Edited by O.L.B. Wolff. Leipzig, Paris: Brockhaus & Avenarius, 1839. (See *GRLMA* vol. 8, item 17780; Wol item 68.)

Girart d'Amiens
Escanor. Edited by Henri Michelant. BLVS 178. Tübingen, Germany: Laupp, 1886. (See *GRLMA* vol. 4, item 220.)

Meliacin ou le cheval de fust. Edited by Antoinette Saly. Senefiance 27. Aix-en-Provence, France: CUER-MA, 1990. (See *GRLMA* vol. 4, item 224.)

Gliglois. Edited by Charles H. Livingston. Harvard Studies in Romance Languages 8. Cambridge: Harvard University Press, 1932. (See *GRLMA* vol. 4, item 228.)

Gogulor. Edited by Ch. H. Livingston. In *Romania* 6 (1940): 85–93.

Graal, Roman du (Post-Vulgate) (See *GRLMA* vol. 4, items 230, 352; Wol item 125; and note 7.)
Large fragments that have been published include:
Abenteuer Gawains, Ywains und Le Morholts mit den drei Jungfrauen aus der Trilogie (Demanda) des Pseudo-Robert de Borron: Die Fortsetzung des Huth-Merlin nach der allein bekannten Hs. Nr. 112 der Pariser National Bibliothek. Edited by H. Oskar Sommer. BZRP 47. Halle, Germany: M. Niemeyer, 1913.
Balain. Edited by M. Dominica Legge. Manchester, England: Manchester University Press, 1942.
Enchantemenz de Bretaigne: An Extract from a Thirteenth-Century Prose Romance "La Suite du Merlin." Edited by Patrick Coogan Smith. UNCSRLL 146. Chapel Hill: University of North Carolina Department of Romance Languages, 1977.

Erec: Roman en prose publié d'après le ms. fr. 112 de la Bibliothèque Nationale. 2d ed. Edited by Cedric E. Pickford. TLF 87. Geneva: Droz/Paris: Minard, 1968.

Folie Lancelot: A Hitherto Unidentified Portion of the Suite du Merlin Contained in MSS. B. N. fr. 112 and 12599. Edited by Fanni Bogdanow. BZRP 109. Tübingen, Germany: Niemeyer, 1965.

Merlin, roman en prose du XIIIe siècle, publié avec la mise en prose du poème de Merlin de Robert de Boron d'après le manuscrit appartenant à M. Alfred H. Huth. 2 vols. Edited by Gaston Paris and Jacob Ulrich. SATF. Paris: Firmin-Didot, 1886.

Graelent. See Lays, Anonymous.

Griseldis. In Elie Golenistscheff-Koutouzoff, *L'histoire de Griseldis en France au XIVe et au XVe siècle.* Paris: Droz, 1933. Version A by Philippe de Mézières, 151–91; version B in prose, 193–222; *Roumant du Marquis de Saluce et de sa femme Griselidys* in verse, 223–48. (See *GRLMA* vol. 8, items 38560, 38580; Wol items 72–74.)

Gui de Cambrai. *Vengement Alixandre.* Edited by Bateman Edwards. Emon 23. Princeton: Princeton University Press, 1928. (See *GRLMA* vol. 4 item 236.)

Gui de Warewic. Edited by Alfred Ewert. CFMA 74–75. Paris: Champion, 1932–33. (See *GRLMA* vol. 4, item 240, vol. 8, item 17860; Wol item 75.)

Guillaume de Lorris and Jean de Meun. *Roman de la rose.* 5 vols. Edited by Ernest Langlois. SATF. Paris: Firmin Didot, 1914–24. (See *GRLMA*, vol. 6, items 4664, 4672, vol. 8, item 50400; Wol items 90, 151.)
———. *Romance of the Rose.* Translated into English by Charles Dahlberg. Princeton: Princeton University Press, 1971.
———. *Roman de la rose.* 3 vols. Edited by Félix Lecoy. CFMA 92, 95, 98. 3 vols. Paris: Champion, 1965–70.
———. *Roman de la rose.* 5 vols. Translated into French by André Lanly. TCFMA 12, 17, 20, 21, 24. Paris: Champion, 1973–76.
———. *Roman de la rose.* Edited by Daniel Poirion. Paris: Garnier-Flammarion, 1974.
———. *Roman de la rose.* Edited and translated into French by Armand Strubel. Lettres gothiques. Paris: Livre de poche.

Guillaume de Palerne. Edited by Alexandre Micha. TLF 384. Paris: Droz, 1990. (See *GRLMA* vol. 4, item 248.)

Guillaume le clerc. *Fergus*. Edited by Wilson Frescoln. Philadelphia: William H.
    Allen, 1982. (*GRLMA* vol. 4, item 244.)
————. *Fergus*. Translated into English by D. D. R. Owen. In *AL* 8 (1989):
    79–183.

Guingamor. See Lays, Anonymous.

Guiron le courtois (Palamèdes): Etude de la tradition manuscrite et analyse critique.
    Edited by Roger Lathuillère. PRF 186. Geneva: Droz, 1966. (See
    GRLMA vol. 4, item 252; Wol item 110.)
Dal Roman de Palamedés ai cantari di Febus-el-Forte. Edited by Alberto Limentani,
    2–168 (even numbered pages), 170–88. Collezione di opere inedite o rare
    124. Bologna, Italy: Commissione per i testi di lingua, 1962.

"The Harley *Brut*: An Early French Translation of Geoffrey of Monmouth's
    Historia regum Britanniae." Edited by Brian Blakey. In *Romania* 82 (1961):
    44–70.

Haveloc and Gaimar's Haveloc Episode. Edited by Alexander Bell. Manchester,
    England: Manchester University Press/New York: Longmans, Green,
    1925.

Hector et Hercule. Edited by Joseph Palermo. TLF 190. Geneva: Droz, 1972. (See
    GRLMA vol. 8, item 24680.)

Heldris de Cornuälle. *Silence*. Edited by Lewis Thorpe. Cambridge, England:
    Heffer, 1972. (See *GRLMA* vol. 4, item 256.)
————. *Silence*. Translated into English by Regina Psaki. GLML 63B. New
    York: Garland, 1991.

Henri d'Andeli. *Lai d'Aristote*. Edited by Maurice Delbouille. BUL 123. Paris:
    Belles Lettres, 1951.

Herbert. *Dolopathos*. Edited by Charles Brunet and Anatole de Montaiglon.
    Paris: P. Jannet, 1856.

Hue de Rotelande
Ipomedon. Edited by A. J. Holden. BFR 17. Paris: Klincksieck, 1979. (See
    GRLMA vol. 4, item 268.)

————. *Protheselaus*. Edited by A. J. Holden. ANTS 47–48. London: ANTS,
    1991. (See *GRLMA* vol. 4, item 272.)

Hunbaut. Edited by Margaret Winters. DMTS 4. Leiden, The Netherlands: Brill, 1984. (See *GRLMA* vol. 4, item 276.)

Huon de Mery. *Tornoiemenz Antecrit*. Edited by Georg Wimmer. AA 76. Marburg, Germany: Elwert, 1888. (See *GRLMA* vol. 6, item 4596.)

Huon le roi. *Vair palefroi*. 2d ed. Edited by Arthur Långfors. CFMA 8. Paris: Champion, 1970.
————. *Vair palefroi*. Translated into French by Jean Dufournet. TCFMA 22. Paris: Champion, 1976.

Huth Merlin. See *Graal, Roman du*.

Ignaure (Lai du prisonnier). Edited by Rita Lejeune. Académie Royale de Langue et de Littérature Françaises de Belgique: Textes anciens 3. Brussels: Palais des Académies/Liège, Belgium: H. Vaillant-Carmanne, 1938.

Ilas et Solvas. Edited by Ernest Langlois. In *Mélanges E. Picot*, 1: 383–89. Paris: Morgand, 1913. (See *GRLMA* vol. 4, item 280.)

Jacques de Longuyon. *Vœux du paon*. In *Buick of Alexander by John Barbour*, edited by R. L. Graeme Ritchie. 4 vols. Scottish Text Society, 17, 21, 25. Edinburgh: Blackwood, 1921–29.

Jakames. *Le Castelain de Couci et la Dame de Fayel*. Edited by John E. Matzke and Maurice Delbouille. SATF. Paris: SATF, 1936. (See *GRLMA* vol. 4, item 288, vol. 8, item 11920; Wol item 34.)
————. *Le Châtelain de Couci et la Dame de Fayel*. Translated into French by A. Petit and F. Suard. Trésors littéraires du Nord de la France 1. Troesnes-La Ferté-Milon, France: Corps 9, 1986.

Jaufré. 2 vols. Edited by Clovis Brunel. SATF 85–86. Paris: SATF, 1943. (See *GRLMA* vol. 4, item 292; Wol item 61.)

Jean d'Arras. *Mélusine*. Edited by Louis Stouff. Publications de l'Université de Dijon, 5. Dijon: Bernigaud et Privat, 1932.

Jean de la Mote. *Parfait du paon*. Edited by Richard J. Carey. UNCSRLL 118. Chapel Hill: University of North Carolina Press, 1972. (See *GRLMA* vol. 8, item 48580.)

Jean de Meun. See Guillaume de Lorris and Jean de Meun.

Jean de Paris. Edited by Edith Wickersheimer. SATF. Paris: Champion, 1923. (See Wol item 87.)

Jean Le Court, dit Brisebarre. *Restor du paon.* Edited by Richard J. Carey. TLF 119. Geneva: Droz, 1966. (See *GRLMA* vol. 8, item 48380.)

Jean Renart. *L'Escoufle.* Edited by Franklin Sweetser. TLF 211. Geneva: Droz, 1974. (See *GRLMA* vol. 4, item 308.)
———. *L'Escoufle.* Translated into French by Alexandre Micha. TCFMA 48. Paris: Champion, 1992.
———. *Lai de l'ombre,* ed. Félix Lecoy. CFMA 104. Paris: Champion, 1983.
———. *Roman de la rose ou de Guillaume de Dole.* Edited by Félix Lecoy. CFMA 91. Paris: Champion, 1979. (See *GRLMA* vol. 4, item 312.)
———. *Guillaume de Dôle ou le Roman de la rose.* Translated into French by Jean Dufournet et al. TCFMA 27. Paris: Champion, 1979.

Jehan. *Mervelles de Rigomer.* 2 vols. Edited by Wendelin Foerster and Hermann Breuer. GRL 19, 39. Dresden, Germany: Niemeyer, 1908–15. (See *GRLMA* vol. 4, item 296.)
———. *"Marvels of Rigomer."* Translated into English by Thomas E. Vesce. GLML 60B. New York: Garland, 1988.

Jehan d'Avennes. Edited by Anna Maria Finoli. Milan, Italy: Cisalpino-Goliardica, 1979. (See *GRLMA* vol. 8, item 18240; Wol item 85.) The romance includes the fifteenth-century version of the *Fille du comte de Pontieu* and *Saladin,* which follow it in manuscript.

Jehan de Tuim. *Hystore de Jules Cesar.* Edited by F. Settegast. Halle, Germany: Niemeyer, 1881.

Jehan le Nevelon. *Venjance Alixandre.* Edited by Edward Billings Ham. Emon 27. Princeton: Princeton University Press, 1931. (See *GRLMA* vol. 4, item 304.)

Joseph d'Arimathie, Prose. (See Wol item 93.)
"The Modena Text of the Prose *Joseph d'Arimathie*." Edited by William Roach. In *RPh* 9 (1956): 313–42.
Joseph d'Arimathie. Edited by Bernard Cerquiglini. In *Roman du graal,* 17–71. Collection 10/18: Bibliothèque Médiévale. Paris: Union Générale d'Editions, 1981.
Joseph von Arimathia. Edited by Georg Weidner. Oppeln: Franck, 1881.

"The Middle French Redaction of Robert de Boron's *Joseph d'Arimathie*." Edited by Richard O'Gorman. In *PAPS* 122 (1978): 261–85.

Joufroi de Poitiers. Edited by Percival B. Fay and John L. Grigsby. TLF 183. Geneva: Droz, 1972. (See *GRLMA* vol. 4, item 316.)
Joufroi de Poitiers. Translated into French by Roger Noël. Studies in the Humanities 7. New York: Lang, 1987.

Lancelot do Lac: The Non-Cyclic Old French Prose Romance. 2 vols. Edited by Elspeth Kennedy. Oxford: Clarendon Press, 1980.
Lancelot. Translated into French by François Mosès. Lettres gothiques. Paris: Livre de poche, 1991.

Lancelot-Grail Cycle. (See Wol item 96.)

Le Saint-Graal ou le Joseph d'Arimathie, première branche des romans de la Table Ronde. 3 vols. Edited by Eugène Hucher. 1874; reprint, Geneva: Slatkine, 1967. (See *GRLMA* vol. 4, item 172.)
Lestoire del saint graal. In vol. 1, *The Vulgate Version of the Arthurian Romances*, edited by H. Oskar Sommer. Washington, D.C.: Carnegie Institution, 1909.
The History of the Holy Grail. Translated into English by Carol J. Chase. In vol. 1, pp.1–163, *Lancelot-Grail: The Old French Arthurian Vulgate and Post-Vulgate in Translation*, general editor Norris J. Lacy. GRLH 941. New York: Garland, 1993.[7]

Merlin. In vol. 2, *The Vulgate Version of Arthurian Romances*, edited by H. Oskar Sommer. Washington, D.C.: Carnegie Institution, 1908. (See *GRLMA* vol. 4, items 350, 352, 356; Wol items 102–03.)
Merlin. Translated into English by Rupert T. Pickens. In vol. 2, pp. 165–424, *Lancelot-Grail: The Old French Arthurian Vulgate and Post-Vulgate in Translation*, general editor Norris J. Lacy. GRLH 941. New York: Garland, 1993. (See note 7.)

Lancelot. 9 vols. Edited by Alexandre Micha. TLF 247, 249, 262, 278, 283, 286, 288, 307, 315. Geneva: Droz, 1978–83. (See *GRLMA* vol. 4, item 324.)
Lancelot. Translated into French by Alexandre Micha. Collection 10/18: Bibliothèque Médiévale. Paris: Union Générale d'Editions, 1983–.
Lancelot [part 1]. Translated into English by Samuel N. Rosenberg and Carleton W. Carroll. In vol. 2, *Lancelot-Grail: The Old French Arthurian Vulgate and Post-Vulgate in Translation*, general editor Norris J. Lacy. GRLH. New York: Garland, 1993. (See note 7.)

Lancelot del Lac. In vols. 3–5, *The Vulgate Version of the Arthurian Romances*, edited by H. Oskar Sommer. Washington, D.C.: Carnegie Institution, 1910–12.

Roman en prose de Lancelot du Lac: Le conte de la charrette. Edited by Gweneth Hutchings. Paris: Droz, 1938.

Queste del saint graal. Edited by Albert Pauphilet. CFMA 33. Paris: Champion, 1980. (See *GRLMA* vol. 4, item 396.)

Quête du graal. Translated into French by Emmanuèle Baumgartner. TCFMA 30. Paris: Champion, 1979.

Quest for the Holy Grail. Translated into English by P. M. Matarasso. London: Penguin, 1969.

Mort le roi Artu. 3d ed. Edited by Jean Frappier. TLF 58. Geneva: Droz/Paris: Minard, 1964. (See *GRLMA* vol. 4, item 364.)

Death of King Arthur. Translated into English by James Cable. London: Penguin, 1971.

Mort du roi Arthur. Translated into French by Monique Santucci. TCFMA 47. Paris: Champion, 1991.

Mort du roi Arthur. Translated into French by Marie-Louise Ollier. Collection 10/18: Bibliothèque Médiévale. Paris: Union Générale d'Editions, 1992.

Lays, Anonymous

Lais anonymes des XIIe et XIIIe siècles. Edited by Prudence Mary O'Hara Tobin. PRF 143. *Graelent*, 83–125; *Guingamor*, 127–55; *Desiré*, 157–205; *Tydorel*, 207–26; *Tyolet*, 227–53; *Espine*, 255–88; *Melion*, 289–318; *Doon*, 319–33; *Lecheor*, 347–58; *Nabaret*, 359–64. Geneva: Droz, 1976.

"Graelent" and "Guingamor": Two Breton Lays. Edited and translated into English by Russell Weingartner. GLML 37A. New York: Garland, 1984.

Lecheor. See Lays, Anonymous.

Lefevre, Raoul. *Histoire de Jason*. Edited by Gert Pinkernell. Frankfurt, Germany: Athenäum, 1971. (See *GRLMA* vol. 8, item 41820; Wol item 134.)

———. *Recoeil des histoires de Troyes*. Edited by Marc Aeschbach. EurH 13, 120. New York: Lang, 1987. (See *GRLMA* vol. 8, item 41840; Wol items 180–84.)

Lorris, Guillaume de. See Guillaume de Lorris and Jean de Meun.

Maillart, Jean. *Comte d'Anjou*. Edited by Mario Roques. CFMA 67. Paris: Champion, 1931. (See *GRLMA* vol. 4, item 298, vol. 8, item 48740.)

Manessier. See *Perceval Continuations*.

Mantel. Edited by F. A. Wulff. In *Romania* 14 (1885): 343–80.

Marie de France. *Les lais*.[8]   Edited by Jean Rychner. CFMA 93. Paris: Champion, 1968.
———. *Les lais*. Translated into French by Pierre Jonin. Paris: Champion, 1972.
———. *Les lais*. Edited by Karl Warnke and translated into French by Laurence Harf-Lancner. Lettres gothiques. Paris: Livre de poche, 1990.
———. *The Lays*. Translated into English by Robert Hanning and Joan Ferrante. Durham, N.C.: Labyrinth Press, 1982.
———. *The Lays*. Translated into English by Glyn S. Burgess and Keith Busby. London: Penguin, 1986.

Marquis de Saluce. See *Griseldis*.

Melion. See Lays, Anonymous.

Melior. Edited by David J. A. Ross. In *MAE* 40 (1971): 104–08.

Melior et Ydoine. Edited by Paul Meyer. In *Romania* 37 (1908): 236–44.

Merlin. Edited by Alexandre Micha. TLF 281. Geneva: Droz, 1980. (See *GRLMA* vol. 4, item 350; Wol item 102. See also *Graal, Roman du*, and *Lancelot-Grail* Cycle.)

Mervelles de Rigomer. See Jehan.

Meun, Jean de. See Guillaume de Lorris and Jean de Meun.

Munich Brut. Edited by Konrad Hofmann and Karl Vollmüller. Halle, Germany: Lippert, 1887.

Nabaret. See Lays, Anonymous.

Narcisus. Edited by M. M. Pelan and N. C. W. Spence. PSTE 147. Paris: Belles Lettres, 1964.
Narcisse. Edited by Martine Thiry Stassin and Madeleine Tyssens. BUL 211. Paris: Belles Lettres, 1976.
Narcisus et Dane. In *Three Ovidian Tales of Love*, edited and translated into English by Raymond Cormier, 85–179. GLML 26A. New York: Garland, 1986.

Noton. Edited by A. Monteverdi. In *AR* 11 (1927): 589–91.

Nouvelles de Sens. In *Nouvelles françaises inédites du XVe siècle,* edited by Ernest Langlois, BXV 6. Paris: Champion, 1908.

Oiselet: Edition and Critical Study. Edited by Lenora D. Wolfgang. TAPS 80.5. Philadelphia: American Philosophical Society, 1990.

Paien de Maisières. *Mule sans frein.* In *Two Old French Gauvain Romances. Part I: "Le chevalier à l'épée" and "La mule sans frein",* edited by R. C. Johnston and D.D.R. Owen. Edinburgh: Scottish Academic Press, 1972. (See *GRLMA* vol. 4, item 368.)

Palamedès. See *Guiron le courtois.*

Parma Venjance Alixandre. Edited by Edward Billings Ham. In *Five Versions of the Venjance Alixandre,* 13–46. Emon 34. Princeton: Princeton University Press, 1935. (See *GRLMA* vol. 4, item 304.)

Partonopeu de Blois. 2 vols. Edited by Joseph Gildea and Leon Smith. Villanova, Pa.: Villanova University Press, 1967–70. (See *GRLMA* vol. 4, item 372.)

Perceforest (See *GRLMA* vol. 8, item 24630; Wol item 112.)
"Etudes sur le roman de *Perceforêt.*" Edited by L.-F. Flutre. In *Romania* 70 (1948–49): 474–522; 71 (1950): 374–92, 482–508; 74 (1953): 44–102; 88 (1967): 475–508; 89 (1968): 355–86; 90 (1969): 341–70; 91 (1970): 189–226. (Contains summary with important extracts.)
Perceforest: Première partie. Edited by Jane H. M. Taylor. TLF 279. Geneva: Droz, 1979.
Perceforest: Troisième partie. Edited by Gilles Roussineau. TLF 365, 409. Geneva: Droz, 1988–91.
Perceforest: Quatrième partie. 2 vols. Edited by Gilles Roussineau. TLF 343. Geneva: Droz, 1987.

Perceval Continuations: The First Continuation. In vol. 1. *Redaction of Mss. TVD.* Edited by William Roach. In vol. 2, *Redaction of Mss. EMQU.* Edited by William Roach and Robert H. Ivy, Jr. In vol. 3.1, *Redaction of Mss, ALPRS.* Edited by William Roach. In vol. 3.2, *Glossary of the First Continuation.* Prepared by Lucien Foulet. Philadelphia, Pa.: American Philosophical Society, 1949–55. (See *GRLMA* vol. 4, item 140.)
Première continuation du roman de Perceval. Translated into French by Henri de Briel. Roi Arthur 3. Paris: Klincksieck, 1972.

Perceval Continuations. In vol. 4, *The Second Continuation.* Edited by William Roach. Philadelphia, Pa.: American Philosophical Society, 1971. (See *GRLMA* vol. 4, item 144.)

Perceval Continuations. In vol. 5, *The Third Continuation by Manessier.* Edited by William Roach. Philadelphia, Pa.: American Philosophical Society, 1983. (See *GRLMA* vol. 4, item 344.)

Gerbert de Montreuil. *La continuation de Perceval* (Fourth Continuation). 3 vols. Edited by Mary Williams and Marguerite Oswald. CFMA 28, 50, 101. Paris: Champion, 1922–75. (See *GRLMA* vol. 4, item 212.)

Perlesvaus: Le haut livre du graal. 2 vols. Edited by William A. Nitze and T. Atkinson Jenkins. 1932–37; reprint, New York: Phaeton, 1972. (See *GRLMA* vol. 4, item 380; Wol item 114.)
High Book of the Grail. Translated into English by Nigel Bryant. Totowa, N.J.: Rowman and Littlefield, 1978.

Philippe de Remi. *Jehan et Blonde.* Edited by Sylvie Lécuyer. CFMA 107. Paris: Champion, 1984. (See *GRLMA* vol. 4, item 384.)
———. *Jehan et Blonde.* Translated into French by Sylvie Lécuyer. TCFMA 35. Paris: Champion, 1986.

———. *La Manekine.* In vol. 1, Philippe de Remi, sire de Beaumanoir, *Œuvres poétiques,* edited by Hermann Suchier. SATF. Paris: Firmin Didot, 1884. (See *GRLMA* vol. 4, item 388; Wol item 92.)
———. *La Manekine.* Translated into French by Christiane Marchello-Nizia. Paris: Stock, 1980.
———. *La Manekine.* Edited and translated into English by Irene Gnarra (Bauer). Garland Publications in Comparative Literature. New York: Garland,

Pierre de la Seppède. *Paris et Vienne.* Edited by Robert Kaltenbacher. In *RF* 15 (1904): 321–688a[a]. (See *GRLMA* vol. 8, item 56280; Wol item 120.)

Pierre de Mézières. See *Griseldis.*

Pierre de Provence: l'ystoire du vaillant chevalier Pierre filz du conte de Provence et de la belle Maguelonne. Edited by Régine Colliot. Aix-en-Provence, France: CUER-MA/Paris Champion, 1977. (See *GRLMA* vol. 8, item 22980; Wol items 121–22.)

Piramus et Tisbé. Edited by C. de Boer. CFMA 26. Paris: Champion, 1921.
Piramus et Tisbé. In *Three Ovidian Tales of Love,* edited and translated into English by Raymond Cormier, 1–83. GLML 26A. New York: Garland, 1986.

Ponthus et la belle Sidoine (livre à gravures imprimé à Lyon, au XVe siècle). Edited by
E. Droz. Paris: Eggiman, 1926. (See *GRLMA* vol. 8, item 23240; Wol
item 124.[9])

Prise de Defur. Edited by Lawton P. G. Peckham and Milan S. La Du. In *La prise
de Defur et Le voyage d'Alexandre au paradis terrestre*, 1–72. Emon 35. New
York: Princeton: Princeton University Press, 1935. (See *GRLMA* vol. 4,
item 392.)

Rambaux de Frise. Edited by B. N. Sargent. UNCSRLL 69. Chapel Hill:
University of North Carolina Press, 1967. (See *GRLMA* vol. 8, item
23800; Wol item 133.)

Raoul de Houdenc, *Meraugis de Portlesguez*. Edited by Mathias Friedwagner.
Halle, Germany: Niemeyer, 1897. (See *GRLMA* vol. 4, item 404.)

Rasse de Brunhamel. *Floridan et Elvide*. Edited by H. P. Clive. Oxford, England:
Blackwell, 1959. (See *GRLMA* vol. 8, item 53240; Wol item 136.)

Reinbert. Edited by Brian Woledge. *MAE* 8 (1939): 85–117, 173–92.

Renart, Jean. See Jean Renart.

Renaut. *Galeran de Bretagne*. Edited by Lucien Foulet. CFMA 37. Paris:
Champion, 1925. (See *GRLMA* vol. 4, item 412.)

Renaut de Beaujeu or de Bagé. *Bel inconnu*. Edited by G. Perrie Williams.
CFMA 38. Paris: Champion, 1929. (See *GRLMA* vol. 4, item 416.)
———. *Bel inconnu*. Translated into French by Michèle Perret and Isabelle
Weill. TCFMA 41. Paris: Champion, 1989.
———. *Bel inconnu*. Edited by Karen Fresco, translated into English by Colleen
P. Donagher, with music edited by Margaret P. Hasselman. GLML 77A.
New York: Garland, 1992.

René d'Anjou. *Livre du cuer d'amours espris*. Edited by Susan Wharton. Collection
10/18: Bibliothèque Médiévale. Paris: Union Générale d'Editions, 1980.
(See *GRLMA* vol. 8, item 57260; Wol item 245.)

Requis. *Richars li biaus*. Edited by Anthony J. Holden. CFMA 106. Paris:
Champion, 1983. (See *GRLMA* vol. 4, item 420.)

Richard sans peur Edited from "Le Romant de Richart" and from Gilles Corrozet's "Richart sans paour." Edited by Denis Joseph Conlon. UNCSRLL 192. Chapel Hill: Department of Romance Languages, University of North Carolina, 1977. (See *GRLMA* vol. 8, item 24420; Wol item 110.)

Richeut. Edited by Philippe Vernay. RH 103. Bern, Switzerland: Francke, 1988.

Robert de Blois
Beaudous. Vol. 1, *Sämtliche Werke*, edited by Jacob Ulrich. Berlin: Mayer & Müller, 1889–95. (See *GRLMA* vol. 4, item 424.)

Floris et Lyriopé. Edited by Paul Barrette. University of California Publications in Modern Philology 92. Berkeley and Los Angeles: University of California Press, 1968. (See *GRLMA* vol. 4, item 428.)

Floris et Liriopé. Vol. 2, *Sämtliche Werke*, edited by Jacob Ulrich. Berlin: Mayer & Müller, 1889–95.

Floris et Liriopé. Edited by Wolfram von Zingerle. AB 12. Leipzig, Germany: Reisland, 1891.

Robert de Boron. *Estoire dou graal.* Edited by William A. Nitze. CFMA 57. Paris: Champion, 1927. (See *GRLMA* vol. 4, item 432.) *Merlin* fragment, pp. 126–30. (See *GRLMA* vol. 4, item 436.)

Robert le diable. Edited by E. Löseth. SATF. Paris: Firmin Didot, 1902. (See *GRLMA* vol. 4, item 440; Wol items 146–47.)

Roi Flore et la belle Jehane. In *Nouvelles françoises en prose du XIIIᵉ siècle*, edited by L. Moland and C. D'Héricault, 83–157. Paris: Jannet, 1856. (Wol item 148).

Rusticien de Pise. See E. Löseth, *Le roman en prose de Tristan, le roman de Palamède et la compilation de Rusticien de Pise: Analyse critique d'après les manuscrits de Paris*, 423–74. BEHE 82. Paris: E. Bouillon, 1890. (See *GRLMA* vol. 4, item 444; Wol item 152.)

Sala, Pierre. *Tristan.* Edited by L. Muir. TLF 80. Geneva: Droz/Paris: Minard, 1958.

Saladin: Suite et fin du deuxième cycle de la Croisade. Edited by Larry S. Crist. TLF 185. Paris: Droz, 1972. (See *Jehan d'Avennes*.)

Sarrasin. *Roman de Hem*. Edited by Albert Henry. TrB 9. Paris: Belles Lettres, 1938. (See *GRLMA* vol. 4, item 448, vol. 6, item 6348.)

Sept sages de Rome Prose Cycle (See *GRLMA* vol. 4, item 452.)
Sept sages Proper (see Wol items 153–57.)
Deux rédactions du roman des Sept sages de Rome. Edited by Gaston Paris. SATF. Paris: Firmin Didot, 1876.
Ystoire de la male marastre: Version M of the Roman des sept sages de Rome. Edited by Hans R. Runte. BZRP 141. Tübingen, Germany: Niemeyer, 1974.

Marques de Rome. Edited by Johann Alton. BLVS 187. Tübingen, Germany: H. Laupp, 1889. (See Wol item 158.)

Laurin fils de Marques le sénéchal: Text of MS. B. N. f. fr. 22548. Edited by Lewis Thorpe. University of Nottingham Research Publication 2. Cambridge, England: W. Heffer, [1958]. (See Wol item 159.)

Cassidorus. Edited by Joseph Palermo. SATF. Paris: Picard, 1963–64. (See Wol item 160.)

Helcanus. Edited by Henri Niedzielski. TLF 121. Geneva: Droz, 1966. (See Wol item 161.[10])

Sept sages de Rome, Verse. Edited by Mary B. Speer. ECAMML 4. Lexington, Ky.: French Forum, 1989.

Sires de Gavres. Edited by E. Gachet. Brussels: Van Dale, 1845. (See *GRLMA* vol. 8, item 17960; Wol item 163.)

Sone de Nausay. Edited by Moritz Goldschmidt. BLVS 216. Tübingen, Germany: Litterarischer Verein, 1899. (See *GRLMA* vol. 4, item 456.)

Suite du Merlin. See *Graal, Roman du*.

Thèbes. 2 vols. Edited by Guy Raynaud de Lage. CFMA 94, 96. Paris: Champion, 1966–71. (See *GRLMA* vol. 4, item 460; Wol items 65–67.)
Thèbes. Translated into French by A. Petit. TCFMA 44. Paris: Champion, 1990.
Thèbes. Translated into English by John Smartt Coley. GLML 44. New York: Garland, 1986.

Thomas. *Horn*. 2 vols. Edited by Mildred K. Pope; revised and completed by T. B. W. Reid. ANTS 9–10, 12–13. Oxford, England: Blackwell, 1955–64.

Thomas d'Angleterre. *Tristan*. 2 vols. Edited by Joseph Bédier. SATF. Paris: Firmin Didot, 1902–05. (See *GRLMA* vol. 4, item 464.)

———. *Les fragments du roman de Tristan*. Edited by Bartina H. Wind. TLF 92. Geneva: Droz/Paris: Minard, 1960.

———. *Tristan*. Edited by Félix Lecoy. CFMA 113. Paris: Champion, 1992.

———. *Tristan*. Edited and translated into English by Stewart Gregory. New York: Garland, 1991.

Thomas of Kent. *The Anglo-Norman "Alexander" ("Le roman de toute chevalerie")*. 2 vols. Edited by Brian Foster and Ian Short. ANTS 29–33. London: ANTS, 1977. (See *GRLMA* vol. 4, item 468.)

Tibaut. *Roman de la poire*. Edited by Christiane Marchello-Nizia. SATF. Paris: Picard, 1984. (See *GRLMA* vol. 6, item 4708.)

Tournoiement aus dames. Edited by Holger Petersen Dyggve. In *Neuphilologische Mitteilungen* 36 (1935): 178–87. (See *GRLMA* vol. 6, item 6144.)

Tresplaisante et recreative hystoire du trespreulx et vaillant cheuallier "Perceual le galloys." In *Der Percevalroman*, edited by Alfons Hilka, 481–614. Halle, Germany: Niemeyer, 1932. (Includes prosification of Chrétien's *Conte du graal* and the *First* and *Second Perceval Continuations*.)

Tristan en prose (See *GRLMA* vol. 4, item 472; Wol item 170.)

Roman de Tristan en prose. 3 vols. Edited by Renée L. Curtis. AS 12–14. Cambridge, England: D. S. Brewer, 1985.

Le Roman de Tristan en prose. Vol. 1 edited by Philippe Ménard, vol. 2 edited by Marie-Luce Chênerie and Thierry Delcourt, vol. 3 edited by Gilles Roussineau, vol. 4 edited by J.-C. Faucon, vol. 5 edited by Denis Lalande with Thierry Delcourt. TLF 353, 387, 398, 408, 416. Geneva: Droz, 1987 to date.

Tristan en prose. Translated into French by Marie-Luce Chênerie and Philippe Ménard. TCFMA 45. Paris: Champion, 1990.

Roman en prose de Tristan, le roman de Palamède et la compilation de Rusticien de Pise: Analyse d'après les manuscrits de Paris. Ed. E. Löseth. BEHE 82. Paris: Bouillon, 1890.

Troie, Prose Versions of. (Wol items 171-85.)

Troie en prose. Edited by L. Constans and E. Faral. CFMA 29. Vol. 1 only appeared. Paris: Champion, 1922.

Troie en prose: version du Cod. Bodmer 147. Edited by Françoise Vielliard. BB 4. Cologny-Geneva, Switzerland: Fondation Martin Bodmer, 1979.

Tydorel. See Lays, Anonymous.

Tyolet. See Lays, Anonymous.

Vallet a la cote mal tailliee (Brunor). Edited by Paul Meyer and Gaston Paris. In *Romania* 26 (1897): 276–80.

Vengeance Raguidel. Edited by Mathias Friedwagner. Halle, Germany: Niemeyer, 1909. (See *GRLMA* vol. 4, item 400.)

Venice Venjance Alixandre. Edited by Edward Billings Ham. In *Five Versions of the Venjance Alixandre*, 1–12. Emon 34. Princeton: Princeton University Press, 1935. (See *GRLMA* vol. 4, item 304.)

Venjance Alixandre in *Renart le contrefait*. Edited by Edward Billings Ham. In *Five Versions of the Venjance Alixandre*, 76–78. Emon 34. Princeton: Princeton University Press, 1935. (See *GRLMA* vol. 4, item 304.)

Voyage d'Alexandre au paradis terrestre. Edited by Lawton P. G. Peckham and Milan S. La Du. In *La prise de Defur and Le voyage d'Alexandre au paradis terrestre*, 73–90. Emon 35. Princeton: Princeton University Press, 1935. (See *GRLMA* vol. 4, item 492.)

Wace. *Brut*. 2 vols. Edited by Ivor Arnold. SATF. Paris: SATF, 1938–40. (See *GRLMA* vol. 4, item 496.)

Waldef (Cod. Bodmer 168). Edited by A. J. Holden. BB 5. Cologny-Geneva, Switzerland: Fondation Martin Bodmer, 1984. (See *GRLMA* vol. 4, item 500.)

Wauquelin, Jean. *Venjance Alixandre*. Edited by Edward Billings Ham. In *Five Versions of the Venjance Alixandre*, 47–75. Emon 34. Princeton: Princeton University Press, 1935. (See *GRLMA* vol. 4, item 304.)

Wistasse le moine, édité d'après le manuscrit, fonds français 1553, de la Bibliothèque Nationale, Paris. Edited by Denis Joseph Conlin. UNCSRLL 126. Chapel Hill: University of North Carolina Press, 1972.

Yder. Edited and translated by Alison Adams. AS 8. Cambridge, England: D. S. Brewer/Totowa, N.J.: Biblio, 1983. (See *GRLMA* vol. 4, item 504.)

Ysaÿe le triste. Edited by André Giacchetti. Publications de l'Université de Rouen 142. Rouen-Maromme, France: Qualigraphie, 1989. (See *GRLMA* vol. 8, item 31900; Wol item 82.)

Incunabula Reprints

Gyron le courtois c. 1501. London: Scolar Press, 1977 (Paris: A. Vérard, ca. 1501). *Lancelot du Lac 1488*. 2 vols. London: Scolar Press, 1973 (Vol. 1, Rouen: Jehan and Gaillard Bourgeois; vol. 2, Paris: Jehan du Pré, 1488). *Meliadus de Leonnoys 1532*. London: Scolar Press, 1980 (Paris: Denis Janet, 1532). *Merlin 1498*. 3 vols. London: Scolar Press, 1975 (Paris: A. Vérard, 1498). *Tristan*. London: Scolar Press, 1976 (Paris: Jehan le Bourgoys, 1489).

Collections

Französische Schicksalsnovellen des 13. Jahrhunderts: La chastelaine de Vergi, La fille du comte de Pontieu, Le roi Flore et la belle Jehanne. Edited and translated into German by Friedrich Wolfzettel. Klassische Texte des Mittelalters in zweisprachigen Ausgaben 26. Munich, Germany: Fink, 1986.
La légende arthurienne: Le graal et la Table Ronde. Edited by Danielle Régnier-Bohler. Paris: Laffont, 1989. Contains translations of Chrétien de Troyes's *Perceval*, *Perlesvaus*, Robert de Boron's *Merlin*, "Caradoc" (from the *First Perceval Continuation*), *Le chevalier à l'épée*, *Hunbaut*, Paien de Maisière's *La demoiselle à la mule*, *L'âtre périlleux*, *Gliglois*, Raoul de Houdenc's *Méraugis de Portlesguez*, *Jaufré*, *Blandin de Cornouaille*, *Les merveilles de Rigomer*, Jean Froissart's *Meliador* (extracts), *Le chevalier du papegau*.
Ludi e spettacoli nel medioevo: I tornei di dame. Edited by Andrea Oulega. Catedra di filologia romanza dell'Università degli studi di Milano. Milan: Cisalpino-La Goliardica, 1970. Includes Pierre Gencien's *Tournoiement aux dames de Paris* and the anonymous *Tournoiement aux dames*.
The Romance of Arthur. Vol. 1, edited by James J. Wilhelm and Laila Zamuelis Gross, includes Chrétien de Troyes's *Lancelot*; vol. 2, edited by James J. Wilhelm, includes all or parts of Wace's *Brut*, *Graelent*, Chrétien de Troyes's *Yvain*, Beroul's *Tristan*, the *Prose Merlin*, and the *Suite du Merlin*; vol. 3, edited by James J. Wilhelm, includes the *Chevalier du papegau*. New York: Garland, 1984, 1986, 1988.
Tristan et Iseut: Les poèmes français—la saga norroise. Edited and translated into French by Daniel Lacroix and Philippe Walter. Lettres gothiques. Paris: Livre de poche, 1989.
Les troubadours: Jaufre, Flamenca, Barlaam et Josaphat. Edited and translated into French by René Lavaud and René Nelli. Bibliothèque européenne. Bruges, Belgium: Desclée de Brouwer, 1960.

Secondary Sources

Given the enormous bibliography on French romance, I have limited this listing to major recent studies. For additional bibliography of critical scholarship, see below. Since critical study of medieval French romance is international in scope, I have included important studies regardless of language.

Bibliographies

Annual

BBSIA: *Bulletin bibliographique de la Société Internationale Arthurienne/Bibliographical Bulletin of the International Arthurian Society.* 1949 to date.

CCM: *Cahiers de civilisation médiévale.* 1958 to date.

Encomia: Bibliographical Bulletin of the International Courtly Literature Society. 1976 to date.

Klapp, Otto, and Astrid Klapp-Lehrmann. *Bibliographie der französischen Literaturwissenschaft-Bibliographie d'histoire littéraire française.* Frankfurt, Germany: Klostermann. 1960 to date.

Modern Humanities Research Association. *Year's Work in Modern Languages.* London: Oxford University Press. 1931 to date.

Modern Language Association of America. *Annual Bibliography.* New York: Modern Language Association. 1921–56.

————. *International Bibliography.* New York: Modern Language Association. 1957 to date.

General

Bossuat, Robert. *Manuel bibliographique de la littérature française du moyen âge.* Melun, France: d'Argences. (See esp. pp. 89–198, 388–413.)

————, with Jacques Monfrin. *Supplément (1949–1953).* Paris: d'Argences, 1956. (See esp. pp. 35–54, 87–90.)

————. *Second supplément (1954–60).* Paris: d'Argences, 1961. (See esp. pp. 31–63, 89–92.)

Vielliard, Françoise, and Jacques Monfrin. *Troisième supplément (1960–1980).* 2 vols. Paris: Editions du Centre National de la Recherche Scientifique, 1986–91. (See esp. pp. 189–392, 701–32.)

Holmes, Urban T., Jr., ed. *The Medieval Period.* Vol. 1 of *A Critical Bibliography of French Literature.* 2d ed. Edited by D. C. Cabeen. Syracuse, N.Y.: Syracuse University Press, 1952. (See esp. pp. 79–140, 193–208.)

Woledge, Brian. *Bibliographie des romans et nouvelles en prose française antérieurs à 1500.* PRF 42. Geneva: Droz, 1954. (Abbreviated as Wol.)

————. *Supplément 1954–73*. PRF 130. Geneva: Droz, 1975. Items use the same number assigned to them in the original volume.

Special

Burgess, Glyn S. *Marie de France: An Analytical Bibliography*. RBC 21. London: Grant & Cutler, 1977.
————. *Supplement No. 1, 1985*. RBC 21, no. 1. London: Grant & Cutler, 1986.
Kelly, Douglas. *Chrétien de Troyes: An Analytic Bibliography*. RBC 17. London: Grant & Cutler, 1976.
Reiss, Edmund, Louise Horner Reiss, and Beverly Taylor. *Arthurian Legend and Literature: An Annotated Bibliography*. Vol. 1: *The Middle Ages*. GRLH 415. New York: Garland, 1984.
Runte, Hans R., J. Keith Wikeley, and Anthony J. Farrell. *"The Seven Sages of Rome" and "The Book of Sindbad": An Analytical Bibliography*. GRLH 387. New York: Garland, 1984.
Sargent-Baur, Barbara Nelson, and Robert Francis Cook. *Aucassin et Nicolete: A Critical Bibliography*. RBC 35. London: Grant & Cutler, 1981.
Shirt, David J. *The Old French Tristan Poems: A Bibliographical Guide*. RBC 28. London: Grant & Cutler, 1980.

Representative or Major Works

Arrathoon, Leigh A., ed. *The Craft of Fiction: Essays in Medieval Poetics*. Rochester, Mich.: Solaris, 1984.
Badel, Pierre-Yves. *Introduction à la vie littéraire du moyen âge*. 2d ed. Bordas Etudes 30. Paris: Bordas, 1984.
Fourrier, Anthime. *Le courant réaliste dans le roman courtois en France*. Vol. 1: *Les débuts (XIIᵉ siècle)*. Paris: Nizet, 1960. (No additional volumes published.)
Frappier, Jean. *Etude sur La mort le roi Artu, roman du XIIIᵉ siècle: Dernière partie du Lancelot en prose*. 2d ed. PRF 70. Geneva: Droz, 1968.
Gallais, Pierre. "Recherches sur la mentalité des romanciers français du moyen âge." *CCM* 7 (1964): 479–93; 13 (1970): 333–47.
Grundriß der romanischen Literaturen des Mittelalters. Heidelberg, Germany: Winter, 1968 to date. Especially vols. 1, 4, 5 (forthcoming), 6, 8 (part 2 forthcoming), and 11 (part 2 forthcoming). (Abbreviated *GRLMA*.)
Haidu, Peter, ed. *Approaches to Medieval Romance*. In *YFS* 51 (1974).
Harf-Lancner, Laurence. *Les fées au moyen âge. Morgane et Mélusine: La naissance des fées*. NBMA 8. Paris: Champion, 1984.
Huchet, Jean-Louis. *Le roman occitan médiéval*. Paris: PUF, 1991.
Kelly, Douglas. *The Art of Medieval French Romance*. Madison: University of Wisconsin Press, 1992.

Köhler, Erich. *Ideal und Wirklichkeit in der höfischen Epik: Studien zur Form der frühen Artus- und Graldichtung.* 2d ed. BZRP 97. Tübingen, Germany: Niemeyer, 1970. Translated as *L'aventure chevaleresque: Idéal et réalité dans le roman courtois. Etudes sur la forme des plus anciens poèmes d'Arthur et du Graal.* Translated by Eliane Kaufholz. Paris: Gallimard, 1974.

Lacy, Norris J., Douglas Kelly, and Keith Busby, eds. *The Legacy of Chrétien de Troyes.* 2 vols. FauxT 31, 37. Atlanta, Ga.: Rodopi, 1987–88. (Abbreviated *LCT.*)

Legge, M. Dominica. *Anglo-Norman Literature and Its Background.* Oxford, England: Clarendon Press, 1963.

Loomis, Roger Sherman, ed. *Arthurian Literature in the Middle Ages: A Collaborative History.* Oxford, England: Clarendon Press, 1959.

Méla, Charles. *La reine et le graal: La "conjointure" dans les romans du graal de Chrétien de Troyes au "Livre de Lancelot."* Paris: Seuil, 1984.

Ménard, Philippe. *Le rire et le sourire dans le roman courtois en France au moyen âge (1150–1250).* PRF 105. Geneva: Droz, 1969.

Poirion, Daniel. *Résurgences: Mythe et littérature à l'âge du symbole (XIIe siècle).* Paris: PUF 1986.

Schmolke-Hasselmann, Beate. *Der arthurische Versroman von Chrestien bis Froissart: Zur Geschichte einer Gattung.* BZRP 177. Tübingen, Germany: Niemeyer, 1980.

Vàrvaro, Alberto. *Il "Roman de Tristan" di Béroul.* PSFM n.s. 3. Turin, Italy: Bottega d'Erasmo, 1963. Translated as *Beroul's "Romance of Tristan."* Translated by John C. Barnes. Manchester, England: Manchester University Press/New York: Barnes & Noble, 1972.

Vinaver, Eugène. *A la recherche d'une poétique médiévale.* Paris: Nizet, 1970.

———. *The Rise of Romance.* Oxford, England: Clarendon Press, 1971.

Zink, Michel. "Une mutation de la conscience littéraire: Le langage romanesque à travers des exemples français du XIIe siècle." *CCM* 24 (1981): 3–27.

———. *La subjectivité littéraire: Autour du siècle de saint Louis.* Paris: PUF, 1985.

Zumthor, Paul. *Essai de poétique médiévale.* Paris: Seuil, 1972.

Selective (since 1975) Updating

Antique Romances

Blask, Dirk Jürgen. *Geschehen und Geschick im altfranzösischen Eneas-Roman.* Romanica et comparatistica 2. Tübingen, Germany: Stauffenberg, 1984.

Donovan, L. G. *Recherches sur "Le roman de Thèbes."* Paris: SEDES, 1975.

Huchet, Jean-Charles. *Le roman médiéval.* Paris: PUF, 1984.

Petit, Aimé. *Naissances du roman: Les techniques littéraires dans les romans antiques du XIIe siècle.* Lille, France: Atelier National Reproduction des Thèses, 1985.

Schöning, Udo. *Thebenroman-Eneasroman-Trojaroman: Studien zur Rezeption der Antike in der französischen Literatur des 12. Jahrhunderts.* BZRP 235. Tübingen, Germany: Niemeyer, 1991.

Lays

Burgess, Glyn S. *The "Lais" of Marie de France: Text and Context.* Athens: University of Georgia Press, 1987.

Clifford, Paula. *Marie de France: Lais.* CGFT 16. London: Grant & Cutler, 1982.

Foulet, Alfred, and Karl D. Uitti. "The Prologue to the *Lais* of Marie de France: A Reconsideration." *RPh* 35 (1981–82): 242–49.

Kroll, Renate. *Der narrative Lai als eigenständige Gattung in der Literatur des Mittelalters: Zum Strukturprinzip der "Aventure" in den Lais.* BZRP 201. Tübingen, Germany: Niemeyer, 1984.

Maréchal, Chantal A., ed. *In Quest of Marie de France A Twelfth-Century Poet.* Medieval and Renaissance Series 10. Lewiston, N.Y.: Mellen, 1992.

Tristan Romances in Verse

Baumgartner, Emmanuèle. *Tristan et Iseut: De la légende aux récits en vers.* Etudes littéraires 15. Paris: PUF, 1987.

Blakeslee, Merritt R. *Love's Masks: Identity, Intertextuality, and Meaning in the Old French Tristan Poems.* AS 15. Cambridge, England: D. S. Brewer, 1989.

Bromiley, Geoffrey. *Thomas's "Tristan" and the "Folie Tristan d'Oxford."* CGFT 61. London: Grant & Cutler, 1986.

Noble, Peter. *Beroul's "Tristan" and the "Folie Tristan de Berne."* CGFT 15. London: Grant & Cutler, 1982.

Chrétien de Troyes

Baumgartner, Emmanuèle. *Chrétien de Troyes: Yvain, Lancelot. La charrette et le lion.* Etudes littéraires 38. Paris: PUF, 1992.

Burgess, Glyn S. *Chrétien de Troyes: Erec et Enide.* CGFT 32. London: Grant & Cutler, 1984.

Chrétien de Troyes: Le Chevalier au lion—approches d'un chef-d'œuvre. Edited by Jean Dufournet. Unichamp 20. Paris: Champion, 1988.

Delcourt, Denyse. *L'éthique du changement dans le roman français du XII⁰ siècle.* HICL 276. Geneva: Droz, 1990.

Freeman, Michelle A. *The Poetics of "Translatio studii" and "Conjointure": Chrétien de Troyes's "Cligés."* FrFM 12. Lexington, Ky.: French Forum, 1979.

Grimbert, Joan Tasker. *"Yvain" dans le miroir: Une poétique de la réflexion dans le "Chevalier au lion" de Chrétien de Troyes.* Purdue University Monographs in Romance Languages 25. Philadelphia: J. Benjamins, 1988.

Halász, Katalin. *Structures narratives chez Chrétien de Troyes.* SRUD 7. Debrecen, Hungary: Kossuth Lajos Tudományegyetem, 1980.

Hunt, Tony. *Chrétien de Troyes: Yvain (Le Chevalier au lion)*. CGFT 55. London: Grant & Cutler, 1986.

Kelly, Douglas, ed. *The Romances of Chrétien de Troyes: A Symposium*. ECAMML 3. Lexington, Ky.: French Forum, 1985.

Lacy, Norris J. *The Craft of Chrétien de Troyes: An Essay on Narrative Art*. DMTS 3. Leiden, The Netherlands: Brill, 1980.

Maddox, Donald. *The Arthurian Romances of Chrétien de Troyes: Once and Future Fictions*. CSML 12. Cambridge: Cambridge University Press, 1991.

——. *Structure and Sacring: The Systematic Kingdom in Chrétien's "Erec et Enide."* FrFM 8. Lexington, Ky.: French Forum, 1978.

Polak, Lucie. *Chrétien de Troyes: Cligés*. CGFT 23. London: Grant & Cutler, 1982.

Topsfield, L. T. *Chrétien de Troyes: A Study of the Arthurian Romances*. Cambridge: Cambridge University Press, 1981.

Grail Romances in Verse and Their Continuations and Adaptations

Corley, Corin F. V. *The Second Continuation of the Old French Perceval: A Critical and Lexicographical Study*. MHRADS 24. London: Modern Humanities Research Association, 1987.

Gallais, Pierre. *L'imaginaire d'un romancier français de la fin du XIIe siècle (description de la "Continuation-Gauvain")*. 4 vols. FauxT 33, 34, 36, 39. Atlanta, Ga.: Rodopi, 1988–89.

Le Rider, Paule. *Le chevalier dans le Conte du graal de Chrétien de Troyes*. Bibliothèque du moyen âge. Paris: PUF, 1978.

Pickens, Rupert T. *The Welsh Knight: Paradoxicality in Chrétien's "Conte del graal."* FrFM 6. Lexington, Ky.: French Forum, 1977.

Schmid, Elisabeth. *Familiengeschichte und Heilsmythologie: Die Verwandtschaftsstrukturen in den französischen und deutschen Gralromanen des 12. und 13. Jahrhunderts*. BZRP 211. Tübingen, Germany: Niemeyer, 1986.

Vial, Guy. *Le Conte du graal: Sens et unité. La Première Continuation: Textes et contenu*. PRF 178. Geneva: Droz, 1987.

Non-Arthurian Verse Romances of the Twelfth Century

Gautier d'Arras. In *BDA* 8 (1990): 5–54 (3 articles).

Legros, Huguette. *La rose et le lys: Etude littéraire du conte de Floire et Blancheflor*. Senefiance 31. Aix-en-Provence, France: CUER MA, 1992.

Pratt, Karen. *Meister Otte's Eraclius as an Adaptation of Eracle by Gautier d'Arras*. GAG 392. Göppingen, Germany: Kümmerle, 1987.

Thirteenth-Century Prose Romance

Der altfranzösische Prosaroman: Funktion, Funktionswandel und Ideologie am Beispiel des "Roman de Tristan en prose." Edited by Ernstpeter Ruhe and Richard Schwaderer. BRPM 12. Munich, Germany: Fink, 1979.

Approches du Lancelot en prose. Edited by Jean Dufournet. Unichamp 6. Paris: Champion, 1984.

Baumgartner, Emmanuèle. *L'arbre et le pain: Essai sur "La Queste del saint graal."* Bibliothèque du moyen âge. Paris: SEDES, 1981.

———. *La harpe et l'épée: Tradition et renouvellement dans le "Tristan en prose."* Bibliothèque du moyen âge. Paris: SEDES, 1990.

———. *Le "Tristan en prose": Essai d'interprétation d'un roman médiéval*. PRF 133. Geneva: Droz, 1975.

Burns, E. Jane. *Arthurian Fictions: Rereading the Vulgate Cycle*. Columbus: Ohio State University Press, 1985.

Kennedy, Elspeth. *Lancelot and the Grail: A Study of the Prose "Lancelot."* Oxford, England: Clarendon Press, 1986.

Leupin, Alexandre. *Le graal et la littérature: Etude sur la Vulgate arthurienne en prose*. Lausanne, Switzerland: Age d'homme, 1982.

Matarasso, Pauline. *The Redemption of Chivalry: A Study of the "Queste del saint graal."* HICL 180. Geneva: Droz, 1979.

Micha, Alexandre. *Essais sur le cycle du Lancelot-Graal*. PRF 179. Geneva: Droz, 1987.

———. *Etude sur le "Merlin" de Robert de Boron: Roman du XIIIᵉ siècle*. PRF 151. Geneva: Droz, 1980.

Nouvelles recherches sur "Le Tristan en prose." Edited by Jean Dufournet. Unichamp 23. Paris: Champion, 1990.

Speer, Mary B. "Recycling the Seven Sages of Rome." *ZRP* 99 (1983): 288–303.

Szkilnik, Michelle. *L'archipel du graal: Etude de l'"Estoire del saint graal."* PRF 196. Geneva: Droz, 1991.

Van Coolput, Colette-Anne. *Aventures querant et le sens du monde: Aspects de la réception productive des premiers romans du graal cycliques dans le "Tristan en prose."* MLov 1:14. Leuven, Belgium: Leuven University Press, 1986.

Thirteenth-Century Verse Romance

Busby, Keith. "*Cristal et Clarie*: A Novel Romance?" In *Convention and Innovation in Literature*, edited by Theo D'Haen, Rainer Grübel, and Helmut Lethen, 77–103. UPAL 24. Philadelphia: Benjamins, 1989.

Carmona, Fernando. *El roman lírico medieval*. Estudios Románicos 1. Barcelona, Spain: Promociones y Publicaciones Universitarias, 1988.

Freeman, Michelle A. "*Fergus*: Parody and the Arthurian Tradition." *FrF* 8 (1983): 197–215.

Gravdal, Kathryn. "*Fergus*: The Courtois Vilain." In her *Vilain and Courtois: Transgressive Parody in French Literature of the Twelfth and Thirteenth Centuries*, 20–50. Regent Studies in Medieval Culture. Lincoln: University of Nebraska Press, 1989.

Kelly, Douglas. *"Tout li sens du monde* dans *Claris et Laris."* *RPh* 36 (1982–83): 406–17.

Un roman à découvrir: "Jehan et Blonde" de Philippe de Remy (XIIIe siècle). Edited by Jean Dufournet. Unichamp 29. Paris: Champion, 1991.

Shepherd, M. *Tradition and Re-Creation in Thirteenth Century Romance: "La Manekine" and "Jehan et Blonde."* FauxT 48. Atlanta, Ga.: Rodopi, 1990.

Zink, Michel. *Roman rose et rose rouge: Le Roman de la rose ou de Guillaume de Dole de Jean Renart.* Paris: Nizet, 1979.

The "Roman de la rose" and Allegorical Romance

Arden, Heather. *The Romance of the Rose.* TWAS 791. Boston: Twayne, 1987.

Etudes sur le Roman de la rose de Guillaume de Lorris. Edited by Jean Dufournet. Unichamp 4. Paris: Champion, 1984.

Hult, David F. *Self-Fulfilling Prophecies: Readership and Authority in the First "Roman de la rose."* Cambridge: Cambridge University Press, 1986.

Pelen, Marc M. *Latin Ironic Poetry in the Roman de la rose.* Vinaver Studies in French 4. Liverpool, England: Cairns, 1987.

Rethinking the "Romance of the Rose": Text, Image, Reception. Edited by Kevin Brownlee and Sylvia Huot. Philadelphia: University of Pennsylvania Press, 1992.

Stakel, Susan. *False Roses: Structures of Duality and Deceit in Jean de Meun's "Roman de la rose."* Stanford French and Italian Studies 69. Saratoga, Calif.: ANMA Libri, 1991.

Strubel, Armand. *La rose, Renard et le graal: La littérature allégorique en France au XIIIe siècle.* NBMA 11. Paris: Champion, 1989.

Romance and "Nouvelle" in the Fourteenth Century and Later

Blumenfeld-Kosinski, Renate. "The Poetics of Continuation in the Old French 'Paon' Cycle." *RPh* 39 (1986): 437–47.

Dembowski, Peter F. *Jean Froissart and His "Meliador": Context, Craft, and Sense.* ECAMML 2. Lexington, Ky.: French Forum, 1983.

Hanly, Michael G. *Boccaccio-Beauvau-Chaucer: Troilus and Criseyde. Four Perspectives on Influence.* Norman, Okla.: Pilgrim Books, 1990.

Huot, Sylvia. "Chronicle, Lai, and Romance: Orality and Writing in the *Roman de Perceforest.*" In *Vox Intexta: Orality and Textuality in the Middle Ages,* edited by A. N. Doane and Carol Braun Pasternack, 203–23. Madison: University of Wisconsin Press, 1991.

Morse, Ruth. "Historical Fiction in Fifteenth-Century Burgundy." *MLR* 75 (1980): 48–64.

Rhétorique et mise en prose au XVe siècle. Actes du VIe Colloque International sur le Moyen Français, Milan, 4–6 May 1988. Vol. 2. Edited by Sergio Cigada and Anna Slerca. Scienze filologiche e letteratura 45: Contributi del

"Centro studi sulla letteratura medio-francese e medio-inglese" 8. Milan, Italy: Vita e Pensiero, 1991.

Stanesco, Michel. *Jeux d'errance du chevalier médiéval: Aspects ludiques de la fonction guerrière dans la littérature du moyen âge flamboyant*. Brill's Studies in Intellectual History 9. New York: Brill, 1988.

Stuip, René E. V. "L'"Histoire des seigneurs de Gavre': Sa popularité à la fin du moyen âge." In *Mélanges J.-R. Smeets*, 281–92. Leiden, The Netherlands: Spiele, 1982.

Suard, François. *Guillaume d'Orange: Etude du roman en prose*. BXV 44. Paris: Champion, 1979. (See especially "L'élément romanesque," pp. 570–91.)

Wallen, Martha. "Significant Variations in the Burgundian Prose Version of *Erec et Enide*." *MAE* 51 (1982): 187–96.

Sources of Romance

Bumke, Joachim. *Mäzene im Mittelalter: Die Gönner und Auftraggeber der höfischen Literatur in Deutschland 1150–1300*. Munich, Germany: Beck, 1979.

Kelly, Douglas. *The Arts of Poetry and Prose*. TSMO 59. Turnhout, Belgium: Brepols, 1991.

Milin, Gaël. *Le roi Marc aux oreilles de cheval*. PRF 197. Geneva: Droz, 1991.

Poirion, Daniel. "Théorie et pratique du style au moyen âge: Le sublime et la merveille." *RHL* 86 (1986): 15–32.

Ruhe, Ernstpeter. "*Inventio* devenue *troevemens*: La recherche de la matière au moyen âge." In *The Spirit of the Court: Selected Proceedings of the Fourth Congress of the International Courtly Literature Society* (Toronto 1983), 289–97. Cambridge, England: Brewer.

Vance, Eugene. *From Topic to Tale: Logic and Narrativity in the Middle Ages*. Theory and History of Literature 47. Minneapolis: University of Minnesota Press, 1987.

Textual Editing

Foulet, Alfred, and Mary Blakely Speer. *On Editing Old French Texts*. ECAMML 1. Lawrence: Regents Press of Kansas, 1979.

Speer, Mary B. "Editing Old French Texts in the Eighties: Theory and Practice." *RPh* 45 (1991): 7–43.

Genre

Carasso-Bulow, Lucienne. *The Merveilleux in Chrétien de Troyes' Romances*. HICL 153. Geneva: Droz, 1976.

Dubost, Francis. *Aspects fantastiques de la littérature narrative médiévale (XIIe–XIIIe siècles): L'autre, l'ailleurs, l'autrefois*. 2 vols. NBMA 15. Paris: Champion, 1991.

Il meraviglioso e il verosimile tra antichità e medioevo. Edited by D. Lanza and O. Longo. BibAR 221. Florence, Italy: Olschki, 1989.

Poirion, Daniel. *Le merveilleux dans la littérature française du moyen âge*. Que sais-je? 1938. Paris: PUF, 1982.

————, ed. *Styles et valeurs: Pour une histoire de l'art littéraire au moyen âge*. Paris: SEDES, 1990.

Scholz, Manfred Günter. *Hören und Lesen: Studien zur primären Rezeption der Literatur im 12. und 13. Jahrhundert*. Wiesbaden, Germany: Steiner, 1980.

Zumthor, Paul. *La lettre et la voix: De la "littérature" médiévale*. Paris: Seuil, 1987.

————. *La poésie et la voix dans la civilisation médiévale*. Collège de France: Essais et conférences. Paris: PUF, 1984.

Adaptation and Intertextuality

Artusroman und Intertextualität. Edited by Friedrich Wolfzettel. Gießen, Germany: Schmitz, 1990

Intertextualités médiévales. Edited by Daniel Poirion. In *Lit* 41 (1981).

Kelly, Douglas. "*Translatio studii*: Translation, Adaptation, and Allegory in Medieval French Literature." *PQ* 57 (1978): 287–310.

Petit, Aimé. *L'anachronisme dans les romans antiques du XIIe siècle*. Lille, France: Atelier National de Reproduction de Thèses, 1985.

Romance: Generic Transformations from Chrétien de Troyes to Cervantes. Edited by Kevin Brownlee and Marina Scordilis Brownlee. Hanover, N.H.: University Press of New England, 1985.

Social and Moral Ideals

Bloch, R. Howard. *Medieval French Literature and the Law*. Berkeley and Los Angeles: University of California Press, 1977.

Chênerie, Marie-Luce. *Le chevalier errant dans les romans arthuriens en vers des XIIe et XIIIe siècles*. PRF 172. Geneva: Droz, 1986.

Duby, Georges. *Les trois ordres ou l'imaginaire du féodalisme*. Paris: Gallimard, 1978.

Hanning, Robert W. *The Individual in Twelfth-Century Romance*. New Haven, Conn.: Yale University Press, 1977.

Keen, Maurice. *Chivalry*. New Haven, Conn.: Yale University Press, 1984.

Lefay-Toury, Marie-Noëlle. *La tentation du suicide dans le roman français du XIIe siècle*. Essais sur le moyen âge 4. Paris: Champion, 1979.

Noble, Peter S. *Love and Marriage in Chrétien de Troyes*. Cardiff: University of Wales Press, 1982.

Scaglione, Aldo. *Knights at Court: Courtliness, Chivalry, and Courtesy from Ottonian Germany to the Italian Renaissance*. Berkeley and Los Angeles: University of California Press, 1991.

The Study of Chivalry: Resources and Approaches. Edited by Howell Chickering and Thomas H. Seller. Kalamazoo, Mich.: Medieval Institute Publications–Western Michigan University, 1988.

Prosody and Prose

The absence of recent studies of prose and versification obliges me to include several important publications that appeared prior to 1975.

Chassé, Dominique. "La mise en mémoire des informations narratives: Le système du vers et le système de la prose." In *Jeux de mémoire: Aspects de la mnémotechnie médiévale*, edited by B. Roy and P. Zumthor, 57–64. Montreal: Presses de l'Université de Montréal, 1985.

Deloffre, Frédéric. *Le vers français.* 3d ed. Paris: SEDES, 1973.

Frappier, Jean. "L'art." In *Etude sur Yvain ou Le Chevalier au lion de Chrétien de Troyes*, 219–72. Paris: SEDES, 1969.

———. "La maîtrise de l'octosyllabe dans le *Conte du graal.*" In *Chrétien de Troyes et le mythe du graal: Etude sur Perceval ou le Conte du graal*, 257–72. Paris: SEDES, 1972.

Poirion, Daniel, ed. *L'écriture romanesque.* In *PerM* 3 (1977). Special issue on lyric and prose in romance.

Rychner, Jean. *Formes et structures de la prose française médiévale: L'articulation des phrases narratives dans la "Mort Artu."* Université de Neuchâtel: Recueil de travaux publiés par la Faculté des Lettres 32. Neuchâtel, Switzerland: Faculté des Lettres/Geneva: Droz, 1970.

Philology and Modern Theories

Aubailly, Jean-Claude. *La fée et le chevalier: Essai de mythanalyse de quelques lais féeriques des XIIe et XIIIe siècles.* Essais 10. Paris: Champion, 1986.

Chandès, Gérard. "Observations sur le champ sémantique de la *recreantise.*" In *Farai chansoneta novele: Hommage à Jean-Charles Payen*, 123–31. Caen: Université de Caen, 1989.

———. *Le serpent, la femme et l'épée. Recherches sur l'imagination symbolique d'un romancier médiéval: Chrétien de Troyes.* FauxT 27. Amsterdam: Rodopi, 1986.

Courtly Ideology and Woman's Place in Medieval French Literature. Edited by E. Jane Burns and Roberta L. Krueger. *Romance Notes* 25, no. 3 (1985). Special Issue.

Gallais, Pierre. *Dialectique du récit médiéval (Chrétien de Troyes et l'hexagone logique).* FauxT 9. Amsterdam: Rodopi, 1982.

Huchet, Jean-Charles. *Littérature médiévale et psychanalyse: Pour une clinique littéraire.* Paris: PUF, 1990.

———. *Tristan et le sang de l'écriture.* Le texte rêve. Paris: PUF, 1990.

Medieval Literature and Contemporary Theory. NLH 10 (1979). Special Issue.

Mittelalterbilder aus neuer Perspektive: Diskussionsanstöße zu amour courtois, Subjektivität in der Dichtung und Strategien des Erzählens. Edited by Ernstpeter Ruhe and Richard Behrens. BRPM 14. Munich, Germany: Fink, 1985.

Modernité au moyen âge: Le défi du passé. Edited by Brigitte Cazelles and Charles Méla. Recherches et rencontres: Publications de la Faculté des Lettres de Genève-Littérature 1. Geneva: Droz, 1990.

The New Medievalism. Edited by Marina S. Brownlee, Kevin Brownlee, and Stephen G. Nichols. Baltimore: Johns Hopkins University Press, 1991.

Virdis, Maurizio. *Perceval: Per un'e(ste)tica del poetico. Fra immaginario, strutture linguistiche e azioni.* Oristano, Italy: S'Alvure, 1988.

Vitz, Evelyn Birge. *Medieval Narrative and Modern Narratology: Subjects and Objects of Desire.* New York: New York University Press, 1989.

Influence of French Romance in Other Languages

GENERAL
Michel Stanesco and Michel Zink. *Histoire européenne du roman médiéval: Esquisses et perspectives.* Paris: PUF, 1992.

CELTIC (See *GRLMA* vol. 1: 163–205, by Wolf-Dieter Lange.)
Rachel Bromwich, A.O.H. Jarman, and Brynley F. Roberts, eds. *The Arthur of the Welsh: The Arthurian Legend in Medieval Welsh Literature.* Cardiff: University of Wales Press, 1991.

DUTCH AND FLEMISH
Arturus rex. 2 vols. Vol. 1: *Catalogus: Koning Artur en de Nederlanden/La matière de Bretagne et les anciens Pays-Bas,* edited by W. Verbeke, J. Janssens, and M. Smeyers. Vol. 2: *Acta conventus Lovaniensis 1987,* edited by Willy Van Hoecke, Gilbert Tournoy, and Werner Verbeke. Leuven, Belgium: Leuven University Press, 1987–91.

Middle Dutch Literature in Its European Context. Cambridge: Cambridge University Press, 1993.

ENGLISH (See *GRLMA* vol. 1: 304–22, by Wolfgang Iser.)
W.R.J. Barron. *English Medieval Romance.* New York: Longman, 1987.

Susan Crane. *Insular Romance: Politics, Faith and Culture in Anglo-Norman and Middle English Literature.* Berkeley and Los Angeles: University of California Press, 1986.

GERMAN (See *GRLMA* vol. 1:264–303, by Joachim Bumke.)
Walter Haug. *Literaturtheorie im deutschen Mittelalter: Von den Anfängen bis zum Ende des 13. Jahrhunderts. Eine Einführung.* Darmstadt, Germany: WB, 1985.

Walter Haug and Burghart Wachinger, eds. *Positionen des Romans im späten Mittelalter*. Tübingen, Germany: Niemeyer, 1991.

HISPANIC (See *GRLMA* vol. 4, part 1: 645–64, by Hans Ulrich Gumbrecht for Spanish; 665–66, by Martin de Riquer for Catalan.)

A. D. Deyermond. "The Lost Genre of Medieval Spanish Literature." *Hispanic Review* 43 (1975): 231–59.

ITALIAN (See *GRLMA* vol. 4, part 1: 667–75, by Henning Krauss.)

Daniela Delcorno Branca. *Il romanzo cavalleresco medievale*. Scuola aperta: Lettere italiane 45. Florence, Italy: Sansoni, 1974.

OCCITAN (See *GRLMA* vol. 4, part 1: 627–44, by Emmanuèle Baumgartner.)

Jean-Charles Huchet. *Le roman occitan médiéval*. Paris: PUF, 1991.

Alberto Limentani. *L'eccezione narrativa: La Provenza medievale e l'arte del racconto*. Turin, Italy: Einaudi, 1977.

Robert A. Taylor. *La littérature occitane du moyen âge: Bibliographie sélective et critique*. Toronto Medieval Bibliographies 7. Toronto: University of Toronto Press, 1977. (Pp. 118–27).

SCANDINAVIAN (See *GRLMA* vol. 1: 333–95, by Knud Togeby.)

Marianne E. Kalinke. "Norse Romance (*Riddarasögur*)." In *Old Norse–Icelandic Literature*, edited by Carol J. Clover and John Lindow, 316–63. Islandica 45. Ithaca, N.Y.: Cornell University Press, 1985.

Reference Works

Flutre, Louis-Ferdinand. *Table des noms propres avec toutes leurs variantes figurant dans les romans du moyen âge écrits en français ou en provençal*. Publications du CESCM 2. Poitiers, France: Centre d'Etudes Supérieures de Civilisation Médiévale, 1962.

Guerreau-Jalabert, A. *Index des motifs narratifs dans les romans arthuriens français en vers (XIIᵉ–XIIIᵉ siècles)*. PRF 202. Geneva: Droz, 1992.

Lacy, Norris J., ed., with Geoffrey Ashe, Sandra Ness Ihle, Marianne E. Kalinke, and Raymond H. Thompson. *The New Arthurian Encyclopedia*. New York: Garland, 1991.

Mölk, Ulrich. *Französische Literarästhetik des 12. und 13. Jahrhunderts: Prologue-Exkurse-Epiloge*. Sammlung romanischer übungstexte 54. Tübingen, Germany: Niemeyer, 1969. (Very useful anthology of author/narrator interventions; see especially sections 23–61, 64–81.)

Le moyen âge. Edited by Robert Bossuat, Louis Pichard, and Guy Raynaud de Lage; revised by Geneviève Hasenohr and Michel Zink. In *Dictionnaire des lettres françaises*. Paris; Fayard, 1992.

Ruck, E. H. *An Index of Themes and Motifs in 12th-Century French Arthurian Poetry*. AS 25. Cambridge, England: Brewer, 1991.

West, G. D. *An Index of Proper Names in French Arthurian Prose Romances.*
University of Toronto Romance Series 35. Toronto: University of
Toronto Press, 1978.

———. *An Index of Proper Names in French Arthurian Verse Romances
1150–1300.* University of Toronto Romance Series 15. Toronto:
University of Toronto Press, 1969.

Notes to Bibliography

1. See also Norris J. Lacy, "Medieval French Arthurian Literature in English,"
Quondam et Futurus n.s. 3, no. 1 (1991): 55–74.

2. On the author's name, see Michael G. Hanly, *Boccaccio-Beauvau-Chaucer:
Troilus and Criseyde. Four Perspectives on Influence* (Norman, Okla.: Pilgrim Books,
1990), 37–80.

3. Complete with T.B.W. Reid, *The Tristan of Beroul: A Textual Commentary*
(Oxford, England: Blackwell, 1972); Tony Hunt, "Textual Notes on Beroul and
Thomas: Some Problems of Interpretation and Emendation," *Tristania* 1
(1975): 29–59; Sven Sandqvist, *Notes textuelles sur le "Roman de Tristan" de Béroul,*
Etudes romanes de Lund 39 (Lund, Sweden: Gleerup, 1984). See also David J.
Shirt, *The Old French Tristan Poems,* RBC 28 (London: Grant & Cutler, 1980),
41–50.

4. No edition of Chrétien is truly critical except Busby's *Perceval*; I have listed
those which are either commonly referred to or are recent.

5. Complete with Brian Woledge, *Commentaire sur "Yvain" ("Le Chevalier au
lion") de Chrétien de Troyes,* 2 vols., PRF 170, 186 (Geneva: Droz, 1986–88).

6. On this and other editions prepared by Wendelin Foerster, see Douglas
Kelly, *Chrétien de Troyes: An Analytic Bibliography,* RBC 17 (London: Grant &
Cutler, 1976), par. Aa1–4. They are useful today for variants.

7. A translation of the entire Vulgate cycle and of the extant parts of the Post-
Vulgate cycle. At the time of publication of my book, the *Estoire,* the *Merlin,*
and the first part of the *Lancelot Proper* had appeared.

8. Complete or partial editions and translations of Marie's *Lais* are too numerous to note completely here. See Glyn S. Burgess, *Marie de France: An Analytical*

Bibliography, RBC 21 (London: Grant & Cutler, 1977), items 1–18, 27–42, 510–11, and Supplement No. 1, RBC 21.1 (1986), items 532–33, 536, 542, 547, 550, 553, 555, 557, 560, 581, 721. The *Bulletin bibliographique de la Société Internationale Arthurienne* (*BBSIA*) reports annually on new editions and translations of the *Lais*.

9. On this romance, see Marie-Claude de Crécy, abstract of her thesis which is an edition of *Ponthus et Sidoine*, *PerM* 15 (1989): 91–93.

10. Includes discussion of the unpublished *Peliarmenus*; see also Wol item 162 on the unpublished *Kanor*.

Index

Works are listed by author unless they are anonymous, in which case they are listed by title.

The Author

Douglas Kelly is the Julian E. Harris Professor of French at the University of Wisconsin–Madison. He is the author of *The Art of Medieval French Romance* (1992); *The Arts of Poetry and Prose* (1991); *Medieval Imagination: Rhetoric and the Poetry of Courtly Love* (1978); *Chrétien de Troyes: An Analytic Bibliography* (1976); and *Sens and Conjointure in the Chevalier de la Charrette* (1966). He has edited *The Legacy of Chrétien de Troyes* (with Norris J. Lacy and Keith Busby); *The Romances of Chrétien de Troyes* and *What Is Literature? France, 1100–1600* (with François Cornilliat and Ullrich Langer) and is the author of numerous articles and reviews on medieval French romance and other topics.